STUDY GUIDE

Katherine M. Demitrakis

SOCIAL PSYCHOLOGY

Fourth Edition

ELLIOT ARONSON
TIMOTHY D. WILSON
ROBIN M. AKERT

PRENTICE HALL, UPPER SADDLE RIVER, NEW JERSEY 07458

©2002 by PEARSON EDUCATION, INC.
Upper Saddle River, New Jersey 07458

ISBN 0-13-060514-X

Printed in the United States of America

TABLE OF CONTENTS

PREFACE TO THE STUDENT

Thank you for considering this study guide. I hope you find that it assists you in your social psychology class. This supplement to the textbook will help you study and prepare to take exams and write papers. I would like to describe the sections for each chapter that you will see in this book. And, I will give you some tips for using the guide and for maximizing your chances for success in the class.

The chapters begin with a Chapter Overview and a Chapter Outline that correspond with the text. These provide you with a framework in which to fit in the details that you will discover in the chapters. Outlines are great memory tools as they help to organize material making it easier to remember. I strongly suggest that you structure all your study materials in this manner. You may want to add subheadings to the general outline. I encourage you to do this. If you make the material personally relevant, that will be a great asset to you when retrieving the information during the exams.

The next section contains the Learning Objectives for the chapter. Use these both to instruct you regarding the important points in the text and as a way to monitor your progress in a chapter. You may not be tested on all of these objectives, but using these to direct your reading and comprehension of the chapters will help you get ready for an exam on any given chapter. Page numbers are indicated for each objective. Therefore, if something sounds unfamiliar, you can refer easily to the text.

The Key Terms sections contain terms that are given special attention in the text. I recommend that you know these well. These important concepts are easy to look up to remind yourself of their definitions. Most instructors consider knowledge of terminology to be a vital objective of the course. Try to do more than memorize the definitions of these terms. Define them in your own words. Apply them to your life (or your friend's). You will improve your recall for the test and acquire language to describe our social world to others.

The Study Questions sections are designed to help you answer essay questions. They also can be helpful for stimulating paper topic ideas. Try to answer these questions even if you only take multiple choice exams in your class. Answering these questions can show you how the material is connected and applied. Read these questions and assess your ability to answer them effectively. Space is provided for your answers.

The next section consists of two Practice Tests for the chapter. Measure your knowledge of the material by taking these tests. Fill in the Blank, Multiple Choice, and Short Answer questions are offered. All the answers to the test questions can be found at the back of the study guide. Chapter and page numbers are provided to reference any material that you need to review.

In the last section, Web Exercise, you will get to explore Internet resources relevant to social psychology. The web activities include writing reaction essays, summarizing articles, and completing self-assessment inventories. The Internet links can be found by going to the web site that accompanies the text.

Finally, good luck in your social psychology class! I hope you enjoy learning about the topics in social psychology. I wish you both academic and personal benefits from this study guide, the textbook, and the course.

Katherine M. Demitrakis

CHAPTER 1

Introduction to Social Psychology

CHAPTER OVERVIEW

The first chapter is an introduction to the field and perspective of social psychology. A main focus of this chapter is to tell you what social psychology is and what it is not. In the first part of the chapter, you will discover similarities between social psychology and other disciplines, but note the important differences that set social psychology apart from fields that study similar phenomena. For example, it may be obvious why social psychology is different from folk wisdom, but distinguishing the perspective from sociology and personality psychology is more challenging. In the second part of the chapter, the important influences of the social situation on people's thoughts, feelings, and behaviors are stressed. This discussion helps to solidify social psychology's unique contribution to the study of social behavior. To understand how the social psychological perspective got started, historical developments that include behaviorism and Gestalt psychology are addressed in this section.

The third part of the chapter describes two fundamental approaches to the study of social behavior. To master the rest of the text it is very important to know the basic assumptions of each approach. These approaches are based on two basic human motives, the need to maintain self-esteem and the need to be accurate. The application of social psychology to solving social problems is considered in the last part of the chapter.

CHAPTER OUTLINE

What is Social Psychology?

      Some Alternative Ways of Understanding Social Influence

      Social Psychology Compared to Other Social Sciences

      Social Psychology Compared to Personality Psychology

The Power of Social Influence

      Underestimating the Power of Social Influence

      The Subjectivity of the Social Situation

Where Construals Come From: Basic Human Motives

      The Self-Esteem Approach: The Desire to Feel Good About Ourselves

      The Social Cognition Approach: The Need to Be Accurate

      Other Motives

Social Psychology and Social Problems

LEARNING OBJECTIVES

After you have read Chapter 1, you should be able to do the following:

1. Define social psychology. Define social influence and state why it is of interest to social psychologists. (p. 6)

2. Define construals. Indicate why social psychologists study these rather than simply the objective environments of people. (pp. 6-7)

3. Indicate how the approach taken by social psychologists is different from that of philosophers and social commentators. Describe why the social psychological approach may lead to more accurate predictions about human behavior compared to these other approaches. (pp. 8-10)

4. Compare and contrast how sociology, personality psychology, and social psychology attempt to understand and predict human behavior. (pp. 10-12)

5. Identify the goals of sociology compared to those of social psychology. (pp. 10-11)

6. Define the term individual differences. Identify the goals of personality psychology compared to those of social psychology. (p. 11-12)

7. Define the term fundamental attribution error. Identify the consequences of making this error and underestimating the power of social influence. (pp. 13-15)

8. Explain how social psychology is influenced by behaviorism and Gestalt psychology. Identify what each school of psychology has contributed to social psychology. (pp. 15-17)

9. Identify the two basic motives that underlie the origins of people's construals. (p. 17)

10. Describe what happens when the two basic human motives conflict. (pp. 18-19)

11. Identify the approaches associated with the two basic human motives. Define the term self-esteem. Define the term social cognition. Describe the assumptions of each approach. (pp. 18-22)

12. Identify the factors that interfere with our attempts to be accurate. (pp. 21-22)

13. Identify other motives that influence the formation of people's construals. (pp. 22-23)

14. Identify some social problems that social psychologists research and try to remedy. (pp. 23-24)

KEY TERMS

social psychology (p. 6)

construal (p. 6)

individual differences (p. 11)

the fundamental attribution error (p. 13)

behaviorism (p. 15)

Gestalt psychology (p. 16)

self-esteem (p. 18)

social cognition (p. 21)

STUDY QUESTIONS

1. What are examples of topics that social psychologists research?

2. What are some examples of social influence?

3. What is contained in a person's construal of the world?

4. Although they may share the same questions, what advantages does social psychology have over folk wisdom and philosophy in answering these questions?

5. What do sociologists study?

6. Which branch of psychology studies how individual differences between people explain their behavior?

7. What are some examples of individual differences?

8.   What is the fundamental attribution error? Why do people commit this error
       when they try to explain other people's behavior?

9.   What are some consequences of committing the fundamental attribution
       error?

10.   According to behaviorism, what do we need to consider to understand human
       behavior?

11.   What has Gestalt psychology contributed to social psychology?

12.   What are the two basic motives that help to form people's construals? What is the definition of each?

13.   Why do people engage in self-justification and what are some of its
       consequences?

14.   What is an assumption of the social cognition approach? What interferes
       with the accuracy of this assumption?

15.   What is the relationship between people's motive to be accurate and their
       expectations about the social world? What can result from people's
       expectations?

PRACTICE TEST 1

Fill in the Blank

1.   The scientific study of the way in which people's thoughts, feelings, and behaviors
       are influenced by the real or imagined presence of other people is called

       _____.

2. The effects of the real or imagined presence of others on people's thoughts, feelings, and behaviors is called _____.

3. The way in which people perceive, comprehend, and interpret the social world is their _____ of the world.

4. A social science concerned with topics such as social class, social structure, and social institutions is called _____.

5. Aspects of people's personalities that make them different from other people are called _____.

6. A discipline in psychology that focuses on individual differences as explanations of social behavior is known as _____.

Multiple Choice

1. Social psychology is not concerned with social situations in any objective sense, but with how people are influenced by:
   a) their construal of the social environment.
   b) abstract social rules and customs.
   c) social situations they've encountered in the past.
   d) their interactions with other people in social situations.

2. The major reason why we have conflicting folk aphorisms like "birds of a feather flock together" and "opposites attract" is that:
   a) one of the sayings does not accurately describe human nature.
   b) for some people one saying applies while for others the opposite is applicable.
   c) there are some conditions under which one saying is correct and other conditions in which the opposite is true.
   d) such sayings were developed in different cultures that taught contrasting values.

3. Psychologists interested in the effects of different personality traits on aggressive behavior are referred to as:
   (a) personality psychologists.
   (b) social psychologists.
   (c) behaviorist psychologists.
   (d) Gestalt psychologists.

4. Why is it difficult for social psychologists to convince people that their behavior is greatly influenced by the social environment?
   a) Because people outside of social psychology are rarely interested in the causes of social behavior.
   b) Because people are motivated to perceive the world accurately.
   c) Because people are inclined to commit the fundamental attribution error in explaining behavior.
   d) all of the above

5

5. Which of the following is NOT a consequence of underestimating the power of social influence?
   a) A false sense of security that "it could never happen to me."
   b An increased risk of succumbing to social influence.
   c) A decrease in one's understanding of the causes of human behavior.
   d) A decrease in one's self-esteem.

6. Behavioral psychologists like Watson and Skinner believed that all human behavior could be understood by examining:
   a) rewards and punishments in the individual's environment.
   b) the impact of broad social and cultural factors on the individual.
   c) how the individual thinks and feels about rewards and punishments.
   d) how the individual is rewarded and punished for having various thoughts and feelings.

7. Research on hazing shows that members like a group better if they had endured unpleasant procedures to get into the group than if they had not. These findings are best accounted for by:
   a) self-justification.
   b) the fundamental attribution error.
   c) principles of reinforcement.
   d) the self-fulfilling prophecy.

8. According to the social cognition approach,
   a) people try to view the world as accurately as possible.
   b) people do their best to understand and predict the social world.
   c) coming up with an accurate picture of the social world is often difficult.
   d) all of the above

9. Social psychologists are primarily concerned that their ideas about human social behavior:
   a) withstand empirical testing.
   b) obey philosophical principles.
   c) adhere to conventional wisdom.
   d) make sense intuitively.

10. Sociologists focus on _____ for explanations of human behavior whereas social psychologists focus on _____ for such explanations.
    a) society; the individual
    b) society; people's past experiences
    c) people's past experiences; the individual
    d) the individual; society

11. When we commit the fundamental attribution error in explaining people's behavior we _____ the power of personality traits and _____ the power of social influence.
    a) overestimate; underestimate
    b) overestimate; overestimate
    c) underestimate; overestimate
    d) underestimate; underestimate

12. By emphasizing the way in which people construe the social world, social psychology has its direct roots more in the tradition of _____ than in behaviorism.
    a) sociology
    b) personality psychology
    c) developmental psychology
    d) Gestalt psychology

13. Whereas the _____ approach emphasizes that behavior is motivated by the desire to feel good about ourselves, the _____ approach emphasizes the need to be accurate.
    a) self-esteem; rational
    b) emotional; rational
    c) social cognition; emotional
    d) self-esteem; social cognition

14. Researchers who attempt to understand social behavior from the perspective of social cognition assume that we:
    a) have a limitless capacity to process information.
    b) try to view the world as accurately as possible.
    c) logically suspend our judgments until we have gathered all the relevant facts.
    d) are primarily motivated to view ourselves as rational.

15. You expect that people at a party will not enjoy your company. Consequently, you spare them the misery of talking with you by being brief and cutting short their conversations with you. Later you learn that your company was not enjoyed. What social psychological phenomenon has occurred in this situation?
    a) social cognition
    b) self-justification
    c) reinforcement
    d) self-fulfilling prophesy

Short Answer

1. Linda, a social psychologist, and Mark, a sociologist, take a walk in a park where they witness a fight between two youths. What explanations are Linda and Mark likely to offer for the aggressive behavior they observed?

2. Compare the self-esteem and social cognition approaches to the study of social behavior. What assumptions are made by each approach?

3. What is the critical distinction between social psychology and folk wisdom philosophy? What is the advantage of social psychology's approach to social behavior?

PRACTICE TEST 2

Fill in the Blank

1. The tendency to overestimate the extent to which people's behavior is due to internal, dispositional factors and to underestimate the role of situational factors is called the _____.

2. A school of psychology that says that human behavior can be understood by examining the reinforcing properties of the environment is called

_____.

3. A school of psychology that stresses the importance of studying the subjective way in which an object appears in people's minds, rather than the objective, physical attributes of the object is called _____.

4. The extent to which people view themselves as good, competent, and decent is called _____.

5. Defending our actions by distorting reality in order to maintain self-esteem is called _____.

6. How people select, interpret, remember, and use social information is called

_____.

7. A social psychological phenomenon whereby people's expectations evoke behavior that confirms their expectations is called _____.

Multiple Choice

1. Social psychologists attempting to convince people to conserve natural resources will first:
   a) delineate the rewards and punishments in the situation which block conservation efforts.
   b) increase people's awareness that natural resources need to be conserved.
   c) identify the motives underlying people's failure to conserve.
   d) adopt a "let's wait and see" approach to the problem of conservation.

2. Which of the following is NOT an example of social influence?
   a) A salesperson convinces someone to buy a set of encyclopedias.
   b) At a party a man feels jealous because his date talks more to his friend than to him.
   c) A student says "thank you" when her professor hands her an exam she doesn't want to take.
   d) A friend tends to be optimistic and views situations in a positive light.

3. Conflicting answers to questions about basic human nature are most likely to be found:
   a) from one generation to the next.
   b) in folk wisdom and philosophy.
   c) from one culture to another.
   d) in personality and social psychology.

4. Which question about aggression is a sociologist most likely to ask?
   a) What universal property of all humans causes them to be aggressive?
   b) What is it about a particular society that produces aggression in its members?
   c) To what extent is human aggression inborn?
   d) Why are humans more aggressive than are other animal species?

5. A personality psychologist interested in studying happiness would most likely wonder:
   a) whether some people are generally happier than other people are.
   b) what the psychological processes are that cause people to be happy.
   c) if people in the U. S. are happier than people in China.
   d) whether happy workers are productive workers.

6. Rather than study how the physical attributes of an object combine to form an impression, Gestalt psychologists study
   a) the whole object itself as it exists in objective reality.
   b) people's subjective perception of the whole object.
   c) the isolated parts without regard to their combination.
   d) parts of the whole that go unnoticed but enter the unconscious mind.

7. To determine the origin of a construal, social psychologists look to:
   a) the social situation itself.
   b) an individual's upbringing and family background.
   c) basic human motives.
   d) broad societal and cultural factors.

8. The main topic of study in social psychology is social:
   a) work.
   b) influence.
   c) behavior.
   d) cognition.

9. According to social psychologists, an individual's behavior in a given situation is best predicted from knowing:
   a) how that individual has behaved in past situations.
   b) the nature of the present situation.
   c) how that individual construes the present situation.
   d) the individual's personality traits.

10. When people observe others behaving in a given situation, they tend to jump to the conclusion that the person rather than the situation caused the behavior. In this, people are most like a(n):
    a) social psychologist.
    b) personality psychologist.
    c) sociologist.
    d) anthropologist.

11. Which of the following would be the most likely to claim that people blindly follow leaders because they are reinforced for such compliance?
    a) Gestalt psychologists
    b) personality psychologists
    c) behavioral psychologists
    d) social psychologists

12. A well-known phrase from Gestalt psychology is:
    a) "The whole is nothing more than the sum of its parts."
    b) "The whole is different from the sum of its parts."
    c) "Opposites attract."
    d) "When the whole is construed, some parts will be deleted."

13. When the need to feel good about oneself clashes with the need to be accurate, people tend to:
    a) put a slightly different spin on the facts so that they are seen in the best possible light.
    b) deny the existence of all information that reflects badly on them.
    c) suffer from low self-esteem and continue to see the world accurately.
    d) remain in conflict since they are willing neither to distort reality nor to perceive themselves negatively.

14. A social psychologist notices that a large number of her students report getting nervous when they have to give presentations in class. In trying to determine the causes of this emotional reaction, the social psychologist will tend to examine:
   a) the dispositional qualities that these students share.
   b) her own commonsense view of why these students become nervous.
   c) the situational factors that could lead to this emotional reaction.
   d) clinical reasons that might explain why students experience nervousness.

15. Which two basic human motives do social psychologists focus on the most?
   a) the desire to reproduce and the desire to maintain one's self-esteem
   b) the desire to reproduce and the desire to achieve a sense of inner peace and harmony
   c) the desire to maintain one's self-esteem and the desire to achieve a sense of inner peace and harmony
   d) the desire to maintain one's self-esteem and the desire to view the world as accurately as possible
   e) the desire to achieve a sense of inner peace and harmony and the desire to view the world as accurately as possible

Short Answer

1. Describe an instance of the self-fulfilling prophecy from your own experiences.

2. Discuss ways in which you are influenced by both the real and imagined presence of others.

WEB EXERCISE

Go to www.prenhall.com/aronson. Click on Chapter 1 then click on the Links icon. Summarize an article by clicking on *Current Research in Social Psychology* or by clicking on the *Journal of Personality and Social Psychology*. What was being studied? How was the study done? What were the findings? What are the implications of the findings? What are your reactions? Or, write a one-page report on graduate school and job opportunities in social psychology and/or psychology in general at www.socialpsychology.org/career.htm.

CHAPTER 2

Methodology: How Social Psychologists Do Research

CHAPTER OVERVIEW

Chapter 2 contains the basic underlying principles of social psychological research. Some of the material may sound familiar, however, it is vital to know the concepts in this chapter well. A firm understanding of this material will increase the enjoyment received from reading the rest of the text. Mastery of these concepts will also help one be more critical of research findings in the text and those one is exposed to in the media.

The first part of the chapter introduces you to the beginning of the research process, the formation of theories and hypotheses. The next part discusses the types, advantages, and disadvantages of the observational method. In the next section, the correlational method is described. The fourth section explains the experimental method. This section contains perhaps the most technical information in the chapter. It is recommended that both definitions and applications of the basic components of this method are learned. Remember that although conclusions about causality may be derived only from experiments, the research method that is used depends on the particular research question being asked. Keep in mind the goals of each method as one reads about each of them. Ethical issues in social psychology are discussed in the next section. Psychological researchers must abide by strict guidelines to insure the welfare of participants in their research. Due to the phenomena that some social psychologists study, ethical research in the field may involve a strong element of creativity. In the last section of this chapter, basic and applied research are compared.

CHAPTER OUTLINE

Social Psychology: An Empirical Science

Formulating Hypotheses and Theories

      Inspiration from Previous Theories and Research

      Hypotheses Based on Personal Observations

The Observational Method: Describing Social Behavior

      Archival Analysis

      Limits of the Observational Method

The Correlational Method: Predicting Social Behavior

      Surveys

      Limits of the Correlational Method: Correlation Does Not Equal Causation

The Experimental Method: Answering Causal Questions

      Independent and Dependent Variables

      Internal Validity in Experiments

      External Validity in Experiments

Cross-Cultural Research

The Basic Dilemma of the Social Psychologist

Ethical Issues in Social Psychology

Basic Versus Applied Research

LEARNING OBJECTIVES

After you read Chapter 2, you should be able to do the following:

1.   Explain why social psychological results sometimes appear obvious. (p. 29)

2.   Explain why it is necessary to translate beliefs into hypotheses. (p. 31)

3.   Describe the process of theory refinement. (p. 31)

4.   Identify the origins of hypotheses. (pp. 31-32)

5.   Identify the three research methods that are used to test hypotheses.
        (p. 32)

6.   Identify the goal of the observational method. Describe ethnography, participant observation and archival analysis. Define interjudge reliability. (pp. 32-35)

7.   Describe the limitations of the observational method in general and a limitation unique to archival analysis. (pp. 35-36)

8.   Identify the goal of the correlational method. Discuss and define the characteristics of a correlation and a correlation coefficient. Define and state possible values of a positive correlation coefficient. Define and state possible values of a negative correlation coefficient. (pp. 36-37)

9.   Identify the role of surveys and samples in conducting correlational research. Explain the importance of selecting samples randomly. Identify potential threats to obtaining accurate survey results. Define random selection. (pp. 37-38)

10.   Distinguish between correlation and causation. Identify three possible causal relationships between variables that are correlated. (pp. 39-42)

11.   Identify the goal of the experimental method. Identify the components of the experimental method. (pp. 41, 43)

12.   Distinguish between independent and dependent variables. (pp. 43-44)

13.   Define internal validity. Identify factors that threaten the internal validity of an experiment. Define random assignment to conditions and explain why it is necessary to internal validity. (pp. 44-46)

14.   Define the term probability value and explain what a p-value tells us. Explain why probability levels are associated with statistics in experimental science. Describe the conditions under which results are considered statistically significant. (p. 45)

15.   Define external validity. Identify the two kinds of generalizability that concern researchers. (pp. 46-48)

16.   Define mundane realism and psychological realism. Discuss the role of the cover story in making experiments realistic. (pp. 46-47)

17.   Explain why randomly selected samples are rarely used in social psychological research. Explain why conducting replications is necessary in social psychological research. (pp. 47-48)

18.   Describe the meta analysis technique. Identify the purpose and goal of this method. (pp. 48-49)

19.   Identify the benefits and goals of cross-cultural research. Discuss precautions researchers should take when doing cross-cultural research. (pp. 49-50)

20.   Compare and contrast lab experiments and field experiments. Describe the relationship between internal and external validity and each type of experimental setting. (pp. 50-51)

21.   Describe the basic dilemma of the social psychologist. Identify a solution to this dilemma. (pp. 50-51)

22.   Describe the ethical dilemma faced by social psychologists and the role of informed consent in resolving this dilemma. (pp. 51-52)

23.   Identify the requirements set forth in the APA guidelines for treating participants ethically. (p. 53)

24.   Identify a deception experiment. Explain the necessity and functions of a debriefing session. Discuss the effects on participants of being deceived. (pp. 52-53)

25.   Contrast the goals of basic and applied research. Discuss the relationship between these types of research. (pp. 53-54)

KEY TERMS

observational method (p. 32)

ethnography (p. 33)

participant observation (p. 33)

archival analysis (p. 33)

interjudge reliability (p. 33)

correlational method (p. 36)

correlation coefficient (p. 36)

surveys (p. 37)

random selection (p. 38)

experimental method (p. 41)

independent variable (p. 43)

dependent variable (p. 43)

random assignment to condition (p. 45)

probability level (p-value) (p. 45)

internal validity (p. 45)

external validity (p. 46)

mundane realism (p. 46)

psychological realism (p. 46)

cover story (p. 46)

replication (p. 48)

meta analysis (p. 48)

field experiments (p. 50)

informed consent (p. 52)

deception (p. 52)

debriefing (p. 52)

basic research (p. 53)

applied research (p. 53)

STUDY QUESTIONS

1.   Why do some conclusions about social behavior seem obvious?

2.   How are theories and hypotheses formulated?

3.   When would it be appropriate to use the ethnography method? Ethnography often involves which kind of observational method?

4.   Why is interjudge reliability necessary in observational studies?

5.   What is an archival analysis?

6.   What are the strengths of the observational method? What are the limits of the observational method?

7.   In addition to describing a relationship between two variables, what do correlations allow us to do?

8.   What is a correlation coefficient? What does it tell us?

9.   What are some criteria for survey data collection in order to help insure that the data are accurate?

10.   What are the necessary components of an experiment?

11.   Regarding an experiment, what does high internal validity imply?

12.   If a researcher used random assignment to conditions and found differences in the dependent variable across conditions, what may account for these differences?

13.   Why might lab experiments lack external validity?

14.   What is a meta analysis? What does it tell us about research findings?

15.   How do replications and cross-cultural research help to increase the external validity of research findings?

16.   What is a trade-off between lab and field experiments? Why are lab experiments conducted in social psychology?

17.   What role do the American Psychological Association (APA) and an Institutional Review Board play in governing research in psychology?

18.   Why is informed consent necessary but sometimes not feasible in social psychological research? What must be done when deception is used in an experiment?

19.   What are the goals of basic research and how do they differ from those of applied research?

PRACTICE TEST 1

Fill in the Blank

1.   A type of observational method used by cultural anthropologists and social psychologists to study and understand a group or culture is _____.

2.   A form of the systematic observational method used by observers who interact with the people being observed is called _____.

3.   A form of the observational method used by researchers who examine the accumulated documents of a culture is called _____.

4.   The level of agreement between two or more people who independently observe and code a set of data is called _____.

5.   The method of research whereby two or more variables are systematically measured and the relationships between them are assessed is called the _____.

6.   A statistic that tells us how well we can predict one variable from another is called a _____.

7. A way of selecting a sample of people from a larger population so that everyone in the population has an equal chance of being selected is called _____.

8. A method whereby under controlled conditions the researcher randomly assigns participants to different conditions, varies a single aspect between these conditions, and measures behavior is called the _____.

9. The variable that is manipulated to determine if it causes changes in another variable is called the _____.

10. The variable that is measured to determine whether it is influenced when another variable is manipulated is called the _____.

11. When the only aspect that varies between experimental conditions is the independent variable, an experiment is said to have _____.

12. The procedure that assures that all participants have an equal chance of taking part in any condition of an experiment is called _____.

13. A research method whereby people are asked questions about their attitudes or behaviors is called _____.

Ch. 2

Multiple Choice

1. From dissonance theory, Leon Festinger was able to make specific predictions about when and how people would change their attitudes. We call these specific predictions:
   a) theories.
   b) hypotheses.
   c) observations.
   d) methods.

2. Using archival analyses, scientists describe a culture by:
   a) surveying a representative sample of members in a culture.
   b) observing the behavior of members in a culture.
   c) manipulating archives and measuring subsequent responses.
   d) examining documents like magazines, diaries, and suicide notes.

3. When INCREASES in the value of one variable are associated with DECREASES in the value of the other variable, then the variables are:
   a) positively correlated.
   b) negatively correlated.
   c) uncorrelated.
   d) independent.

4. As long as the sample is selected randomly, we can assume that the sampled responses:
   a) are a reasonable match to responses of the whole population.
   b) correlate with one another.
   c) reflect the true beliefs and opinions of the individuals sampled.
   d) are determined by chance factors.

17

5. From studies which indicate that viewing television violence is correlated with aggressive behavior in children, we can conclude that:
   a)   watching violence on television may cause aggressive behavior.
   b)   the aggressive personalities of some children may cause them to prefer violence on television.
   c)   some third factor like a hostile home environment may cause some children to both prefer violence on television and to behave aggressively.
   d)   all the above are possible causal relationships.

6. A "____ experiment" is identical in design to a laboratory experiment except that it is conducted in a real-life setting.
   a)   savanna
   b)   field
   c)   bush
   d)   real-life

7. How should research be conducted in order to resolve the basic dilemma of the social psychologist?
   a)   By doing replications, conduct some experiments that have internal validity and others that have external validity.
   b)   Conduct carefully designed experiments that have both internal and external validity.
   c)   Do all research in the field.
   d)   Conduct applied rather than basic research.

8. Which of the following is true of the three basic types of methods used to answer questions about social behavior?
   a)   One of the methods is better than the other two for answering all kinds of questions.
   b)   Each method causes the researcher to make identical statements about the research findings.
   c)   Different strengths and weaknesses make each method unsuitable for answering any question completely.
   d)   Different strengths and weaknesses make each method the most suitable to answer a different kind of question.

9. Which of the following is a statistical technique that allows researchers to test how reliable the effects of an independent variable are over many replications?
   a)   correlation coefficient
   b)   deception
   c)   meta analysis
   d)   double blind

10. Two individuals independently observe the same behavior at a playground. If one reports seven instances of "aggression" and the other records seventeen such instances, then ____ will be low.
   a)   interjudge reliability
   b)   internal validity
   c)   generalizability
   d)   external validity

11. If you found the correlation coefficient between height and weight to be +.74, you could conclude that:
   a)   you made a mistake in your calculations.
   b)   as height increases, weight increases.
   c)   as height increases, weight decreases.
   d)   height and weight are uncorrelated.

12. Latane and Darley (1968) varied the number of witnesses to an emergency and measured helping behavior. In this experiment _____ was the independent variable and _____ was the dependent variable.
    a) helping behavior; the number of witnesses
    b) the number of witnesses; helping behavior
    c) the emergency; helping behavior
    d) number of witnesses; the emergency

13. When the only aspect that varies across conditions in an experiment is the independent variable(s), the experiment is said to have:
    a) internal validity
    b) external validity
    c) reliability
    d) generalizability

14. Social psychologists are most concerned with generalizability across:
    a) independent and dependent variables.
    b) theories and hypotheses.
    c) identical experiments.
    d) situations and people.

15. In an experiment on how anonymity affects aggression (Zimbardo, 1970), participants wore bags on their heads and administered shocks to a victim in another room. Assuming that wearing bags gave participants a sense of anonymity, this procedure:
    a) had mundane realism but not psychological realism.
    b) had psychological realism but not mundane realism.
    c) had both mundane realism and psychological realism.
    d) lacked both mundane realism and psychological realism.

Short Answer

1. Why must the independent variable be the only thing that varies between the groups in an experiment?

2. What is the primary limitation of carefully controlled laboratory experiments and how can this limitation be overcome?

3. Under what conditions can deception experiments be conducted, and what procedures must be followed if deception is used?

PRACTICE TEST 2

Fill in the Blank

1. A number, calculated with statistical techniques, which indicates the likelihood that the results of an experiment occurred by chance and were not due to the independent variable, is called the _____.

2. The extent to which the results of a study can be generalized to other situations and to other people is known as _____.

3. The extent to which an experiment captures psychological processes like those that occur in everyday life is called _____.

4. A study repeated again, often with different subject populations or in different settings, is called a(n) _____.

5. A statistical technique which allows researchers to assess the strength of the effects of the independent variable by looking at its effects over many replications is called _____.

6. An experiment that is conducted in a real-life setting is called a _____.

7. Research conducted to solve a particular social problem is known as _____.

8. An individual's willingness to participate in an experiment after receiving a description of the kinds of experiences that participants will go through is called _____.

9. Misleading or concealing from participants the true purpose of the study or the events that will actually transpire is called _____.

10. Explaining to participants, at the end of an experiment, the purpose of the study and exactly what transpired is called _____.

11. The technique whereby a researcher watches people and keeps track of their behaviors is the _____ method.

12. If participants are performing tasks or in situations which occur frequently in the real world, the experiment may be considered high in _____ realism.

13. To achieve psychological realism in an experiment, the experimental participants may be told a _____ story.

Multiple Choice

1. The basic dilemma of the social psychologist is that:
    a) there is usually a tradeoff in experiments between internal and external validity.
    b) individual differences among participants can never be ruled out as alternative explanations for experimental results.
    c) there is a tradeoff between mundane and psychological realism.
    d) people behave differently when they are being observed.

2. While ____ research aims to solve a specific problem, ____ research tries to understand human social behavior purely for reasons of intellectual curiosity.
    a) basic; applied
    b) applied; basic
    c) theoretical; practical
    d) practical; theoretical

3. Which of the following is among the American Psychological Association's list of guidelines for conducting ethical research in psychology?
    a) The results of the study must be revealed during a debriefing.
    b) No research procedures may be used to deceive subjects about the true nature of the study.
    c) No research procedures may be used that are likely to cause serious or lasting harm to participants.
    d) All participants must agree to complete the experiment once it has begun.

4. What is the best research method to use to find out if watching violent pornography affects men's attitudes toward women?
   a) case study
   b) participant observation
   c) experiment
   d) survey

5. Why is the experiment considered the method of choice by most social psychologists?
   a) It is the least expensive method.
   b) It is the only method that describes human behavior.
   c) It is the only method that discovers correlational relationships between variables.
   d) It is the only method that can determine causal relationships.

6. Which of the following do social psychologists calculate to determine whether or not the results of their study are statistically significant?
   a) the significance level (s-value)
   b) the probable level (p-value)
   c) the probability level (p-value)
   d) the correlational value (c-value)

7. Dr. Gomez studies different cultures by becoming a part of the cultural group being investigated. Dr. Gomez most likely is using the _____ method.
   a) experiment
   b) case study
   c) ethnography
   d) archival analysis

8. The purpose of the cover story is:
   a) to deceive participants to make them give researchers data that supports their hypotheses.
   b) to maintain psychological realism.
   c) to decrease mundane realism.
   d) to increase external validity.

9. According to the text, it is more important that an experiment is higher in _____ realism than in _____ realism.
   a) mundane; internal
   b) psychological; mundane
   c) external; psychological
   d) real world; mundane

10. What must follow the research study, especially when deception is used?
    a) informed consent
    b) debunking
    c) debriefing
    d) none of the above

11. Which statement is true regarding theory refinement in social psychology?
    a) Once a theory is developed, it cannot be modified.
    b) Social psychologists continuously refine theories based on their observations of how society is changing.
    c) Social psychologists continuously refine theories based on empirical tests of their theories.
    d) Once a hypothesis derived from a theory is disproved, the theory cannot be refined.

12. An experiment has external validity when:
    a) the only aspect that varies across conditions in the experiment is the independent variable.
    b) the experimental situation is similar to events that often happen in everyday life.
    c) the results of the experiment generalize across situations and people.
    d) the experiment satisfies the researcher's goal to solve a specific problem..

13. Dr. Sanchez conducted an experiment to find out how facial expressions affect impressions of people. Participants had a discussion with someone (the experimenter) who either smiled a lot, frowned a lot, or kept a neutral facial expression throughout the interaction. The participants then filled out a questionnaire to indicate their gender, ethnicity, and how much they liked the experimenter. The independent variable is ____ and the dependent variable is ____.
    a) gender; liking
    b) ethnicity; liking
    c) liking; facial expression
    d) facial expression; liking
    e) liking; gender

14. Two studies were conducted on the topic of test anxiety. One was a field experiment and the other was a laboratory experiment. In the field experiment, the anxiety of students who took an easy test in a different section of a calculus class was measured. For the lab experiment, students were administered randomly either a difficult exam or an easy exam, and the amount of anxiety they experienced was compared. Which of the following is true about these studies?
    a) The field study is higher in mundane realism.
    b) If people in the laboratory study did not take the exams all that seriously, then the field study was higher in psychological realism.
    c) Only the laboratory study can address the question of whether difficult tests cause more anxiety than easy tests.
    d) The laboratory study was higher in internal validity.
    e) All the above are true.

15. Suppose that a study assessing the relationship between alcohol consumption and students' grade point average (GPA) found a correlation of -.73 between the amount of alcohol that students drink and their GPA. The best conclusion from this study would be:
    a) something about drinking alcohol tends to make people have a lower GPA.
    b) something about drinking alcohol tends to make people have a higher GPA.
    c) if one knows how much alcohol a student drinks, one can predict quite well the student's GPA.
    d) having a high GPA tends to cause people to drink less.
    e) students who are insecure or depressed tend to drink more and study less than other students do.

Short Answer

1. What kinds of behaviors do observational methods best assess? What questions are addressed by the use of the observational method?

2. A local news program asks viewers to place a 50-cent call to the station in order to survey opinions on gun control. Near the end of the program a reporter announces "Our survey results indicate that community members overwhelmingly support gun control." Why should you be skeptical about the conclusion drawn?

WEB EXERCISE

Go to www.socialpsychology.org/link. Click on Online Social Psychology Studies. Participate in an online study. Summarize your experience. What did you learn about yourself? What did you discover about online research compared to the research methods discussed in the textbook? Or, go to www.prenhall.com/aronson, click on the links for Chapter 2, and click on The Problem with Statistics by Richard F. Taflinger. What questions should one consider when reading about research findings and statistics?

CHAPTER 3

Social Cognition: How We Think About the Social World

CHAPTER OVERVIEW

Chapter 3 informs readers of the procedures, strategies, and problems people exhibit when they perceive and judge the social world. A main theme of this chapter concerns the biases that may color people's perceptions and judgments of others. The major influence of schemas on the processing of information about the social world is addressed in the first section of the chapter. Other mental shortcuts people use to conserve cognitive resources also are examined. Examples of judgmental heuristics (availability, representativeness, and anchoring and adjustment) and the functions and problems associated with their use are significant topics in this section.

The chapter also describes the distinction between automatic and controlled thinking. This distinction helps explain the flexibility of the social thinker. The effects of motivation and cognitive load figure prominently on people's ability to be accurate perceivers and judges. The last section of the chapter tells about the utility of teaching people to improve their reasoning skills. Educating people about the errors that are characteristic of human thinking has proven useful in the goal of improving people's perceptions and judgments of others.

CHAPTER OVERVIEW

On Automatic Pilot: Low-Effort Thinking

      People as Everyday Theorists: Automatic Thinking with Schemas

      Mental Strategies and Shortcuts

Controlled Social Cognition: High-Effort Thinking

      Automatic Believing, Controlled Unbelieving

      Ironic Processing and Thought Suppression

      Mentally Undoing the Past: Counterfactual Reasoning

A Portrayal of Social Thinking

Improving Human Thinking

LEARNING OBJECTIVES

After reading Chapter 3, you should be able to do the following:

1.   Identify the characteristics of automatic thinking. Discuss the advantages and disadvantages of automatic thinking. (p. 59)

2.   Define a schema. Identify which mental processes are affected by the use of schemas. (p. 59)

3.   Identify the functions of schemas. Describe conditions when schemas are very important. (pp. 59-62)

4.   Identify problems with schema use. Discuss how schemas may lead to memories that are inaccurate. (pp. 61-63)

5.   Define the processes of accessibility and priming. Describe the influence of accessibility and priming on schema use. (pp. 63-66)

6.   Define the perseverance effect. Discuss the role of schemas in producing the perseverance effect. (pp. 66-67)

7.   Explain how the self-fulfilling prophecy makes schemas resistant to change. Outline the steps involved in the self-perpetuating cycle of a self-fulfilling prophecy. (pp. 67-71)

8.   Describe the relationship between culture, schema content, and memory. (pp. 71-74)

9.   Define judgmental heuristics and the advantages and limitations of using these heuristics. (p. 74)

10.   Define the availability heuristic. Discuss reasons why the availability heuristic may result in faulty judgments. Identify conditions that increase the availability of information in memory. (pp. 74-76)

11.   Define the representativeness heuristic. Define base rate information. Discuss why the use of the representativeness heuristic results in the underuse of base rate information. (pp. 76-77)

12.   Define the anchoring and adjustment heuristic and the consequences of its use. Describe the process by which anchoring and adjustment are used to make judgments. (pp. 77-80)

13.   Define biased sampling. Describe the consequences of generalizing information from a biased sample to the population. (pp. 79-80)

14.   Identify the characteristics of controlled thinking. Describe the effects of motivation on people's judgments and decisionmaking. Discuss the effects of cognitive load on human thinking and judgment formation. Explain what is meant by automatic believing and controlled unbelieving. (pp. 82-85)

15.   Describe the two-part process involved in successful thought suppression. (pp. 85-87)

16.   Define counterfactual thinking. Give an example of a statement that is indicative of this type of reasoning. Discuss conditions that facilitate counterfactual thinking. Identify consequences, both positive and negative, of counterfactual reasoning. (pp. 87-88)

17.   Describe the portrayal of the social thinker. Define the meaning of the metaphor "flawed scientist" for the human thinker. (pp. 88-89)

18.   Define the overconfidence barrier. Describe how this barrier can be overcome. Discuss the effectiveness of teaching people basic statistical and methodological reasoning principles. (pp. 89-91)

KEY TERMS

social cognition (p. 58)

automatic thinking (p. 59)

schemas (p. 59)

accessibility (p. 63)

priming (p. 64)

perseverance effect (p. 66)

self-fulfilling prophecy (p. 67)

judgmental heuristics (p. 74)

availability heuristic (p. 74)

representativeness heuristic (p. 77)

base rate information (p. 77)

anchoring and adjustment heuristic (p. 78)

biased sampling (p. 79)

controlled thinking (p. 82)

thought suppression (p. 85)

counterfactual thinking (p. 87)

overconfidence barrier (p. 89)

STUDY QUESTIONS

1.   What is social cognition? What do researchers in this area study?

2.   What are the advantages of automatic thinking? When is automatic thinking problematic?

3.   Why are schemas so important to study? What role do they play in people's understanding and interpretations of themselves and the social world? What are examples of cognitive processes that are influenced by schemas?

4.   What functions do schemas serve? Why does their use sometimes have adaptive value? How is their use maladaptive? How do accessibility and priming affect schema use?

5.   What is the relationship between schemas and the perseverance effect?

6.   Why does the self-fulfilling prophecy occur? What function does it serve? How can it affect resistance to schema change?

7.   How do cultures influence schema content?

8.   Why do people use judgmental heuristics? What are three heuristics that people use to make judgments? When people rely on these heuristics what kind of information are they not taking into account?

9.   What are the effects of motivation on judgment formation? How is automatic thinking different from controlled thinking? What effects does cognitive load have on these two types of thinking?

10.   How do automatic thinking and controlled thinking interact to allow for successful thought suppression?

11.   What is the relationship between the occurrence of counterfactual thinking and emotional reactions to events?

12.   What is perhaps the best metaphor for the social thinker? Why?

13.   What can we teach people so that they overcome the overconfidence barrier and increase their reasoning ability?

PRACTICE TEST 1

Fill in the Blank

1. Cognitive structures people have to organize their knowledge about the social world by themes or subjects are called _____.

2. Mentally changing some part of the past to imagine what might have been is called _____.

3. Thinking that is _____ is nonconscious, effortless, involuntary, and unintentional.

4. The ease with which schemas can be brought to mind is called _____.

5. Two processes, one automatic and the other controlled, are involved in successful thought _____.

6. The persistence of people's beliefs after evidence supporting these beliefs has been discredited is called the _____.

7. An expectation about what another person is like which influences how one acts toward that person and causes that person to behave in a way that is consistent with the expectation is called a(n) _____.

8. Mental shortcuts people use to make judgments quickly and efficiently are called _____.

Multiple Choice

1. Social cognition is the study of:
    a)   the way people think, feel, and act toward others.
    b)   the way in which people's thoughts, feelings, and behaviors are influenced by the real or imagined presence of others.
    c)   how people's behavior is motivated by the need to perceive and present themselves favorably.
    d)   how people select, interpret, remember, and use information to make judgments and decisions .

2. Because we notice and think about behavior that is consistent with our schemas,
    a)   schemas become stronger and more impervious to change.
    b)   schemas are very frail structures that can be easily toppled.
    c)   behavior that is even slightly inconsistent with our schemas becomes highly noticeable.
    d)   we are frequently attending to redundant, useless information.

3. We are most likely to use schemas to "fill in the blanks" when we:
    a)   observe uninteresting stimuli.
    b)   observe familiar stimuli.
    c)   are uncertain what it is that we're observing.
    d)   fail to attend to what we are observing.

4.   Evidence is more likely to be noticed, recalled, and given greater weight if it:
        a)   confirms our expectations.
        b)   is objectively verifiable.
        c)   threatens our self-esteem.
        d)   presents a plausible alternative to our beliefs.

5.   Which process affects whether or not a schema will be used to guide social perception?
        a)   accountability
        b)   accessibility
        c)   priming
        d)   both b and c

6.   People's beliefs about themselves and the social world persist even after the evidence supporting their beliefs is discredited. This finding has been labeled the:
        a)   persistence problem.
        b)   perseverance effect.
        c)   self-fulfilling prophesy.
        d)   overconfidence barrier.

7.   The self-fulfilling prophecy makes schemas resistant to change because:
        a)   it distorts our perceptions of disconfirming evidence.
        b)   it produces the evidence the individual needs to confirm the schema.
        c)   it provides a theme or topic around which a schema can be structured.
        d)   all of the above

8.   When we base our judgments on the ease with which we can bring something to mind, we are using the ____ heuristic.
        a)   availability
        b)   representativeness
        c)   anchoring/adjustment
        d)   retrievability

9.   Given information about a specific person that contradicts base rate information, people tend to:
        a)   ignore the information about the person and use only the base rate information.
        b)   integrate the information about the individual and the base rate information.
        c)   look for another heuristic.
        d)   ignore the base rate, judging only how representative the information about the person is of a general category.

10.   Which of the following is most likely performed using controlled thinking?
        a)   tying one's shoes
        b)   calculating the answer to a difficult math problem
        c)   walking around one's house
        d)   using established stereotypes to form an impression of someone

11.   Because people think that their reasoning processes are less fallible than they actually are, anyone trying to improve people's accuracy is up against a(n):
        a)   certainty threshold.
        b)   perseverance effect.
        c)   illusory correlation.
        d)   overconfidence barrier.

29

12. Kelley (1950) had students read different descriptions of a guest lecturer who they evaluated at the end of class. Results indicated that:
   a) the descriptions influenced how students rated the lecturer's unambiguous behaviors.
   b) the descriptions influenced students to such an extent that they failed to differentiate between ambiguous and unambiguous behaviors.
   c) the descriptions had no effect on the students' ratings.
   d) the descriptions influenced how students rated the lecturer's ambiguous behaviors.

13. Which of the following is NOT an advantage of viewing the world through schema-tinted glasses?
   a) Schemas allow us to interpret the meaning of ambiguous behavior.
   b) Schemas facilitate the unbiased processing of information.
   c) Schemas facilitate smooth social interactions.
   d) Schemas allow us to deal with experiences in a manner that requires little cognitive effort.

14. The process by which recent experiences increase accessibility of a schema is called:
   a) retrieval.
   b) priming.
   c) availability.
   d) perseverance.

15. Any time people act on their schemas in a way that makes the schema "come true," a(n) ____ results.
   a) stereotype
   b) self-fulfilling prophesy
   c) illusory correlation
   d) perseverance effect

Short Answer

1. Describe three heuristics that aid our judgments. Give examples of each one.

2. What approach has been demonstrated to reduce people's overconfidence? The effectiveness of this approach suggests that overconfidence results from what?

3. Describe the influence of culture on the content of schemas.

PRACTICE TEST 2

Fill in the Blank

1. A heuristic whereby judgments are based on the ease with which something can be brought to mind is called the _____.

2. A heuristic whereby things are classified according to how similar they are to a typical case is called the _____.

3. Information about the frequency of members of different categories in the population is called _____.

4. A heuristic whereby judgments are made by adjusting an answer away from an initial value is called the _____.

5. Making generalizations from samples of information known to be a biased or atypical is called _____.

6. The finding that people usually have too much confidence in the accuracy of their own judgments has been labeled the _____.

7. The process by which recent experiences make schemas, traits, or concepts come to mind more readily is called _____.

8. Thinking that is conscious, voluntary, and effortful is referred to as _____ thinking.

9. How people pick, explain, retrieve, and use social information to make judgments and decisions is called _____.

Multiple Choice

1. Making judgments by comparing someone to a stereotype demonstrates the use of a(n) ____ heuristic.
   a) anchoring
   b) representative
   c) adjustment
   d) unavailable

2. Which is NOT a characteristic of counterfactual thinking?
   a) It decreases the strength of emotional reactions to a negative event.
   b) It increases the strength of emotional reactions to a negative event.
   c) It occurs in response to an unexpected outcome.
   d) Its likelihood is influenced by the ease of mentally undoing an actual outcome.

3. When people are faced with judgmental tasks which have important consequences for them
   a) they use more complex strategies and make more accurate judgments.
   b) they experience heightened arousal which interferes with their normal cognitive processes.
   c) they rely more heavily on cognitive shortcuts and make fewer accurate judgments.
   d) they experience heightened arousal which enables them to use cognitive shortcuts especially efficiently.

4. Samantha bought a make of car highly recommended by many people she knows and a leading consumer magazine. The particular car she bought broke down many times and cost her a great deal of money on repairs. Based on her experience, Samantha generalizes to all cars of the same make and says that they are all poorly made and unreliable. Since she is using incomplete information in her judgment, she is committing:
   a) the self-fulfilling prophecy.
   b) the perseverance effect.
   c) the base rate error.
   d) biased sampling.

5. Nonconscious and unintentional is to ____ thinking as conscious and effortful is to ____ thinking.
   a) automatic; controlled
   b) heuristic; automatic
   c) controlled; heuristic
   d) automatic; conditioned

6. When are people likely to act in accordance with their expectations of others?
    a)   when schemas are very accessible
    b)   when they are motivated
    c)   when people are distracted
    d)   both a and c

7. Regarding our ability to engage in thought suppression, the ____ process is the automatic part of the system and the ____ process is the controlled part of the system.
    a)   operating; checking
    b)   distracting; monitoring
    c)   monitoring; operating
    d)   operating; monitoring

8. Which of the following is FALSE about thought suppression?
    a)   It involves two processes, one automatic and the other controlled.
    b)   It is more difficult to suppress unwanted thoughts when one is preoccupied or tired.
    c)   It is healthier for people to suppress thoughts about negative events than to discuss them.
    d)   It is healthier for people to discuss their problems than it is to suppress thoughts about them.

9. Natasha expects men to be rude. She meets her roommate's boyfriend, and he acts somewhat rude to Natasha because she is cold toward him. This is an example of the:
    a)   hindsight bias.
    b)   expectation bias.
    c)   self-fulfilling prophecy.
    d)   perseverance effect.

10. Like other types of automatic thinking, priming occurs:
    a)   slowly.
    b)   deliberately.
    c)   voluntarily
    d)   none of the above

11. Which of the following is true about counterfactual reasoning?
    a)   It is an effortful thought process.
    b)   It consumes mental energy.
    c)   It can be a useful thought process.
    d)   All the above are true about counterfactual reasoning.
    e)   None of the above are true about counterfactual reasoning.

12. If people are influenced by arbitrary numbers when making judgments regarding, for instance, a convicted defendant's prison sentence, they are using the:
    a)   representativeness heuristic.
    b)   availability heuristic.
    c)   anchoring and adjustment heuristic.
    d)   base rate information.

13. Which of the following is NOT true regarding judgmental heuristics?
    a)   They usually do not produce as good a decision compared to considering every piece of information.
    b)   They allow people to make judgments quickly and efficiently.
    c)   They may be inadequate or misapplied.
    d)   They are more likely to be used when our self-esteem has been threatened.

14. There is reason to believe that people can become more skilled at making social judgments and inferences because:
    a) the history of human evolution makes this inevitable.
    b) humans are especially prone to make errors and can only improve at this process.
    c) students who take statistics classes historically do much better on the Graduate Record Exam.
    d) people can be trained to make fewer judgmental errors when making inferences about others.

15. A highly accessible schema is one that:
    a) people can bring to mind easily.
    b) most people have developed.
    c) is very easy to develop.
    d) others will know is being used.

Short Answer

1. Contrast automatic and controlled thinking. Describe how these processes are involved in thought suppression.

2. Amy's taking out an ad in the classified to sell her old car. She knows that if she prints "Make offer" people will offer her about $2000 for the car. Instead, she prints "$3000 or best offer." Why might she expect to receive higher bids for her car using this strategy?

3. You have noticed that a friend of yours seems especially prone to jump to conclusions about people on the basis of very little information about them. Naturally, you suspect that he/she is committing errors in inference. Using what you learned in Chapter 3, describe how you would attempt to correct your friend's errors.

WEB EXERCISE

Visit www.prenhall.com/aronson and go to Chapter 3 links. Click on Social Cognition Paper Archive and summarize an article of your choice. Or, click on Counterfactual Research News or Being Human and the Illusory Correlation and summarize what you learned. Or, go to the Chapter 3 Try It!, A Social-Cognitive Magic Trick, click on the link, then write up your answers to the questions provided.

CHAPTER 4

Social Perception: How We Come to Understand Other People

CHAPTER OVERVIEW

The topic of Chapter 4 is how people attempt to understand and explain the behaviors of others. The first section of the chapter depicts the ability people have to decode and encode nonverbal behavior. Cultural and gender differences in nonverbal behavior display and interpretation also are discussed. In the next section the use of heuristics to understand other people is identified. How these heuristics often can bias social perceptions is examined. Research confirms that people's perceptions of others are not as accurate as they may think.

The third section consists of research in the area of attribution theory. Causal attributions are reasons people formulate to explain the behavior of others. Social psychologists have proposed several attribution theories. For example, the covariation model focuses on how people make internal (dispositional) or external (situational) attributions to explain other people's behaviors. According to this model, this involves considering three types of information: consensus, distinctiveness, and consistency. Another main focus of this chapter is on the role of culture in the attribution process. Cultural differences in the tendency to commit various attribution errors are explored. The attribution process can lead to inaccurate attributions for both others' and our own behaviors. Why these errors occur is discussed. The final section of this chapter addresses the accuracy of people's attributions and impressions. Like other perceptions of the social world, people's perceptions of others may be somewhat inaccurate. People's behavior can be influenced powerfully by other people's preconceptions. In fact, the perpetuation of the behaviors that others expect often occurs.

CHAPTER OUTLINE

Nonverbal Behavior

      Facial Expressions of Emotion

      Other Channels of Nonverbal Communication

      Multichannel Nonverbal Communication

      Gender Differences in Nonverbal Communication

Implicit Personality Theories: Filling in the Blanks

      The Role of Culture in Implicit Personality Theories

Causal Attribution: Answering the "Why" Question

      The Nature of the Attribution Process

      The Covariation Model: Internal Versus External Attributions

      The Fundamental Attribution Error: People as Personality Psychologists

      The Actor/Observer Difference

      Self-Serving Attributions

The Role of Culture in the Attribution Process

        Culture and the Fundamental Attribution Error

        Culture and the Correspondence Bias

        Culture and Other Attribution Biases

How Accurate Are Our Attributions and Impressions?

        Why Are Our Impressions Of Others Sometimes Wrong?

        Why Do Our Impressions Seem Accurate?

LEARNING OBJECTIVES

After reading Chapter 4, you should be able to do the following:

1.   Define social perception. (p. 97)

2.   Define nonverbal communication. Identify the different channels of nonverbal communication. (p. 97)

3.   Identify the various functions of nonverbal behavior and discuss the effects nonverbal communication can have on verbal communication. (pp. 97-98)

4.   Discuss Darwin's theory of universal facial expressions of emotion and research that supports this theory. Define encode and decode. (pp. 99-101)

5.   Identify factors than decrease decoding accuracy. Define affect blends. Define display rules. Define emblems and list examples of them. Discuss cross-cultural differences in nonverbal communication. (pp. 101-104)

6.   Describe how we gather information from multichannel nonverbal communication. (pp. 103-105)

7.   Identify gender differences in the ability to decode nonverbal communication that is sincere versus deceptive. Explain Eagly's social-role theory and how it explains the above differences. (p. 106)

8.   Define and discuss the origins, functions, and drawbacks of implicit personality theories. Discuss cross-cultural differences in the content of implicit personality theories. (pp. 107-109)

9.   Identify the focus of attribution theory. Describe the nature of the attribution process according to Fritz Heider. Distinguish between internal and external attributions. List examples of each type of attribution. (pp. 109-111)

10.   Describe the covariation model of Kelley and the process it attempts to describe. Identify and define the three kinds of information Kelley claims we use to make attributions. Identify the types of attributions we make when these kinds of information are combined in different ways. (pp. 111-113)

11.   Define the fundamental attribution error. Define perceptual salience. Describe the two-step process of attribution. Discuss why the fundamental attribution error is so prevalent. Describe people's intuitive beliefs about others' tendencies to make the fundamental attribution error. Define the spotlight effect. (pp. 113-119)

12. Define the actor/observer difference and its relationship to the fundamental attribution error. Discuss the causes of the actor/observer difference. Identify the influences of perceptual salience and information availability on the actor/observer difference. (pp. 119-122)

13. Define self-serving attributions. Identify self-serving attributions for success and for failure. Discuss why people make self-serving attributions. (pp. 122-125)

14. Discuss the motives underlying defensive attributions. Identify and define two forms of defensive attributions. Discuss the relationship between defensive attributions and "blaming the victim" of misfortune. Identify when blaming the victim fails to defend our belief in a just world. (pp. 125-126)

15. Describe the findings from research on the role of culture in the attribution process. Discuss cultural differences in the prevalence of the fundamental attribution error. Define the correspondence bias. Describe the role that culture plays in the prevalence of the correspondence bias. Summarize cultural differences in the attribution process that relate to the fundamental attribution error. (pp. 126-131)

16. Discuss cultural differences in the frequency of other attribution biases including the actor/observer difference, the self-serving bias, the belief in the just world, and the spotlight effect. (pp. 131-132)

17. Discuss the accuracy of our attributions and impressions of strangers and friends. Explain why our impressions of others are sometimes wrong and why we might not realize it. (pp. 132-135)

KEY TERMS

social perception (p. 97)

nonverbal communication (p. 97)

encode (p. 99)

decode (p. 99)

affect blends (p. 101)

display rules (p. 102)

emblems (p. 103)

social-role theory (p. 106)

implicit personality theory (p. 107)

attribution theory (p. 110)

internal attribution (p. 110)

external attribution (p. 110)

covariation model (p. 111)

consensus information (p. 112)

distinctiveness information (p. 112)

consistency information (p. 112)

fundamental attribution error (p. 114)

perceptual salience (p. 115)

two-step process of attribution (p. 116)

spotlight effect (p. 119)

actor/observer difference (p. 119)

self-serving attributions (p. 122)

defensive attributions (p. 125)

unrealistic optimism (p. 125)

belief in a just world (p. 126)

correspondence bias (p. 129)

STUDY QUESTIONS

1. What are the most diagnostic channels of nonverbal communication? What are other channels of nonverbal communication? What functions do nonverbal cues serve?

2. What is the relationship between encoding and decoding? What are the six major emotional expressions that are universally encoded and decoded?

3. What are affect blends? What are display rules? What are examples of cross-cultural differences in display rules?

4. What are emblems? What are examples of these?

5. Who may be better at decoding nonverbal cues, extroverts or introverts, men or women?

6. How does the social-role theory explain gender differences in encoding and decoding nonverbal communication?

7. What is an implicit personality theory? What are functions of implicit personality theories?

8. What is attribution theory? What does it try to describe and explain? How do internal attributions differ from external ones?

9. What is the premise of the covariation model? What information do we examine for covariation when we form attributions? When are people most likely to make an internal attribution or an external attribution according to the covariation model?

10. What is the fundamental attribution error? Why does it occur? What is perceptual salience? What is the two-step process of attribution? What are people's intuitive beliefs regarding how often others commit the fundamental attribution error? What is the spotlight effect?

11. What is the actor/observer difference? Why does it occur?

12. When we form self-serving attributions, to what do we attribute our successes and our failures?

13. What are defensive attributions? What is unrealistic optimism? What is the belief in a just world? What functions do these defensive attributions serve?

14.   What are cultural differences in the occurrence of the fundamental attribution error? What is the correspondence bias? What cultural differences exist in the tendency to engage in the actor/observer difference, the self-serving bias, the belief in the just world, and the spotlight effect?

15.   What are some reasons why our impressions of others are sometimes incorrect? Why don't we know when our impressions of others are wrong?

PRACTICE TEST 1

Fill in the Blank

1.   The study of how we form impressions of and make inferences about other people is called _____.

2.   The ways in which people communicate without spoken language is called _____.

3.   To _____ is to express emotions and to _____ is to interpret them.

4.   Culturally determined rules about the nonverbal behaviors that are appropriate to display are called _____.

5.   Facial expressions where parts of the face are displaying different emotions are referred to as _____.

6.   Nonverbal gestures that have clear, well-understood definitions within a given culture are called _____.

7.   The theory which maintains that division of labor between the sexes produces gender-role expectations as well as sex-typed skills and beliefs which are responsible for differences in social behavior is known as _____.

8.   Schemas that people use to group various kinds of personality traits together are called _____.

9.   A theory concerned with the way in which people explain the causes of their own and other people's behavior is called _____.

10.   The inference that an individual's behavior is caused by something about the person is called a(n) _____.

11.   The inference that an individual's behavior is caused by something about the situation that the person is in is called a(n) _____.

12.   The _____ effect occurs when one overestimates the extent to which one's behaviors and appearance are noticed by other people.

13.   The inclination to conclude that people's behaviors match their personality is the _____ bias.

Multiple Choice:

1.   Which of the following is an example of multi-channel nonverbal communication?
        a)   averting ones eyes while speaking with a flat tone and twisting on one foot
        b)   exhibiting sadness in one part of the face and disgust in another
        c)   interpreting a compliment as false flattery when you're in a bad mood
        d)   all of the above

2.   Greg has recently taken in a stray dog. If you make an external attribution for Greg's behavior, you will conclude that:
        a)   Greg likes dogs.
        b)   Greg felt sorry for the dog.
        c)   the dog is probably cute and friendly.
        d)   others will perceive Greg as an animal lover.

3.   The perception that our own behaviors are caused by the situation but that others' behaviors are dispositionally caused is known as the:
        a)   fundamental attribution error.
        b)   attribution difference.
        c)   actor/observer difference.
        d)   anchoring adjustment heuristic.

4.   A consequence of our belief in a just world is that we:
        a)   blame the victims of misfortune.
        b)   focus on situational causes of others' behavior.
        c)   make accurate attributions and impressions.
        d)   are more likely to attribute our own behavior to dispositional causes.

5.   Facial expressions, tone of voice, and the use of touch are all examples of:
        a)   context dependent attributional cues.
        b)   affect blends.
        c)   display rules.
        d)   nonverbal communication.

6.   Japanese women less often exhibit a wide, uninhibited smile than women in Western cultures because Japanese and Western cultures prescribe different:
        a)   display rules.
        b)   values.
        c)   affect blends.
        d)   implicit personality theories.

7.   Which of the following is an example of an emblem?
        a)   a road sign
        b)   the written explanation of a nonverbal cue
        c)   the "okay" sign created with the thumb and forefinger
        d)   averted eye gaze

8.   _____ are more likely to detect lies through nonverbal communication and _____ are more likely to accurately interpret such communication when it is sincere.
   a)   Males; males
   b)   Females; females
   c)   Males; females
   d)   Females; males

9.   The display of different emotions on different parts of the face is called a(n):
   a)   affect emblem.
   b)   nonverbal blend.
   c)   facial incongruity.
   d)   affect blend.

10.   According to Fritz Heider (1958), the attributions we make for people's behavior can be either _____ or _____.
   a)   target-based; category based
   b)   internal; external
   c)   perceptual; physical
   d)   accurate; biased

11.   The study of how we form impressions and make judgments of others is called:
   a)   judgmental heuristics.
   b)   social perception.
   c)   attribution theory.
   d)   social cognition.

12.   The three types of information central to Kelly's (1967) covariation model are:
   a)   consensus, correspondence, and distinctiveness.
   b)   consensus, consistency, and correspondence.
   c)   correspondence, distinctiveness, and consistency.
   d)   consensus, distinctiveness, and consistency.

13.   Research on cultural differences in attribution styles indicates that people from Western cultures are:
   a)   less skilled at forming impressions of behavior.
   b)   taught to prefer dispositional explanations of behavior.
   c)   taught to prefer situational explanations of behavior.
   d)   reluctant to publicly state dispositional explanations of behavior.

14.   The automatic formation of an internal attribution followed by a situational one given time and effortful thought describes the:
   a)   fundamental attribution error.
   b)   multi-step process of attribution.
   c)   actor-observer difference.
   d)   two-step process of attribution.

15.   Research on the accuracy of our first impressions of strangers reveals that:
   a)   we are surprisingly accurate in our estimates of people who are similar to us.
   b)   we are surprisingly accurate in our estimates of people in general.
   c)   we are surprisingly inaccurate when we have little information on which to base our impressions.
   d)   our impressions of others become no more accurate the more we get to know them.

Short Answer

1.   Describe Eagly's social-role theory. How does it explain why women lose their superiority at deciphering someone's nonverbal cues when that person is lying? Describe research that supports this theory.

2.   Describe Kelley's covariation model of attribution including the types of information people use to make attributions about an actor's behavior.

3.   You meet John at a fraternity party and quickly form an impression of him as a wild, fun-loving, and perhaps irresponsible person. In fact, John is a hard working and determined chemistry major. Discuss causes of your erroneous impression of John and two reasons why you might be able to accurately predict John's behavior nevertheless.

PRACTICE TEST 2

Fill in the Blank

1.   The notion that we make attributions about a person's behavior by observing the things that covary with that behavior is called the _____.

2.   Information about the extent to which other people behave the same way toward the same stimulus as the actor does is called _____.

3.   Information about the extent to which an actor behaves in the same way toward different stimuli is called _____.

4.   Information about the extent to which the behavior of an actor toward a stimulus is the same across time and circumstances is called _____.

5.   The tendency to overestimate the extent to which people's behavior is due to internal, dispositional factors and to underestimate the role of situational factors is called the _____.

6.   The tendency to see others' behavior as dispositionally caused and our own behavior as situationally caused is known as the _____.

7.   Explanations for one's successes that credit internal, dispositional factors, and explanations for one's failures that blame external, situational factors are called _____.

8.   A form of defensive attribution wherein people think that good things are more likely to happen to them than to their peers, and that bad things are less likely to happen to them than to their peers is called _____.

9.   A form of defensive attribution wherein people assume that bad things happen to bad people and that good things happen to good people is called _____.

10.   Both _____, or the focus of people's attention, and the availability of information account for the actor/observer effect.

11.   First making an internal attribution about someone's behavior and then adjusting it to consider the situation is part of the _____ process of attribution formation.

12.   Explanations for behavior that protect people from feeling vulnerable and mortal are called _____ attributions.

2 step proc   attrib
consensus/distinm/con
FAE

Multiple Choice

1. Though you may have an inaccurate impression of Jane, you may be good at predicting her behavior when you are together if:
   a) you treat her in a manner that makes her behavior confirm your expectancies.
   b) you maintain a high degree of confidence in your predictions.
   c) you make internal attributions for her behaviors.
   d) all the above

2. To express emotions is to _____ and to interpret emotions is to _____.
   a) display; perceive
   b) decode; encode
   c) encode; decode
   d) display; decode

3. A theory that has been used to explain gender differences in nonverbal communication is:
   a) gender-role theory.
   b) sex-expectation theory.
   c) social-role theory.
   d) gender-differences theory.

4. Which of the following is FALSE regarding implicit personality theories?
   a) The implicit personality theories of different individuals can share common components.
   b) Implicit personality theories are influenced by cultural factors.
   c) Implicit personality theories influence how people form impressions of others.
   d) An individual's implicit personality theory is unique and does not share common components with others.

5. Which of the following focuses on how we make inferences about the causes of other people's behaviors?
   a) implicit personality theory
   b) attribution theory
   c) social-role theory
   d) social perception theory

6. According to Kelley's (1967) covariation model, when people use information about whether or not the actor acts the same way toward everyone, not just the target, they are using _____ information to make an attribution about the actor's behavior.
   a) distinctiveness
   b) consensus
   c) discriminating
   d) consistency

7. According to Kelley's (1967) covariation model, when people use information about whether or not others, not just the actor, act the same way toward the target, they are using _____ information to make an attribution about the actor's behavior.
   a) distinctiveness
   b) consensus
   c) discriminating
   d) consistency

8. According to Hansen and Hansen (1988), we are faster at decoding and locating faces in a crowd that express ____ than faces that express ____.
   a) sadness; happiness
   b) anger; fear
   c) anger; happiness
   d) happiness; fear

9. Richards and Gross (1999) found that people who suppressed unpleasant emotions compared to people who did not suppress unpleasant emotions experienced:
   a) better memory for the information provided to them.
   b) poorer memory for the information provided to them.
   c) higher blood-pressure readings.
   d) both b and c.

10. Which of the following helps explain why people commit the fundamental attribution error?
    a) perceptual salience
    b) lack of situational information
    c) the spotlight effect
    d) both a and b
    e) all the above

11. Our tendency to overestimate the degree to which our behaviors and appearance are noticed and focused on by others is called the:
    a) fundamental attribution error.
    b) spotlight effect.
    c) actor-observer difference.
    d) self-serving bias.

12. When people make ____ attributions for successes and ____ attributions for failures, they are making self-serving attributions.
    a) external; dispositional
    b) internal; dispositional
    c) internal; external
    d) external; internal

13. All of the following are reasons why people make self-serving attributions EXCEPT WHICH ONE?
    a) to maintain self-esteem
    b) because we want to present ourselves to others in a positive way
    c) because of the information we have available to us
    d) because we are motivated to be accurate

14. Which of the following is a type of defensive attribution?
    a) realistic hopefulness
    b) unrealistic optimism
    c) belief in an unjust world
    d) illusion of vulnerability

15. Which of the following is true about the correspondence bias?
    a) It is the tendency to believe that people's behavior matches their personalities.
    b) It occurs across cultures.
    c) People in collectivist cultures are more likely to adjust it to take into account situational information compared to people from individualist cultures.
    d) All the above are true about the correspondence bias.

Short Answer

1.   Why are our attributions influenced by perceptual salience?

2.   Give a recent example of self-serving attributions that you have made for success and failure.

WEB EXERCISE

Go to www.prenhall.com/aronson. Click on the Chapter 4 Try It!, Test Your Nonverbal Skills. Click on the link. How well did you perform on the tests of your ability to decode nonverbal information? In what ways does what you learned correspond with the textbook's material on nonverbal behavior?

CHAPTER 5

Self-Knowledge: How We Come to Understand Ourselves

CHAPTER OVERVIEW

The first part of Chapter 5 considers the nature of the self and how definitions of the self differ according to gender and culture. The remainder of the chapter documents major theories in social psychology that help readers understand how they may find out information about themselves. Each theory focuses on a different method of discovering self-knowledge. Another difference between the theories presented in the chapter is that some deal with finding out who people are and others deal with finding out how people feel and why they feel the way they do. An assumption of these theories is that people do not always know how they feel and why they feel the way they do. Some theories acknowledge that people may be incorrect about their feelings and the origins of them.

One way to gain self-knowledge is through introspection. Self-awareness theory proposes that by becoming aware of oneself, one can increase self-knowledge. Sometimes self-awareness can be unpleasant, however. A second theory proposes that people gain self-knowledge by examining their own behaviors. The self-perception theory helps readers understand how rewards influence people's motivation to perform tasks. Two theories in the chapter, the two-factor theory of emotion and the cognitive appraisal theories of emotion, help explain how people experience emotions and how they interpret the causes of their emotions.

The last section in this chapter focuses on how and why people present themselves to other people. People's need to engage in impression management is examined as are strategies that allow people to present their desired impressions to others. These strategies include ingratiation and self-handicapping.

CHAPTER OUTLINE

The Nature of the Self

     The Functions of the Self

     Cultural Differences in the Definition of the Self

     Gender Differences in the Definition of the Self

Knowing Ourselves Through Introspection

     Focusing on the Self: Self-Awareness Theory

     Judging Why We Feel the Way We Do: Telling More than We Can Know

     The Consequences of Introspecting About Reasons

Knowing Ourselves Through Observations of Our Own Behavior

     Inferring Who We Are from How We Behave: Self-Perception Theory

     Intrinsic versus Extrinsic Motivation

     Understanding Our Emotions: The Two-Factor Theory of Emotion

     Finding the Wrong Cause: Misattribution of Arousal

Interpreting the Social World: Cognitive Appraisal Theories of Emotion

Knowing Ourselves Through Observations of Other People

Knowing Ourselves By Comparing Ourselves to Others

Impression Management: All the World's a Stage

LEARNING OBJECTIVES

After reading Chapter 5, you should be able to do the following:

1.   Define self-concept. Define self-awareness. Discuss animal and human research on the sense of self. Discuss how our self-concepts change with age. (pp. 141-142)

2.   Discuss the functions of the self. Describe how successful people's attempts at self-control are. Identify factors that hinder self-control and those that foster self-control. (pp. 142-143)

3.   Describe different conceptions of the self across cultures. Contrast the independent view of the self with the interdependent view of the self. (pp. 143-145)

4.   Discuss the research findings on gender differences in the definition of the self. (pp. 145-146)

5.   Identify basic self-motives that are common across cultures and gender. (p. 146)

6.   Discuss introspection as a source of self-knowledge. Describe self-awareness theory and what kinds of information self-awareness reveals. Identify the emotional and behavioral consequences of self-awareness. Discuss when self-awareness is aversive and how we attempt to stop being self-aware. (pp. 146-150)

7.   Distinguish between thoughts people have about how they feel or what kind of person they are, and why they feel the way they do. Discuss the role of causal theories in telling more than we can know. (pp. 150-153)

8.   Identify the consequences of introspecting about reasons and the kinds of information that come to mind when people introspect about reasons. Define reasons-generated attitude change and discuss its consequences. Discuss why analyzing reasons may change a person's feelings. (pp. 153-154)

9.   Describe Daryl Bem's self-perception theory. Identify when and how people use observations of their own behavior as a source of self-knowledge. (pp. 154-155)

10.   Describe the relationship between intrinsic motivation, external rewards, and the overjustification effect. Define task-contingent and performance-contingent rewards. Identify conditions under which overjustification can be avoided. (pp. 155-158)

11.   Identify the two factors or steps required to understand our own emotional states according to Schachter's two-factor theory of emotion. Discuss the implications of Schachter's theory for the idea that emotions are somewhat arbitrary. Discuss how the two-factor theory explains the misattribution of arousal. (pp. 158-162)

12.   Identify the central idea of cognitive appraisal theories of emotion. List the two kinds of appraisals that are important in determining our emotions in response to an event. Compare and contrast Schachter's two-factor theory with the cognitive appraisal theories. (pp. 162-163)

13. Identify the postulates of social comparison theory. Discuss when people engage in social comparison and with whom they choose to compare themselves when their goal is to construct an accurate self-image. Discuss the motives underlying upward and downward social comparisons and the consequences of engaging in each. (pp. 164-166)

14. Identify the relationship between self-presentation and impression management. Discuss Goffman's theory of social interaction. Identify two self-presentation strategies that people use in everyday life. Define ingratiation. (pp. 166-168)

15. Distinguish between two ways that people self-handicap. Discuss the advantages and disadvantages of self-handicapping. (pp. 168-169)

KEY TERMS

self-concept (p. 141)

self-awareness (p. 141)

independent view of the self (p. 143)

interdependent view of the self (p. 144)

introspection (p. 146)

self-awareness theory (p. 148)

causal theories (p. 152)

reasons-generated attitude change (p. 154)

self-perception theory (p. 154)

intrinsic motivation (p. 155)

extrinsic motivation (p. 155)

overjustification effect (p. 156)

task-contigent rewards (p. 157)

performance-contingent rewards (p. 157)

two-factor theory of emotion (p. 159)

misattribution of arousal (p. 161)

cognitive appraisal theories of emotion (p. 163)

social comparison theory (p. 164)

upward social comparison (p. 165)

downward social comparison (p. 166)

self-presentation (p. 166)

impression management (p. 166)

ingratiation (p. 168)

self-handicapping (p. 168)

STUDY QUESTIONS

1.   What is a self-concept and how does it change from childhood to adulthood?

2.   What are the functions of the self? How successful are people's attempts at self-control? What factors influence self-control?

3.   How do self-concepts differ in Western cultures compared to Eastern cultures?

4.   How do self-concepts differ according to gender?

5.   What is similar about self-concepts across cultures and gender?

6.   How often do people rely on introspection for self-knowledge?

7.   According to self-awareness theory, what are the consequences of becoming self-aware? What are strategies people use to become less self-aware?

8.   When is self-knowledge difficult to obtain? Why do causal theories fall short of explaining why we feel or did something? Why is it a problem to rely on language to describe the origins of our feelings? What is reasons-generated attitude change?

9. According to self-perception theory, what besides introspection is a source of self-knowledge? When are we most likely to seek out this source of self-knowledge?

10. What is the overjustification effect? What type of motivation is adversely affected by the overjustification effect? Why is this problematic? Which type of rewards are less likely to result in the overjustification effect?

11. According to the two-factor theory of emotion, how do we understand our emotional states? What is the significance of the main findings of the Schachter and Singer (1962) experiment? What is misattribution of arousal?

12. What is the main difference between the two-factor theory of emotion and cognitive appraisal theories of emotion?

13. Why do we engage in social comparison? What are the consequences of making upward and downward social comparisons? What are motives underlying each type of comparison?

14. How is impression management different from self-presentation? How do we manage our impressions?

15. Why do people self-handicap? What are two ways that we self-handicap?

PRACTICE TEST 1

Fill in the blank

1. The "known" aspect of the self or the self-definition is called _____.

2. The process whereby people look inward and examine their own thoughts, feelings, and motives is known as _____.

3. A theory which states that when people focus their attention on themselves they evaluate and compare their behavior to their internal standards and values is called _____.

4.   A theory about the causes of one's own feelings and behaviors is called a(n) _____.

5.   One theory maintains that when our attitudes and feelings are uncertain or ambiguous we infer these states by observing our behavior and the situation in which it occurs. This theory is called _____.

6.   Rewards that are based on the quality of one's work are called _____ rewards.

7.   Incentive to engage in an activity because it is enjoyable or interesting is called _____.

8.   The finding that people view their behavior as caused by compelling extrinsic reasons and underestimate the extent to which their behavior is caused by intrinsic reasons is termed the _____.

9.   One theory says that people infer what their emotions are by first experiencing physiological arousal and then by using situational cues to suggest an emotional label for that arousal. This theory is called the _____.

10.   Attributing one's arousal to the wrong source, resulting in a mistaken or exaggerated emotion is called _____.

11.   Theories of emotion that state that emotional experiences depend on how one explains and construes an event and do not require feeling physiological arousal are called _____ theories of emotion.

12.   A theory that holds that people learn about their own abilities and attitudes by comparing themselves to others is called _____.

Multiple Choice

1.   When asked "Who am I?" a child is most likely to respond:
      a)   "I'm a nine-year-old."
      b)   "I'm a happy person."
      c)   "My friends think I'm friendly."
      d)   "I'm against corporal punishment."

2.   What is most likely an accurate view of the self in people in Eastern cultures?
      a)   the independent view
      b)   the correspondent view
      c)   the interdependent view
      d)   the individualistic view

3.   Nisbett and Wilson (1977) asked shoppers which pair of identical pantyhose on a display table they preferred and why. Shoppers failed to recognize that the position of the pantyhose caused them to prefer items on the right side of the display because:
      a)   their causal schemas told them that presenting items on the left causes more favorable evaluations.
      b)   participants failed to use causal schemas to make their evaluations.
      c)   participants failed to introspect when making their evaluations.
      d)   their causal schemas told them that the position of items does not affect preference.

51

4. According to Daryl Bem's (1972) self-perception theory, when internal cues about attitudes or personality are weak, ambiguous, or uninterpretable, people:
   a) cannot form accurate self-perceptions.
   b) engage in introspection to determine how they feel and so clarify the meaning of their internal cues.
   c) compare their behaviors to stronger internal cues such as values and standards for behavior.
   d) infer their own internal states by observing their own overt behavior.

5. The act of thinking about ourselves is called:
   a) self-perception.
   b) self-concept.
   c) self-schemas.
   d) self-awareness.

6. Giving teenagers extra privileges in exchange for doing household chores will probably not produce the overjustification effect because:
   a) extrinsic interest in this activity is initially high.
   b) intrinsic interest in this activity is initially low.
   c) teenagers have already learned to operate within a system of rewards and punishments.
   d) extra privileges are not extrinsic motivators for teenagers.

7. Which type of rewards are more likely to lead to the overjustification effect?
   a) performance-contingent rewards
   b) task-contingent rewards
   c) instrinsic-contingent rewards
   d) response-contingent rewards

8. The two factors in Schachter's (1964) two-factor theory of emotion are:
   a) physiological arousal and introspection.
   b) overt behavior and observing that behavior from an external perspective.
   c) physiological arousal and seeking a label that explains the arousal.
   d) overt behavior and seeking an explanation for the behavior.

9. Which of the following demonstrates the misattribution of arousal?
   a) You rarely pet cats and infer that you do not like them.
   b) You panic in the belief that you will fail an exam after taking two caffeine tablets to get you through an "all-nighter."
   c) You find your job at the bookstore less enjoyable following a substantial raise in pay.
   d) All of the above demonstrate the misattribution of arousal.

10. What is the main difference between the two-factor theory of emotion and the cognitive appraisal theories of emotion?
   a) The two-factor theory does not acknowledge the existence of physiological arousal.
   b) The cognitive appraisal theories do not acknowledge the role of cognitive interpretations of events in the experience of emotion.
   c) The cognitive appraisal theories acknowledge biological influences on emotional experience.
   d) The cognitive appraisal theories do not acknowledge the existence of physiological arousal in the experience of emotion.

11. The ____ function of the self regulates our behavior while the ____ function of the self helps us interpret information about ourselves and the social world.
    a) emotional; organizational
    b) spiritual; executive
    c) organizational; executive
    d) executive; organizational

12. Which of the following is true about self-control?
    a) We are better at it when we are well rested.
    b) Being under stress increases people's self-control.
    c) People are better at self-control if they haven't been practicing it very long.
    d) Alcoholics who stop drinking have a worse than average chance of quitting smoking.

13. Which of the following theories begins with the supposition that people have a need to evaluate their opinions and abilities?
    a) impression management theory
    b) the two factor theory of emotion
    c) social comparison theory
    d) self-perception theory

14. Which of the following is an example of ingratiation?
    a) boasting that the school's track star is your roommate
    b) setting out to impress your psychology classmates with the knowledge you gained over the summer working at a clinic
    c) partying rather than studying the night before a difficult exam
    d) complementing your professor on his choice of ties today

15. Which of the following is true about introspection?
    a) Males are more introspective than females.
    b) Introspection is useful in explaining why we feel or behave the way we do.
    c) As an internal process, it cannot be initiated by external factors.
    d) We do not rely on this source of information as often as we think we do.

Short Answer

1. Argue that self-perception theory is a variation on attribution theory discussed in Chapter 4.

2. You have been dating someone for a week now and have decided that before the relationship goes any further that it would be a good idea to introspect about the reasons WHY you like this person. What is likely to happen as you introspect? What negative consequence might arise from your introspection?

3. What are the advantages and disadvantages of self-awareness?

PRACTICE TEST 2

Fill in the Blank

1. Comparing ourselves to people who are better than we are on a particular trait or ability, in order to determine the standard of excellence, is called _____.

2. Providing others with an image of who you are or who you want others to believe you are through your words, nonverbal behaviors, and your actions is called _____.

3. Consciously or unconsciously orchestrating a carefully designed presentation of self that will create a certain impression that fits your goals or needs in social interaction is called _____.

4. The process whereby people flatter, praise, and generally try to make themselves likable to another, often higher status person, is a self-presentational strategy known as _____.

5. Creating obstacles and excuses to explain potentially poor performance is a self-presentational strategy called _____.

6. Defining oneself in terms of one's relationships to other people and recognizing that one considers others' thoughts and feelings prior to making a decision or performing an action indicates an _____ view of the self.

7. Research has found that people in many Western cultures have an _____ view of the self.

8. Incentive to engage in a behavior because of the external rewards one receives is called _____.

9. Attitude change that results from thinking about the reasons behind one's attitudes is called _____ attitude change.

10. Rewards that are based on the performance of a job are called _____ rewards.

11. When people want to protect or enhance their self-concepts by comparing themselves to others who are doing worse in a pertinent area, they are making _____ social comparisons.

Multiple Choice

1. Deciding that you are in a bad mood because it is Monday is an example of a(n)
   a) availability heuristic.
   b) causal theory.
   c) perceptual set.
   d) self-schema.

2. Which of the following demonstrates the overjustification effect?
   a) A band member enjoys her job as a guitarist in a band and decides to go solo.
   b) Hugo loves to read and joins a book club that requires a monthly fee.
   c) Pamela quits her job as a secretary because she finds it boring and goes back to school.
   d) An engineer who loved to solve mechanical problems as a child now views them as dreary tasks.

3. Participants in a study by Schachter and Singer (1962) who unwittingly took epinephrine, a drug that causes arousal, felt angry when filling out an insulting questionnaire in the presence of another angry individual because:
   a) epinephrine made them angry.
   b) they experienced arousal and sought out an explanation or label for that arousal in the situation.
   c) the epinephrine heightened the feeling of annoyance produced by the questionnaire.
   d) heightened arousal enabled subjects to experience empathy for the other individual and so experience his anger.

4. According to _____ theory, when we attend to ourselves we compare our current actions to our internal values.
   a) self-perception
   b) self-awareness
   c) attribution
   d) self-evaluation maintenance

5. Writing a list of explanations for why people chose their romantic partners may decrease temporarily their love for their partners due to:
   a) cognitive dissonance.
   b) reasons-generated attitude change.
   c) self-awareness.
   d) overjustification effect.

6. Lewis and Brooks (1978) found that self-recognition, a rudimentary self-concept, develops at around _____ of age.
   a) two months
   b) six months
   c) one year
   d) two years

7. In order to gain important self-knowledge, people choose to compare themselves to:
   a) others who are similar to them on the important attribute or dimension.
   b) individuals regarded as "typical" on the important attribute or dimension.
   c) individuals regarded as "the best" on the important attribute or dimension.
   d) others who are inferior to them on the important attribute or dimension.

8. While self-handicapping may prevent unflattering attributions for our failures, it often has the negative consequence of
   a) creating the impression that one is a pompous, arrogant braggart.
   b) creating the impression that one is "kissing up."
   c) causing the poor performance that is feared in the first place.
   d) increasing dependence on others for self-esteem.

9. Enjoyment is to _____ motivation as reward is to _____ motivation.
   a) intrinsic; extrinsic
   b) internal; external
   c) extrinsic; intrinsic
   d) external; internal

10. We use _____ social comparison when we want to better ourselves and we use _____ social comparison when we want to feel better about ourselves.
    a) downward; upward
    b) upward; downward
    c) external; internal
    d) biased; unbiased

11. When we want people to form a particular impression of ourselves we engage in:
    a) self-presentation.
    b) self-appraisal.
    c) impression management.
    d) self-management.

12.   According to Festinger's social comparison theory, when will people compare themselves with other people and with whom do they compare themselves?
        a)   when they have an objective standard for comparison and with people who are dissimilar to them
        b)   when they have an objective standard for comparison and with people who are similar to them
        c)   when they DO NOT have an objective standard for comparison, when they are uncertain about themselves, and with people who are dissimilar to them
        d)   when they DO NOT have an objective standard for comparison, when they are uncertain about themselves, and with people who are similar to them
        e)   when they DO NOT have an objective standard for comparison, when they are certain about themselves, and with people who are similar to them

13.   Wilson et al. (1993) found that the decisions people make following reasons-generated attitude change:
        a)   are usually accurate.
        b)   are ones that people tend to regret.
        c)   reveal valuable information about their self-concepts.
        d)   tend to be consistent with their true attitudes.

14.   Participants in Nisbett and Wilson's (1977) experiment reported that a distracting noise had affected their ratings of a film when, in fact, it had not. These results may be explained by concluding that participants:
        a)   failed to use causal theories.
        b)   failed to use introspection.
        c)   exhibited reasons-generated attitude change.
        d)   generated a faulty causal theory.

15.   Rose Marie once found painting to be an enjoyable hobby. Now that she works as a commercial artist, however, she rarely paints in her spare time. Rose Marie might begin to enjoy painting again if she:
        a)   focuses on the external rewards that painting offers her.
        b)   learns new painting techniques.
        c)   focuses on the intrinsic reasons for painting and distances herself from the external rewards she receives from her job.
        d)   quits her job and becomes a self-employed artist.

Short Answer

1.   Compare and contrast self-perception theory and the two-factor theory of emotion.

2.   You have worked in the library for two years. One year ago, if someone had asked you how much you liked your job, you would have said that you liked it very much. Since then, you have received a large raise in pay. Why, if you overjustify your reason for working at the library, will you claim to like the job less following your raise?

WEB EXERCISE

Go to www.socialpsychology.org. Click on Online Social Psychology Studies, then click on Social Topics, followed by clicking on Self and Social Identity, and finally click on the link to the National Association for Self-Esteem. Take the Self-Esteem Self-Evaluation Survey and write up your reactions. Or, instead of the National Association for Self-Esteem, click on the link to the International Society for Self and Identity. Check out the abstracts of research papers on these topics and summarize the three you find the most interesting.

CHAPTER 6

Self-Justification and the Need to Maintain Self-Esteem

CHAPTER OVERVIEW

Chapter 6 focuses on the consequences of the need people have to justify their actions in order to maintain their self-esteem. Cognitive dissonance explains why some people's feelings and behaviors seem counterintuitive. One main finding of this research area is that making irrevocable decisions, expending effort to attain a goal, and counterattitudinal advocacy can all result in dissonance. Since dissonance is perceived as unpleasant, different ways to reduce dissonance exist and are described.

The second part of the chapter is concerned with recent research and theories on self-justification and self-esteem maintenance. For example, the focus of self-discrepancy theory is on how inconsistencies within aspects of one's self can result in dissonance. In addition, self-completion theory, self-evaluation maintenance theory, and self-affirmation theory also have arisen based on cognitive dissonance theory and research. These theories offer qualifications and additions to cognitive dissonance theory. The chapter also explains individual differences in people's need to self-verify versus self-enhance. Lastly, the chapter shows how dissonance reduction can result in a rationalization trap and that this tendency depends on cultural influences.

CHAPTER OUTLINE

The Need to Justify our Actions

    The Theory of Cognitive Dissonance

    Rational Behavior Versus Rationalizing Behavior

    Decisions, Decisions, Decisions

    The Justification of Effort

    The Psychology of Insufficient Justification

    The Aftermath of Good and Bad Deeds

    The Evidence for Motivational Arousal

New Directions in Research on Self-Justification

    Self-Discrepancy Theory

    Self-Completion Theory

    Self-Evaluation Maintenance Theory

    Self-Affirmation Theory

Self-Justification Versus Self-Maintenance: The Role of Negative Self-Beliefs

    Self-Verification versus Self-Enhancement

Dissonance Reduction and Culture

Avoiding the Rationalization Trap

Learning from Our Mistakes

Heaven's Gate Revisited

LEARNING OBJECTIVES

After reading Chapter 6, you should be able to do the following:

1.   Describe the theory of cognitive dissonance. Discuss the conditions that elicit dissonance and what strategies we use to reduce dissonance. Explain what is meant by rational behavior versus rationalizing behavior. (pp. 174-178)

2.   Identify the consequences of making important decisions. Define post-decision dissonance. Explain how changing our attitudes after a decision serves to reduce dissonance. (pp. 178-179)

3.   Identify the role played by the irrevocability of decisions in producing dissonance. Define "lowballing" and explain why the technique is effective. (pp. 179-180)

4.   Describe the effects of deciding to behave morally or immorally on the experience of dissonance and the reduction of dissonance. (pp. 180-182)

5.   Define what is meant by justification of effort. Identify the consequences of working hard to attain something worthless and the importance of volunteering such effort. (pp. 182-184)

6.   Distinguish between internal and external justification. Define counter-attitudinal advocacy. Describe the effects of inducing counter-attitudinal advocacy with minimum external justification. Discuss the application of counter-attitudinal advocacy to race relations and AIDS prevention. (pp. 184-187)

7.   Explain how insufficient punishment and insufficient justification lead to self-persuasion. Describe the effects of self-persuasion on behavior. (pp. 188-192)

8.   Discuss the effects of doing favors for people we don't like. Define the Ben Franklin effect. Describe the effects of harming others. Identify the causes and consequences of dehumanizing victims. (pp. 192-196)

9.   Discuss evidence for a physiological component of dissonance and its consequences. (pp. 196-197)

10.   Define self-discrepancy theory. Discuss consequences of conflict between the actual self and the ideal self and ought selves. Describe how dissonance due to self-discrepancy can be reduced. (pp. 198-200)

11.   Define self-completion theory. Describe how a positive self-image can be maintained according to this theory. (pp. 200-201)

12.   Distinguish between dissonance theory and self-evaluation maintenance theory. Identify the three important predictors of dissonance according to self-evaluation maintenance theory. Describe the conditions when we bask in the reflected glory of a friend's achievements and when we experience dissonance. Identify strategies to reduce dissonance. Describe the implications of dissonance for helping strangers and helping friends according to self-evaluation maintenance theory. (pp. 201-204)

13.   Define self-affirmation theory. Describe the conditions under which self-affirmation will be used to reduce dissonance and discuss how self-affirmation differs from other strategies we use to reduce dissonance. (pp. 204-206)

14. Define self-verification theory. Identify two reasons why people with negative self-views might be motivated to maintain this negative view. Describe the conditions when people with negative self-views prefer self-verifying information over self-enhancing information. (pp. 206-208)

15. Discuss the effects of culture on dissonance reduction. Define a "rationalization trap." Describe the relationship between self-affirmation and the rationalization trap. (pp. 208-210)

KEY TERMS

cognitive dissonance (p. 174)

post-decision dissonance (p. 178)

lowballing (p. 179)

justification of effort (p. 182)

external justification (p. 184)

internal justification (p. 185)

counterattitudinal advocacy (p. 185)

insufficient punishment (p. 189)

self-persuasion (p. 190)

self-discrepancy theory (p. 198)

self-completion theory (p. 200)

self-evaluation maintenance theory (p. 201)

self-affirmation theory (p. 204)

self-verification theory (p. 207)

self-justification (p. 207)

rationalization trap (p. 209)

STUDY QUESTIONS

1. What are conditions that may result in cognitive dissonance? Why does cognitive dissonance occur?

2. What is the relationship between making important decisions and experiencing dissonance? What happens to attitudes toward the chosen alternative and the alternative that is not chosen? How does the permanence of the decision affect the experience of dissonance?

3. Why is lowballing an effective persuasion technique? How does dissonance reduction after a moral decision affect people's tendency to behave ethically or unethically in the future?

4. What is the relationship between the justification of effort and dissonance reduction?

5. Why can insufficient justification result in dissonance? What are the consequences of reducing dissonance through external justification compared to internal justification? When does counterattitudinal advocacy result in private attitude change?

6. What are the effects of insufficient punishment on the judgments of an object or entity? What are the effects of mild versus severe threats on the level of dissonance experienced?

7. Why is self-persuasion a long-lasting form of attitude change?

8. What are the consequences of doing something unpleasant for a friend compared to doing something unpleasant for someone who is disliked? What are the effects of doing a favor for someone on how much this person is liked? How and why does dehumanizing victims occur?

9. What does self-discrepancy theory explain? How is dissonance reduced according to this theory?

10. What is self-completion theory? How is dissonance reduced according to this theory?

11. What is self-evaluation maintenance theory? What are two necessary factors for the occurrence of dissonance according to this theory? How does this theory explain why people may help strangers more than they help their friends?

12. What causes dissonance according to self-affirmation theory? How is dissonance reduced according to this theory?

13. When do people prefer self-verification more than self-enhancement?

14. What is a rationalization trap and how does one develop? How can this trap be avoided? What can other cultures teach us about avoiding this trap?

PRACTICE TEST 1

Fill in the Blank

1. A feeling of discomfort caused by performing an action that is discrepant from one's conception of oneself as a decent and sensible person is called _____.

2. Dissonance that is aroused after a person makes a decision is called _____.

3. Raising the price of a product after inducing the customer to agree to pay a very low price is an unscrupulous sales strategy called _____.

4. The tendency for people to increase their liking for something they have worked hard to attain is called _____.

5. A person's reason or explanation for his/her dissonant behavior that resides outside the individual is known as _____.

6. Reducing dissonance by changing something about oneself is called _____.

7. A process by which individuals are induced to state an opinion or attitude that runs counter to their own private belief or attitude is called a _____.

8. The theory that predicts people will get distressed when their sense of their actual self conflicts with their desired self-conceptions is called _____.

Multiple Choice

1. An individual who strongly opposes helmet laws is excited to find a study which shows that neck injuries are a more common outcome of motorcycle accidents when helmets are worn than when helmets are not worn. This individual is reducing dissonance by:
    a) changing behavior to bring it in line with the dissonant cognition.
    b) adding cognitions that justify the behavior.
    c) modifying dissonant cognitions to justify the behavior.
    d) adopting a self-concept that is consistent with the behavior.

2. If a participant in Brehm's (1956) study claimed that an iron and an electric can opener were equally desirable appliances, she was asked to choose one of these as a gift. Later she was asked to rerate the two appliances. If she chose the can opener, her second rating of the appliances were typically:
    a) lower for the can opener and higher for the iron.
    b) lower for the can opener and lower for the iron.
    c) higher for the can opener and higher for the iron.
    d) higher for the can opener and lower for the iron.

3. An insurance salesperson offers a home insurance policy to customers at a very low rate. Just before the sale, however, he claims to have realized an error in his calculations. The actual cost of the policy, he claims, is substantially greater than he originally estimated. What is the name of the unscrupulous strategy used by the insurance salesperson?
    a) lowballing
    b) hard selling
    c) counter-attitudinal advocacy
    d) rationalizing

4. Mills (1958) had children compete on a difficult exam under conditions that made cheating easy and presumably undetectable. The children's attitudes toward cheating were measured the next day and revealed that:
    a) children who cheated adopted a harsher attitude toward cheating while those who resisted cheating became more lenient toward cheating.
    b) children adopted a more lenient attitude toward cheating after competing with each other.
    c) children who cheated became more lenient toward cheating while those who resisted cheating adopted a harsher attitude toward cheating.
    d) children became more lenient toward cheating after competing with each other.

5. In the Festinger and Carlsmith (1959) experiment, participants who were paid $20.00 to lie felt less dissonance than subjects paid $1.00 because receiving $20.00:
    a) put participants in a good mood that counteracted dissonance.
    b) provided self-verification cues that participants were in fact moral people.
    c) was sufficient external justification for lying.
    d) allowed subjects to affirm their worth and circumvented dissonance.

6. Dehumanizing the victim increases:
    a) dissonance caused by our cruel treatment of others.
    b) the likelihood that cruel treatment will continue or even escalate.
    c) empathy for the victim.
    d) the likelihood that hostilities will end.

7. While most dissonance research has focused on how our own behavior threatens our self-image, research on self-evaluation maintenance theory focuses on:
    a) how our own behavior threatens the image other people have of us.
    b) how other people's behavior threatens their self-image.
    c) how other people's behavior threatens our self-image.
    d) how our own behavior reveals our self-image to others.

8. According to self-evaluation maintenance theory, we want our friends to do well on tasks of low self-relevance so that we can:
    a) bask in the reflected glory of our friends' achievements.
    b) distract our friends from excelling on tasks of high self-relevance.
    c) make the task more relevant to ourselves.
    d) provide some distance between ourselves and our friends.

9. Which of the following best characterizes the role of self-enhancement needs in people with poor opinions of themselves?
    a) People with poor opinions of themselves are not motivated by self-enhancement needs.
    b) People with poor opinions of themselves feel an especially great need for self-enhancement.
    c) Among people with poor opinions of themselves, the need for self-enhancement is likely to conflict with self-verification needs.
    d) Among people with poor opinions of themselves, self-enhancement is likely to be self-verifying.

10. In order to learn from our mistakes, we must be able to:
    a) circumvent dissonance by affirming our positive qualities.
    b) find both internal and external justification for our behaviors.
    c) deny the existence of inconsistent beliefs.
    d) tolerate dissonance long enough to examine the situation objectively.

11. In general, the most rational way to reduce dissonance that follows foolish or immoral behavior is to:
    a) justify the behavior by adding cognitions to support it.
    b) justify the behavior by modifying dissonant cognitions.
    c) change the behavior to bring it in line with the dissonant cognition.
    d) adopt a self-concept that is consistent with the behavior.

12. Imagine that you've agreed to buy a notoriously unreliable but attractive sports car instead of a less attractive but dependable station wagon. Which of the following will reduce dissonance in this situation?
    a) knowing that you've purchased an unreliable car
    b) thinking that you could rely on the station wagon
    c) putting a substantial down payment on the sports car
    d) imagining how good you'll look in the sports car

13. When a counter-attitudinal advocacy is accomplished with a minimum of external justification,
    a) private attitudes change in the direction of public statements.
    b) public statements change in the direction of private attitudes.
    c) private attitudes and public statements tend to spread apart.
    d) private attitudes are subtly revealed in public statements.

14.　Aronson and Carlsmith (1963) told children that they were not allowed to play with a highly desirable toy and measured the children's liking for the toy after this rule was obeyed in the experimenter's absence. They found that children's liking for the toy:
 a)　increased when the rule was accompanied by a mild threat.
 b)　decreased when the rule was accompanied by a severe threat.
 c)　decreased when the rule was accompanied by a mild threat.
 d)　increased when the experimenter left the room.

15.　Dissonance theory predicts that if we do a favor for someone we dislike, we will:
 a)　expect a favor in return.
 b)　come to like that person.
 c)　feel that we are weak.
 d)　expect to be taken advantage of.

Short Answer

1.　How do groups ensure the loyalty of their members by requiring them to endure severe initiation procedures before joining?

2.　Contrast the sources of dissonance described in self-completion theory compared to self-discrepancy theory.

3.　The announcer on the radio congratulates caller number ten. She's just won a prize and is asked what her favorite radio station is. Ecstatically, she states the station's call letters. Why is her subsequent opinion of the station likely to be higher if her prize was a T-shirt than if her prize was $100?

PRACTICE TEST 2

Fill in the Blank

1.　External justification that is insufficient for having resisted a desired activity or object and which usually results in individuals devaluing the activity or object is called _____.

2.　A long-term form of attitude change that results from attempts at self-justification is called

_____.

3.　A theory of dissonance in interpersonal relationships maintains that dissonance is a function of how we perform on a task relative to another person, how close we are to that person, and how relevant the task is to our self-image. This theory is called _____.

4.　A theory suggesting that people will reduce the impact of a dissonance arousing threat by focusing on and affirming their competence on some dimension unrelated to the threat is called _____.

5.　A theory suggesting that people have a need to seek confirmation of their self-concept, whether the self-concept is positive or negative, is called _____.

6.　The web of distortion that we trap ourselves in by rationalizing past behaviors and that prevents us from seeing things as they really are is called the _____.

7.　The tendency to justify one's actions in order to maintain one's self-esteem is called

_____.

8. The prediction that when people experience a threat to an important part of their self-concept they will be motivated to achieve social recognition for that aspect of their identity is made by _____.

Multiple Choice

1. Aronson et al. (1991) found that students who composed arguments in favor of the use of condoms, recited them on videotape, and were made aware of their own failure to use condoms were:
   a) less likely to buy condoms than the students in the other conditions.
   b) more likely to buy condoms than the students in the other conditions.
   c) less likely to report using condoms than the students in the other conditions.
   d) equally likely to buy condoms as the students in the other conditions.

2. If we cannot rationalize away a threat to our self-esteem we can avoid dissonance by asserting our competence and integrity in some other area. This is the rationale of _____ theory.
   a) self-affirmation
   b) self-evaluation maintenance
   c) self-verification
   d) cognitive dissonance

3. The combined findings of research on dissonance, self-evaluation maintenance, and self-affirmation theories suggest that humans:
   a) generally suffer from low self-esteem induced by a constant state of tension.
   b) are limited in their abilities to restore esteem.
   c) are flexible in finding ways to restore esteem.
   d) generally take a rational approach to the restoration of their self-esteem.

4. Through the reduction of dissonance, there is a tendency to catch ourselves up in a web of distortion that prevents us from seeing things as they really are. This phenomenon is known as the:
   a) distortion web.
   b) rationalization trap.
   c) ego-defensive snare.
   d) self-verification lure.

5. People may say that they like a boring task on which they spent a lot of time and expense due to:
   a) justification of effort.
   b) post-decision dissonance.
   c) lowballing.
   d) insufficient punishment.

6. The success of the lowballing technique is due to:
   a) the commitment already made to the purchase.
   b) the illusion of irrevocability.
   c) dissonance reduction techniques.
   d) all the above.

7. The tendency to validate one's actions to maintain one's self-esteem is called:
   a) self-verification.
   b) self-justification.
   c) self-affirmation.
   d) self-evaluation.

8. According to self-discrepancy theory, the type of person we hope to be reflects our _____ self and the type of person we believe we should be reflects our _____ self.
   a) actual; ideal
   b) ideal; ought
   c) ideal; actual
   d) actual; ought

9. Large rewards and severe punishments are examples of _____ justification for behavior and result in _____ attitude change.
   a) internal; great
   b) external; great
   c) internal; little
   d) external; little

10. According to self-discrepancy theory, when people are made aware of a discrepancy between their actual and their ideal selves they are likely to experience which emotion(s)?
   a) anxiety
   b) sadness
   c) dejection
   d) both sadness and dejection
   e) anxiety, sadness, and dejection

11. Carla considers herself a good actress and recently was turned down for a part in a community production. Carla would take the first opportunity to prove her acting ability according to which theory?
   a) self-completion theory
   b) self-affirmation theory
   c) self-discrepancy theory
   d) self-perception theory

12. Which of the following is true about dissonance reduction and culture?
   a) Only Westerners feel dissonance and therefore the need to reduce it.
   b) Only Easterners feel dissonance and therefore the need to reduce it.
   c) Both Westerners and Easterners feel dissonance but only Westerners need to reduce it.
   d) Both Westerners and Easterners feel dissonance and both need to reduce it.

13. Charles loves to go drag racing. One day, he comes across an article indicating how dangerous the sport can be. He starts to feel tense. How might Charles get rid of this uneasy feeling, according to cognitive dissonance theory?
   a) decide that he does not want to drag race in the future
   b) convince himself that the source of the article is not credible
   c) selectively expose himself to information that says that drag racing can be safe
   d) decide that the reason he feels uncomfortable is that he is being evaluated at his job tomorrow and not that he is upset about how dangerous drag racing can be
   e) any of the above may reduce dissonance

14. Ann Marie supports drilling in the Alaskan wilderness. Shawn wants to convince her that drilling there should be banned. According to cognitive dissonance theory, what could Shawn do to change her attitude?
   a) Give her a large reward to openly endorse a ban on drilling.
   b) Provide her with many strong arguments and facts that support a ban on drilling.
   c) Create the illusion that everyone else favors a ban on drilling, so that going against them makes her feel uncomfortable.
   d) Offer her a small, but adequate, reward to openly endorse a ban on drilling.

15. Cognitive dissonance is:
    a) the sense of well-being that arises when self-esteem needs and needs for accuracy are satisfied.
    b) the confusion that occurs when situations evoke emotions that do not seem appropriate for the given situation.
    c) the discomfort caused by engaging in a behavior that is discrepant from one's conception of oneself as a decent and sensible person.
    d) a change in attitude that follows the careful analysis of arguments relevant to an issue.

Short Answer

1. Experimental participants who voluntarily wrote a counter-attitudinal essay showed the most attitude change when they had taken a placebo that was supposed to relax them. How does this finding support the existence of physiological arousal in dissonance?

2. Argue that humans are very flexible in maintaining their self-esteem by discussing the various strategies we may use to reduce dissonance according to the theory of cognitive dissonance, self-evaluation theory, and self-affirmation theory.

WEB EXERCISE

Go to www.prenhall.com/aronson. Click on the links for Chapter 6. Click on the Media's Perception of Self-esteem Research. What points is the author making in the U.S. News and World Report article? Based on your reading of this chapter, what are your reactions to the article? Explain.

CHAPTER 7

Attitudes and Attitude Change: Influencing Thoughts and Feelings

CHAPTER OVERVIEW

In Chapter 7, the topics of attitudes and attitude change are examined. The reasons why it is useful to know whether an attitude is affectively, cognitively, or behaviorally based are explained. The concepts of attitude strength and accessibility also are mentioned in this section.

Attitude change models are discussed in the next section. The precursors and consequences of two routes to persuasion, the central and the peripheral, are addressed. In addition to informing readers about how to change attitudes, the chapter provides information on how to resist attitude change and peer pressure through attitude inoculation procedures.

Attitudes also are studied for their predictive value. Conditions that increase the consistency between attitudes and spontaneous and deliberative behaviors are reviewed. Lastly, the chapter discusses why and how advertising is effective at changing the buying behavior of consumers. The controversial topic of subliminal advertising is presented.

CHAPTER OUTLINE

The Nature and Origin of Attitudes

       Where Do Attitudes Come From?

       Attitude Strength and Attitude Accessibility

Attitude Change

       Changing Attitudes by Changing Behavior: Cognitive Dissonance Theory Revisited

       Persuasive Communications and Attitude Change

       Emotion and Attitude Change

How to Make People Resistant to Attitude Change

       Attitude Inoculation

       Resisting Peer Pressure

       When Persuasion Attempts Boomerang: Reactance Theory

When Will Attitudes Predict Behavior?

       Predicting Spontaneous Behaviors

       Predicting Deliberative Behaviors

The Power of Advertising

> How Advertising Works

> Subliminal Advertising: A New Form of Mind Control?

LEARNING OBJECTIVES

After reading Chapter 7, you should be able to do the following:

1. Define an attitude and identify its components. Discuss the differences between cognitively based attitudes and affectively based attitudes. (pp. 217-219)

2. Explain how affectively based attitudes are formed via classical conditioning and operant conditioning. (pp. 219-220)

3. Define a behaviorally based attitude and discuss how it is formed. (p. 220)

4. Identify different determinants of attitude strength. Discuss the relationship between an attitude's strength and its accessibility and the resistance to change the attitude. Discuss the conditions that increase accessibility and resistance to attitude change. (pp. 220-222)

5. Discuss the role of cognitive dissonance in attitude change. Identify the conditions under which attitude change via cognitive dissonance is most likely. Distinguish between internal and external justification and discuss the role of "counter-attitudinal advocacy" in producing dissonance and attitude change. (pp. 222-223)

6. Explain why advertisers favor persuasive communications over dissonance techniques to change attitudes. (p. 223)

7. Describe the Yale Attitude Change Approach. Identify and define the three factors in an influence setting emphasized by this approach. Provide examples of each factor. Identify a problem with the Yale Attitude Change Approach. (pp. 223-225)

8. Describe the aim of attitude change models like Petty and Cacioppo's elaboration likelihood model and Chaiken's heuristic-systematic model of persuasion. (pp. 225-232)

9. Identify the two routes to persuasion described in the elaboration likelihood model. Identify the factors that determine the route people take. Identify factors that increase people's motivation and ability to pay attention to the arguments. Discuss how attitudes changed by the central route to persuasion differ from attitudes changed by the peripheral route. (pp. 225-230)

10. Discuss the influence of different moods on persuasion. Identify the role of fear-arousing communications in persuasion. Describe the conditions under which fear appeals foster or inhibit attitude change. (pp. 230-232)

11. Describe the process whereby emotions act as heuristics to persuasion according to the heuristic-systematic model of persuasion. Identify the problem with using emotions as a guide to attitude formation. (pp. 232-233)

12. Identify the most effective means of changing affectively and cognitively based attitudes. (pp. 233-234)

13. Discuss cross-cultural differences in the kinds of attitudes people have and how these attitudes are changed. (pp. 234-235)

14. Identify the purpose of attitude inoculation. Identify a potential disadvantage of making people resistant to attitude change. Discuss the role of reactance when persuasion attempts "boomerang." (pp. 235-237)

15. Describe the conditions under which attitudes predict spontaneous and deliberative behaviors. Discuss the role of attitude accessibility in predicting spontaneous behaviors. Discuss the role of people's intentions and other variables outlined in the theory of planned behavior in predicting deliberative behaviors. Define and explain the relationship between attitudes toward behaviors, subjective norms, and perceived behavioral control that is outlined in the theory of planned behavior. (pp. 237-240)

16. Identify the most effective advertising strategies for changing affectively and cognitively based attitudes when personal relevance is high, for changing cognitively based attitudes when personal relevance is low, and for selling bland products that evoke few emotions. (pp. 241-243)

17. Discuss the controversial topic of subliminal advertising and evaluate the claim that subliminal messages are effective. Describe evidence for subliminal influence from laboratory experiments. Identify what research has found regarding the power of advertising that is consciously perceived. (pp. 243-248)

KEY TERMS

attitude (p. 217)

cognitively based attitude (p. 218)

affectively based attitude (p. 218)

classical conditioning (p. 219)

operant conditioning (p. 219)

behaviorally based attitude (p. 220)

attitude accessibility (p. 221)

persuasive communication (p. 223)

Yale Attitude Change approach (p. 224)

elaboration likelihood model (p.225)

central route to persuasion (p. 225)

peripheral route to persuasion (p. 225)

need for cognition (p. 227)

fear-arousing communications (p. 231)

heuristic-systematic model of persuasion (p. 232)

attitude inoculation (p. 235)

reactance theory (p. 237)

theory of planned behavior (p. 239)

subjective norms (p. 240)

subliminal messages (p. 243)

STUDY QUESTIONS

1.   What is an attitude and what are its components? Why is it important to consider each of these components?

2.   What are the origins and aspects of affectively based attitudes?

3.   When do people infer their attitudes from their behavior?

4.   What is the relationship between attitude accessibility and attitude strength? How does an attitude become accessible?

5.   When does counterattitudinal advocacy lead to private attitude change? What is the process underlying this change?

6.   According to the Yale Attitude Change Approach, what are the three main elements in a persuasive situation?

7.   What are the major differences between the central and peripheral routes to persuasion? What are people attending to when they use each route? When are people more likely to use the central route compared to the peripheral route? What are two motives for the use of the central route, according to the elaboration likelihood model?

8.   What are some examples of peripheral cues? What route to persuasion leads to lasting attitude change?

9. How do emotions, like moods, influence persuasion? How do emotions act as a heuristic to persuasion and what route to persuasion are people taking when they use their emotions as a guide to attitude formation?

10. What level of fear is most effective in a persuasive communication? What is the best strategy if you are hoping to arouse fear in your persuasive communication? Why?

11. What are important factors to consider when designing a persuasive communication?

12. What is the purpose of attitude inoculation and how should this process be implemented? What are ways to resist peer pressure? What is reactance and how may it occur?

13. Under what conditions do attitudes predict spontaneous and deliberative behaviors? How does the theory of planned behavior predict deliberative behaviors?

14. Is there evidence that subliminal messages in a persuasive communication influence our behavior in everyday life?

15. How do ads perpetuate stereotypical patterns of thinking? Provide examples.

PRACTICE TEST 1

Fill in the Blank

1. An enduring evaluation--positive or negative--of people, objects, and ideas is called a(n) _____.

2. The component of an attitude comprised of the emotions and feelings people associate with an attitude object is called the _____ component.

3. The component of an attitude comprised of people's beliefs about the properties of the attitude object is called the _____ component.

4. The component of an attitude comprised of people's actions toward the attitude object is called the
    _____ component.

5. A communication advocating a particular side of an issue is called a(n)
    _____.

6. The study of the conditions under which people are most likely to change their attitudes in response to
    persuasive messages is called the _____.

7. A theory that specifies when people will take the central or peripheral route to persuasion when presented with
    a persuasive communication is called the _____.

8. The route to persuasion people take when they carefully think about and process the content of a persuasive
    communication is called the _____ route.

9. The route to persuasion people take when they are persuaded by surface characteristics of a persuasive
    communication is called the _____ route.

10. The extent to which a topic has important consequences for people's well-being is referred to as
    _____.

11. Persuasive messages that attempt to change people's attitudes by arousing their fears are called
    _____.

12. Attitudes that are based primarily on people's beliefs about the properties of the attitude object are called
    _____.

Multiple Choice

1. Responding to a "puppies for sale" ad, you arrive at the seller's home and immediately fall in love with the first
    puppy you see. The component of your attitude toward the puppy that is exemplified by such a reaction is
    called the ____ component.
    a)   behavioral
    b)   cognitive
    c)   affective
    d)   heuristic

2. While studying the conditions under which people are most likely to be influenced by persuasive
    communications, Hovland and colleagues at Yale repeatedly asked:
    a)   who says what to whom?
    b)   when will logical arguments persuade people and when will more
            superficial characteristics do so?
    c)   why are communications persuasive?
    d)   what condition produces the most influence?

3. Distraction during a persuasive message and message complexity prevent the careful consideration of relevant
    arguments by decreasing the:
    a)   motivation to attend to relevant arguments.
    b)   ability to attend to relevant arguments.
    c)   personal relevance of the message.
    d)   degree of association between message characteristics and internal
            response cues.

4. Though fear-arousing communications are threatening, people will reduce this threat by changing their attitudes and behaviors only when:
    a)   the communication produces an extremely high level of fear.
    b)   the fear-arousing message can be easily ignored.
    c)   the fear-arousing communication is directed at individuals with high levels of self-esteem.
    d)   the fear-arousing communication offers suggestions about how to avoid the threat.

5. Children may adopt prejudiced attitudes through operant conditioning if their parents:
    a)   associate such attitudes with emotionally positive stimuli.
    b)   punish them for expressing such attitudes.
    c)   reward them for expressing such attitudes.
    d)   present arguments favoring such attitudes.

6. Which of the following is true regarding when attitudes will predict spontaneous or deliberative behaviors?
    a)   Attitudes will predict spontaneous behaviors when they are very accessible.
    b)   Attitude-behavioral consistency is high among people with accessible attitudes.
    c)   Deliberate behaviors are predicted by people's intentions.
    d)   Both a and b are true.
    e)   All the above are true.

7. A personality variable that has been linked to the use of the central route to persuasion is:
    a)   need for emotion.
    b)   need for reason.
    c)   need for explanation.
    d)   need for cognition.

8. Good moods are most likely to result in taking the ____ route to persuasion.
    a)   central
    b)   heuristic
    c)   peripheral
    d)   cognitive

9. Words or pictures that are not consciously perceived but may be influential are:
    a)   exceptional messages.
    b)   subliminal messages.
    c)   reactance messages.
    d)   unconscious messages.

10. The theory of planned behavior states that all of the following are predictors of people's planned, deliberative behaviors EXCEPT:
    a)   subjective norms.
    b)   perceived behavioral control.
    c)   attitudes toward the specific behavior.
    d)   social norms.

11. According to Petty and Cacioppo's (1986) elaboration likelihood model, when people are persuaded by surface characteristics of a message, such as how long the message is, they have taken the ____ route to persuasion.
    a)   central
    b)   peripheral
    c)   heuristic
    d)   subjective

12. Attitudes changed by the central route to persuasion are:
    a) maintained over time.
    b) consistent with behaviors.
    c) resistant to counterpersuasion.
    d) all the above.

13. Shavitt (1990) presented participants with cognitively or affectively oriented ads for products about which people had either cognitively or affectively based attitudes. Results indicated that participants were most influenced by:
    a) cognitively based ads.
    b) affectively based ads.
    c) ads that "matched" the type of attitude they had.
    d) cognitively based ads that were self-relevant and affectively based ads that were not relevant.

14. When you encounter an object and your attitude toward that object comes immediately to mind, your attitude is said to be highly:
    a) resistant.
    b) accessible.
    c) deliberative.
    d) intentional.

15. After strongly prohibiting the reading of banned books, professor Jones has noticed an increased interest by her students in the books. Which of the following theories best explains this outcome?
    a) theory of reasoned action
    b) elaboration likelihood model
    c) reactance theory
    d) classical conditioning theory

Short Answer

1. Give examples of cognitively, affectively, and behaviorally based attitudes.

2. When do persuasive attempts "boomerang" and why?

3. As a marketing specialist, what advertising approach would you recommend to the maker of greeting cards?

PRACTICE TEST 2

Fill in the Blank

1. Attitudes that are based primarily on people's emotions and values that are evoked by the attitude object are called _____.

2. The process of repeatedly pairing an emotion-evoking stimulus with a neutral stimulus until the neutral stimulus takes on the emotional properties of the first stimulus is called _____.

3. Changing the frequency of freely chosen behaviors by positively reinforcing or punishing the behavior is called _____.

4. Attitudes that are based primarily on people's observations of how they behave toward the attitude object are called _____.

5.   The strength of association between an object and a person's evaluation of that object is known as _____.

6.   Making people immune to attitude change attempts by initially exposing them to small doses of the arguments against their position is called _____.

7.   According to one theory, when people feel that their freedom to perform a certain behavior is threatened, they will reduce the threat by performing that behavior. This theory is called _____.

8.   According to one theory, the best predictors of people's planned, deliberative behaviors are people's attitudes toward the specific behavior, their subjective norms, and their perceived behavioral control. This theory is called the _____.

9.   People's beliefs about how other people they care about will view their behavior are called their _____.

10.   Words and pictures that are not consciously perceived but supposedly influential are called _____.

11.   People high in the need for _____ tend to take the central route to persuasion and pay careful attention to the quality of arguments in a persuasive communication.

12.   According to the _____ model of persuasion, people taking the peripheral route to persuasion use mental shortcuts to process a persuasive communication.

Multiple Choice

1.   Responses to which of the following questions will best predict whether someone donates clothes to the Salvation Army next Sunday at noon?
    a)   "How much are you willing to help others"?
    b)   "How do you feel about making donations to charities"?
    c)   "How do you feel about donating clothes to the Salvation Army"?
    d)   "How do you feel about donating clothes to the Salvation Army next Sunday at noon"?

2.   A(n) ____ communication is a communication that advocates a particular side of an issue.
    a)   attitude change
    b)   influential
    c)   persuasive
    d)   subjective

3.   An attitude change theory that states that we can satisfy our need to justify engaging in attitude-discrepant behaviors by changing our attitudes is:
    a)   self-evaluation maintenance theory.
    b)   cognitive dissonance theory.
    c)   elaboration likelihood theory.
    d)   self-affirmation theory.

4.   Fear-evoking persuasive appeals fail if they are too strong and threatening because:
    a)   people become defensive.
    b)   people deny the threat.
    c)   people will not think rationally about the issue.
    d)   All the above are reasons.

5. Heuristic processing is to the _____ route to persuasion as systematic processing is to the _____ route to persuasion.
   a) primary; secondary
   b) secondary; primary
   c) peripheral; central
   d) central; peripheral

6. Making people immune to persuasion attempts by exposing them to small doses of arguments against their position is called:
   a) attitude inoculation.
   b) attitude vaccination.
   c) attitude reactance.
   d) attitude prevention.

7. Regarding attitude-behavior consistency, it is important to measure people's beliefs about how others will view the given behavior. These beliefs are called:
   a) subjective norms.
   b) objective norms.
   c) injunctive norms.
   d) social norms.

8. Advertisers, cable television companies, and grocery stores work together to test the effects of advertising campaigns by conducting:
   a) cable split market tests.
   b) cable market tests.
   c) split cable market tests.
   d) mail surveys.

9. Which of the following is FALSE regarding subliminal messages?
   a) There is no evidence that subliminal messages, both those used in everyday life and those manipulated in the lab, influence people's attitudes.
   b) Subliminal tapes, for example to boost self-esteem or improve memory, are ineffective.
   c) Ads that are consciously perceived exert more influence on people's attitudes than do those that are not consciously perceived.
   d) All the above are false.

10. According to the elaboration likelihood model of persuasion, the _____ of persuasive arguments has more impact when people's personal involvement in the issue is _____.
    a) strength; low
    b) strength; high
    c) quantity; high
    d) both a and c
    e) none of the above

11. According to the Yale Attitude Change approach, which of the following is true?
    a) Distracted audiences are persuaded less often than are audiences not distracted.
    b) People with moderate self-esteem are less persuadable than are people with low or high self-esteem.
    c) It is best to present a one-sided persuasive communication.
    d) People are more susceptible to attitude change when they are between the ages of 18 and 25.

12. An attitude is a(n):
    a) temporary judgment of complex social stimuli.
    b) enduring evaluation of people, objects, and ideas.
    c) influence to the real or imagined presence of others.
    d) belief about how other people will view one's behavior.

13.   The two fundamental means of changing attitudes that are considered in this chapter include:
       a)   changing behavior and persuasive communication.
       b)   social influence and introspection.
       c)   reinforcement and advertising.
       d)   inoculation and fear-arousing communication.

14.   Participants in a study by Petty et al. (1981) were told that their university was thinking about requiring senior comprehensive exams either immediately or in 10 years. Participants paid greater attention to arguments favoring the exams when they believed that the exam policy might take effect immediately because:
       a)   the issue was personally relevant.
       b)   a decision had to be made very soon.
       c)   the participants knew friends who were seniors.
       d)   the participants were opposed to the exam policy.

15.   When we can find little external justification for behavior that is inconsistent with an attitude, changing the attitude so that it is consistent with the behavior is one way to reduce:
       a)   reactance.
       b)   personal relevance.
       c)   attitude accessibility.
       d)   cognitive dissonance.

Short Answer

1.   Describe Petty and Cacioppo's (1986) elaboration likelihood model. What are the two routes to persuasion that people may take? What determines the route taken? What are the effects of persuasion by each route?

2.   Describe the "attitude inoculation" technique used to help people resist attempts to persuade them. How has this technique been adapted in order to make individuals resistant to peer pressure?

WEB EXERCISE

Go to www.prenhall.com/aronson. Visit a site devoted to the analysis of propaganda by clicking on Chapter 7 links and clicking on the link to the Propaganda Analysis Homepage of the Institute of Propaganda Analysis. How is propaganda different from scientific analysis? Go to the Propaganda Gallery and write a paragraph about your reactions. Identify the seven techniques that propaganda involves. What questions should be asked when we encounter each of these techniques?

CHAPTER 8

Conformity: Influencing Behavior

CHAPTER OVERVIEW

This chapter deals with the powerful influence that people have in getting others to do what they are doing or what they want others to do. The first section of the chapter describes one type of influence that increases conformity, informational social influence. The motivation to be right underlies informational social influence. Informational social influence helps to explain the phenomena of contagion and mass psychogenic illness. Although it is adaptive to follow others when they are right, the chapter warns that resisting informational social influence may be best sometimes. Steps to do this are outlined.

Another type of influence linked with conformity is normative social influence. Classic studies are depicted in this section that make readers aware of people's concern with adhering to social norms and being liked by others. This is the motivation that underlies normative social influence. As with informational social influence, resisting normative pressures is possible. Another topic addressed in this section is minority influence. Minority influence research studies how small groups can influence larger ones.

The next section of this chapter considers compliance. Compliance involves changing one's behavior as a result of a direct request from someone. In addition to mindless conformity, two successful compliance techniques are detailed here. Lastly a particular kind of conformity, obedience to authority, is addressed. The findings of Milgram comprise the bulk of this material. His studies of obedience have contributed greatly to the understanding of how people can commit inhumane acts as a result of situational constraints.

CHAPTER OUTLINE

Conformity: When and Why

Informational Social Influence: The Need To Know What's "Right"

> The Importance of Being Accurate

> When Informational Conformity Backfires

> When Will People Conform to Informational Social Influence?

> Resisting Informational Social Influence

Normative Social Influence: The Need to Be Accepted

> Conformity and Social Approval: The Asch Line Judgment Studies

> The Importance of Being Accurate, Revisited

> The Consequences of Resisting Normative Social Influence

> Normative Social Influence in Everyday Life

> When Will People Conform to Normative Social Influence?

> Resisting Normative Social Influence

LEARNING OBJECTIVES

After reading Chapter 8, you should be able to do the following:

1.   Define conformity. Identify the motivation underlying informational social influence. (p. 255)

2.   Describe Sherif's (1936) experiment. Discuss why Sherif chose to use the autokinetic effect in his experiment. Describe the results of Sherif's experiment. (pp. 255-257)

3.   Distinguish between private acceptance and public compliance. Identify which of these is produced by informational social influence. (pp. 256-257)

4.   Explain the relationship between conformity due to informational social influence and the importance of being accurate. (pp. 257-258)

5.   Describe the conditions under which informational social influence backfires. Identify examples of contagion and mass psychogenic illnesses. Discuss the role of the mass media in the spread of modern mass psychogenic illness. (pp. 258-261)

6.   Identify three situations that produce conformity to informational social influence. (p. 261)

7.   Identify the steps people can take to determine whether other people provide accurate information and to resist other people's information when it is inaccurate. (pp. 262-263)

8.   Identify the motivation underlying normative social influence. Define and give examples of social norms. (pp. 263-264)

9.   Describe Asch's (1956) experiment. Identify how the situation in Asch's experiment differed from the situation in Sherif's experiment. Describe the basic findings of Asch's experiment. Explain why these findings were surprising. (pp. 264-267)

10. Identify whether private acceptance or public compliance usually results from normative social influence. Describe Asch's variation of his original experiment and explain how this resulted in strong evidence for normative influence. (pp. 266-267)

11. Explain the relationship between conformity due to normative social influence and the importance of being accurate. (pp. 267-268)

12. Discuss the consequences of resisting normative social influence. Describe Schachter's (1951) experiment and discuss its results. (pp. 268-270)

13. Discuss examples of normative social influence from harmless trends and fads to more sinister forms of conformity including many women's attempts to conform to an extremely thin standard of feminine physical attractiveness. Describe the changes in cultural standards for feminine physical attractiveness in the last century. (pp. 270-273)

14. Discuss the relationship between social influence and men's body image and how cultural norms regarding men's body image have changed in the second half of the last century. (pp. 273-275)

15. Identify when people will conform to normative social influence. Describe social impact theory. Identify the relationships between the strength, immediacy, and number of influence sources, and subsequent conformity. List some predictions made by the theory when strength, immediacy, and the number of influence sources are manipulated. (p. 275)

16. Identify three characteristics of the group that increase conformity to normative social influence. Identify what size group induced maximum conformity in Asch's experiments. Discuss why it might be dangerous to have policy decisions made by highly cohesive groups. Discuss the effects of having an ally on conformity to normative social influence. Discuss the findings of cross-cultural research on conformity and the results of conformity studies replicated in the same culture after many years. (pp. 275-279)

17. Identify two characteristics of the individual that may affect conformity to normative social influence. Discuss why the relationship between personality traits and conforming behavior is not always clear-cut. Discuss the results of meta-analyses conducted to determine whether women conform more than men. Identify when gender differences in conformity are especially likely. Discuss why male researchers are more likely to find gender differences in conformity than female researchers. (pp. 279-280)

18. Identify the steps people can take to resist normative social influence. Discuss the role of idiosyncrasy credits in resisting normative social influence. (p. 280)

19. Discuss the necessity of minority influence for introducing change within groups. Identify how a minority must express its views if it is to exert influence. Identify the kind of social influence minorities exert and what effect this has on the majority. (pp. 280-281)

20. Discuss how social influence can be used to promote constructive behavior. Define injunctive and descriptive norms. Describe how injunctive and descriptive norms can reduce problematic behaviors such as littering and increase beneficial social behavior. (pp. 281-284)

21. Define compliance. Define mindless conformity. List advantages and disadvantages of mindless conformity. (pp. 284-285)

22. Discuss the relationship between the door-in-the-face technique and the reciprocity norm. Identify a disadvantage of the door-in-the-face technique. (pp. 285-287)

23. Define the foot-in-the-door technique and discuss why it is effective. (p. 287)

24. Describe Milgram's obedience studies. Identify what percentage of participants in Milgram's studies obeyed the experimenter completely. Discuss variations of the original study which demonstrate the kinds of social influence that caused obedience. Discuss the roles of normative and informational influence in explaining Milgram's findings. (pp. 288-293)

25. Identify two key aspects of the situation that caused participants in Milgram's obedience studies to continue following an "obey authority" norm long after it was appropriate to do so. Discuss the evidence that suggests participants in Milgram's experiments were not expressing a universal aggressive urge. (pp. 293-295)

KEY TERMS

conformity (p. 253)

informational social influence (p. 255)

private acceptance (p. 256)

public compliance (p. 257)

contagion (p. 259)

mass psychogenic illness (p. 260)

social norms (p. 263)

normative social influence (p. 264)

social impact theory (p. 275)

idiosyncrasy credits (p. 280)

minority influence (p. 281)

injunctive norms (p. 282)

descriptive norms (p. 282)

compliance (p. 284)

mindless conformity (p. 284)

door-in-the-face technique (p. 285)

reciprocity norm (p. 286)

foot-in-the-door technique (p. 287)

STUDY QUESTIONS

1.   What is conformity? What are two main reasons why we conform? What advantages does conforming provide?

2.   When are we likely to conform to informational social influence? What are the differences between private acceptance and public compliance? Which one is more likely when we conform due to informational social influence?

3.   What is the relationship between conformity due to informational social influence and the importance of being accurate? What happens to rates of conformity when the situation is ambiguous and the importance of the task is high?

4.   What is contagion? How do the mass media influence the likelihood of mass psychogenic illness?

5.   What are three main factors that make conforming due to informational social influence very likely? Why?

6.   Why is the decision whether or not to conform so important? What are some questions we should ask ourselves when we are deciding whether we should conform due to informational social influence?

7.   What are the differences between informational social influence and normative social influence? What are social norms? Why are they followed so often?

8.   Why were the findings of Asch's conformity study surprising? Were Asch's participants more likely conforming due to informational social influence or normative social influence? Why?

9.   What is the relationship between normative social influence and the importance of being accurate? What happens to rates of conformity when the situation is unambiguous and the importance of the task is high?

10. According to Schachter's (1951) study, how do people deal with a nonconformist?

11. What are historical and contemporary examples of normative social influence? What do they tell us about the power and consequences of conforming due to social pressures? How has social influence affected women's and men's body image?

12. What does social impact theory attempt to explain? To what do the variables of strength, immediacy, and number of influence sources refer? What is the relationship between these variables and conformity?

13. When will people conform due to normative social influence? What are the main conditions that increase this conformity?

14. What are cross-cultural differences in conformity? Has conformity increased or decreased since the 1950's?

15. Do personality traits readily predict who will conform due to normative social influence? Why or why not?

16. What is the magnitude of sex differences in ability to be influenced? Under what conditions are women more likely to conform than men are? Why?

17. What are two steps toward nonconformity? What are idiosyncrasy credits?

18. What are important conditions for the occurrence of minority influence? How do minorities tend to influence majorities? What is more likely a result of minority influence, public compliance or private acceptance?

19. What are injunctive and descriptive norms and how can they be used to foster beneficial behavior?

20.   How does mindless conformity happen?

21.   What is the relationship between the door-in-the-face technique and the reciprocity norm?

22.   What is the foot-in-the-door technique? Why is it effective?

23.   What are the basic findings of the Milgram obedience study? What percentage of participants delivered the highest voltage of shock possible? Why was it difficult for participants in Milgram's studies to disobey authority? How do informational social influence and normative social influence help us understand Milgram's findings?

24.   What do variations of Milgram's study tell us about limits to obedience to authority?

PRACTICE TEST 1

Fill in the Blank

1.   A change in behavior due to the real or imagined influence of other people is called _____.

2.   An influence to conform to other people's behavior because it defines an ambiguous situation for us and helps us choose appropriate courses of action is called _____.

3.   Conforming to other people's behavior out of a genuine belief that what they are doing or saying is right is called _____.

4.   Conforming to other people's behavior publicly, without necessarily believing in what you are doing or saying is called _____.

5.   The rapid transmission of emotions or behavior through a crowd is called _____.

6.   The occurrence in a group of people of similar physical symptoms with no known physical cause is known as _____.

7.   Implicit or explicit rules a group has for the acceptable behaviors, values, and beliefs of its members are called _____.

8.   An influence to conform to other people's behavior in order to be liked or accepted by others is called _____.

9.   Obeying internalized social norms without deliberating about one's actions is called
       _____.

Multiple Choice

1.   Why did individual estimates of a light's apparent motion converge when participants in Sherif's (1951)
       experiment called out their estimates in a group?
       a)   Because participants used each other as a source of information.
       b)   Because participants wanted to be liked by the others.
       c)   Because participants badgered each other until everyone agreed.
       d)   Because the mere presence of others had subtle effects on participants'
              visual processes.

2.   Which of the following are recommended steps for resisting informational social influence?
       a)   Remember that resistance is possible and determine the sensibility of the
              available information.
       b)   Remember that unanimous majorities are rarely wrong and determine the
              strength of agreement within the majority.
       c)   Remember that people's opinions differ and search out advice from a
              similar individual.
       d)   Remember that you can't please everybody and that membership in some
              groups is more important than membership in others.

3.   How was Asch's conformity study different from Sherif's?
       a)   Asch created an ambiguous situation while Sherif created an unambiguous
              one.
       b)   Asch created an unambiguous situation while Sherif created an ambiguous
              one.
       c)   The subjects in Asch's study were better problem-solvers than those in
              Sherif's study.
       d)   Accomplices in Asch's study imposed greater pressure on participants than did accomplices in Sherif's
              study.

4.   When participants in Asch's (1956) study indicated which of three comparison lines matched a standard line by
       writing their responses on a piece of paper rather than by saying them out loud, conformity:
       a)   increased somewhat.
       b)   remained the same.
       c)   dropped dramatically.
       d)   dropped slightly.

5.   While stopped at a traffic light in a large city, a man appears from nowhere and, without asking, sprays your
       windshield with cleaner and wipes off the glass. The man realizes that you are likely to tip him if you, like
       most people, obey the _____ norm.
       a)   generosity
       b)   morality
       c)   obedience
       d)   reciprocity

6.   According to Latane's (1981) social impact theory, the amount of influence that people whose opinions differ
       from your own will exert will be greatest if they are in a group that is:
       a)   comprised of 3 people.
       b)   important.
       c)   unanimous.
       d)   b and d

7. Replications of Asch's (1956) conformity research across many cultures and different time periods indicate that amounts of conformity:
   a) are constant culture to culture and over time in a given culture.
   b) vary from culture to culture but are constant over time in a given culture.
   c) vary from culture to culture and over time in a given culture.
   d) are constant culture to culture but vary over time in a given culture.

8. Which of the following is true about people's susceptibility to conforming due to informational social influence?
   a) People are more likely to conform due to informational social influence when the situation is straightforward than when it is not straightforward.
   b) People are more likely to conform due to informational social influence when it is important to be accurate than when it is unimportant.
   c) People are more likely to conform due to informational social influence when accuracy is unimportant than when it is important.
   d) People are less likely to conform due to informational social influence when the situation is unclear than when it is straightforward.

9. The first step in resisting normative social influence is to:
   a) ignore the source of influence.
   b) take action to avoid being influenced.
   c) find an ally to assist in resisting influence.
   d) become aware of the norms guiding behavior.

10. In Milgram's obedience studies participants played the role of "teacher" in what they believed was an experiment on the effects of punishment on learning. Throughout the experiment they feared they might kill a "learner" with increasingly strong electrical shocks. Mild prods by an authority to "please continue" were nonetheless enough to get ___% of Milgram's participants to obey completely.
   a) 1.0
   b) 12.5
   c) 36.0
   d) 62.5

11. Which of the following forms of social influence induced the participants in Milgram's obedience studies to administer the maximum level of shock possible to a helpless learner?
   a) normative social influence
   b) informational social influence
   c) both normative and informational social influence
   d) neither normative nor informational social influence

12. Conformity is:
   a) the spread of emotions and behaviors throughout a large group.
   b) the occurrence of similar physical symptoms in a group of people with no known physical cause.
   c) a rule for acceptable social behavior.
   d) a change in behavior due to the real or imagined influence of other people.

13. Whereas normative social influence leads to ____, informational social influence produces ____.
   a) private acceptance; public compliance
   b) public compliance; private acceptance
   c) conformity; minority influence
   d) minority influence; conformity

14. Temporary dizziness and paralysis experienced by citizens of Mattoon, Illinois following reports of a phantom anesthetist were attributed to _____ after scientists found no trace of a mystery gas.
    a) hypochondriasis
    b) mass psychogenic illness
    c) schizophrenia
    d) conversion

15. Asch (1956) presented participants with three comparison lines and a standard line that clearly matched one of the comparison lines. When participants were asked to publicly identify the matching line they went along with a rigged majority and made incorrect judgments:
    a) almost every time.
    b) about half of the time.
    c) about a third of the time.
    d) almost never.

16. Bibb Latane's social impact (1981) theory describes:
    a) characteristics that make a source influential.
    b) the type of people who are most likely to conform.
    c) when conformity is foolish and when it is wise.
    d) cognitive processes involved in "mindless" conformity.

17. Personality traits have been found to be poor predictors of conformity because:
    a) the social situation is often as important in understanding how someone will behave as is his or her personality.
    b) personality traits that might influence conformity have not been identified.
    c) gender is often as important in understanding how someone will behave as is his or her personality.
    d) all of the above

18. Alice Eagly (1987) believes that women may exhibit more conforming behavior than men only when an audience is present because:
    a) women are less confident of themselves in front of an audience than men.
    b) women are more easily influenced than men.
    c) women are less socially adept than men.
    d) gender roles dictate that men should be individualists while women should be cooperative.

Short Answer

1. You are an advertiser and a client approaches you for advice. She has a warehouse full of anchovy pizzas that will go bad in a month if they are not sold. Knowing that people are likely to conform to a particular social norm mindlessly, what sales strategy would you recommend?

2. Give three reasons why participants obeyed the experimenter in Milgram's studies.

3. Make two columns with the headings "informational social influence" and "normative social influence." List the following names and terms under the appropriate heading: Asch, Schachter, Milgram, Sherif, minority influence, "mindless" conformity, contagion.

4. Compare and contrast informational and normative social influence. Why are they called "social" influences? What motives underlie each type of influence and what effects does each type have on our behavior?

PRACTICE TEST 2

Fill in the Blank

1. A technique to induce compliance whereby people are presented with a large request and are expected to refuse it, and then presented with a smaller request is called the _____.

2. A social norm that dictates that we should do something nice for someone who has done something nice for us is called the _____.

3. A theory that states that conformity to social influence depends on the strength, immediacy, and number of others in the group is known as _____.

4. The credits a person earns, over time, by conforming to group norms are called _____.

5. The effect that a minority of group members has on the behavior or beliefs of the majority is called _____.

6. The compliance technique whereby people are first asked a small request and then are asked a larger one is called the _____.

7. Norms that motivate behavior by informing people about what behaviors are adaptive in a situation are called _____ norms.

8. Norms that motivate behavior by offering rewards for conforming to these norms are called _____ norms.

9. When someone engages in a behavior as a result of a direct request from another, _____ has occurred.

Multiple Choice

1. After hearing a minority opinion, majority members may come to realize that there are different perspectives from their own and consider the issue more carefully. Subsequent change in the majority's opinion will be the result of _____ social influence.
    a)   consensual
    b)   informational
    c)   responsive
    d)   normative

2. A change in behavior that is a result of a direct request from another is:
    a)   mindless conformity.
    b)   private acceptance.
    c)   compliance.
    d)   obedience.

3. The reciprocity norm has been linked with which of the following compliance techniques?
    a)   the foot-in-the-face technique
    b)   the door-in-the-face technique
    c)   the foot-in-the-door technique
    d)   minority influence technique

4. Why did obedience by participants in Milgram's studies drop drastically when two accomplices, acting as fellow teachers, refused to obey the experimenter?
   a) Because the participant could not continue without the help of the accomplice teachers.
   b) Because similar peers exert more normative social influence than do dissimilar authority figures.
   c) Because the accomplices served as allies which enabled participants to resist normative social influence.
   d) Because the two accomplices outnumbered the experimenter and formed an influential majority.

5. The "escalation" of shocks that subjects administered in Milgram's studies resulted because:
   a) participants found it difficult to stop shocking the learner after justifying the administration of each previous level of shock.
   b) participants became desensitized to shocking the learner.
   c) participants convinced themselves that the experimenter was solely responsible and simply followed his requests.
   d) participants became convinced that it was acceptable to shock the learner and their natural aggressive tendencies took over.

6. Mass psychogenic illness is a form of:
   a) normative social influence.
   b) contagion.
   c) informational social influence.
   d) both b and c.

7. Which of the following is a good question to ask oneself when determining whether or not to conform to informational social influence?
   a) Do the behaviors of others seem rational?
   b) If I conform, will my behaviors violate my common sense or values?
   c) Do others know any more than I do?
   d) All the above are good questions to ask oneself.

8. Normative social influence involves conformity to a group's social norms. These norms are rules for acceptable:
   a) behaviors.
   b) values.
   c) beliefs.
   d) all the above.

9. Baron et al. (1996) found that people are _____ likely to conform due to normative social influence when an unambiguous task is an _____ one.
   a) less; important
   b) more; important
   c) less; unimportant
   d) none of the above

10. People learn what body type is considered attractive in their culture due to _____, and their attempts to create this ideal body type are an example of conformity due to _____.
    a) contagion; normative social influence
    b) informational social influence; normative social influence
    c) informational social influence; mass psychogenic illness
    d) normative social influence; informational social influence

11.   Resisting the normative social influence of a group is easier if one has built up ____ with the group.
       a)   reciprocity credits
       b)   conformity credits
       c)   influence credits
       d)   idiosyncrasy credits

12.   Knowing that lying is wrong is a(n) ____ norm, while knowing that there are situations when people lie is a(n) ____ norm.
       a)   social; injunctive
       b)   descriptive; social
       c)   injunctive; descriptive
       d)   descriptive; injunctive

13.   According to Kallgren et al. (2000), injunctive norms are:
       a)   more likely to produce desirable behaviors than are descriptive norms.
       b)   less likely to produce desirable behaviors than are descriptive norms.
       c)   equally effective as descriptive norms in producing desirable behaviors.
       d)   equally ineffective as descriptive norms in producing desirable behaviors.

14.   The phrase "operating on automatic pilot" is used to describe:
       a)   normative social influence.
       b)   informational social influence.
       c)   contagion.
       d)   mindless conformity.

15.   Asking for a small request followed by asking for a larger request describes the ____ compliance technique.
       a)   door-in-the-foot
       b)   foot-in-the-door
       c)   door-in-the-face
       d)   mindless conformity

16.   Ramona held relatively anti-environmental views in high school. Last year, she began attending a college where pro-environmental attitudes and people are the norm. Gradually, Ramona starts to express more pro-environmental views than in the past. Her new attitudes are likely due to:
       a)   her authoritarian personality.
       b)   the psychology of inevitability.
       c)   having to compete with other women for dates.
       d)   conformity processes.

17.   According to research on informational social influence, which of the following would be the best way to help a child overcome his fear of escalators?
       a)   carefully explain the safety features of escalators
       b)   offer him a small reward for riding the escalator
       c)   let him watch while you enjoy riding the escalator
       d)   have him watch as some of his classmates ride up and down the escalator.

18.   Tyrone works for a nonprofit agency that is seeking donations. He is visiting local business officials hoping to raise their commitment to support his agency. Which of the following approaches is likely to work the best?
       a)   Ask for $1000 a month and leave it at that.
       b)   First ask for $5000, and if they refuse, ask for $500.
       c)   Ask for $200 a month and leave it at that.
       d)   First for a small donation, such as $200. Then, visit later and ask for a larger amount, such as $500 a month

Short Answer

1. Why is Asch's conformity study "one of the most dramatic illustrations of blindly going along with the group, even when the individual realizes that by doing so he turns his back on reality and truth"? (Moscovici, 1985, p. 349)

2. Describe Bibb Latane's (1981) Social Impact Theory. What are the sources of social impact and what characteristics of these sources determine the amount of impact a group will have?

3. Describe means of resisting informational and normative social influence.

WEB EXERCISE

Go to www.prenhall.com/aronson. Go to the News Clips for Chapter 8. Write your reactions to what you read regarding the issues relevant to this chapter. These include conformity, mass psychogenic illness, minority influence, and obedience. Or, click on the Links for the chapter and go to The Asch Conformity Effect. Summarize the research that has been done on conformity to normative social influence since Asch's studies.

CHAPTER 9

Group Processes: Influence in Social Groups

CHAPTER OVERVIEW

Chapter 9 considers how groups influence the behaviors of their members. Groups exist in a wide variety of forms. Groups are defined in the first section of this chapter and why people join groups is addressed. Descriptions of the influences of social norms, social roles, and group cohesiveness on group processes are given. Phenomena that occur in groups, social facilitation, social loafing, and deindividuation are considered. Social loafing and social facilitation are closely related. Arousal due to the presence of others can facilitate or hinder people's performance. The complexity of the task also must be considered. This section outlines these corresponding conditions. Deindividuation helps explain the behavior of people in large groups when they feel anonymous and unaccountable for their actions.

The next section discusses research on how well groups make decisions. Topics in this area include process loss, groupthink, and group polarization. Leadership theories also are addressed in this section. Two theories concerned with leadership effectiveness are examined. The last section of this chapter focuses on the utility of communication and negotiation to reduce conflict. The phenomenon of social dilemmas is explored. Conditions that foster trust and cooperation are discussed.

CHAPTER OUTLINE

Definitions: What Is a Group?

>   Why do People Join Groups?

>   The Composition of Groups

How Groups Influence the Behavior of Individuals

>   Social Facilitation: When the Presence of Others Energizes Us

>   Social Loafing: When the Presence of Others Relaxes Us

>   Gender and Cultural Differences in Social Loafing: Who Slacks Off the Most?

>   Deindividuation: Getting Lost in the Crowd

Group Decisions: Are Two (or More) Heads Better Than One?

>   Process Loss: When Group Interactions Inhibit Good Problem Solving

>   Group Polarization: Going to Extremes

>   Leadership in Groups

Conflict and Cooperation

>   Social Dilemmas

>   Using Threats to Resolve Conflict

Effects of Communication

Negotiation and Bargaining

LEARNING OBJECTIVES

After reading Chapter 9, you should be able to do the following:

1. Provide a definition of groups and state reasons why people join groups. Define social norms and social roles, including gender roles, and the function they serve in groups. Identify two possible costs to social roles and discuss their implications. Discuss the influence of group cohesiveness on group processes. (pp. 301-305)

2. Describe the relationship between social facilitation and the mere presence of others. Explain why the presence of others causes arousal. Discuss the effects of social facilitation on the performance of simple and complex tasks. (pp. 305-308)

3. Describe social loafing and discuss why it occurs. Identify how the setting in which social loafing occurs is different from the setting in which social facilitation occurs. Identify factors that increase and decrease social loafing. (pp. 308-310)

4. Identify gender and cultural differences in the occurrence of social loafing. Explain these differences. (pp. 310-311)

5. Identify the two factors important for predicting the effects of the presence of others on performance. (p. 311)

6. Define deindividuation and describe the effects of deindividuation on behavior. Identify conditions that increase deindividuation. Describe the conditions that determine whether deindividuation will lead to positive or negative behaviors. (pp. 311-314)

7. Identify sources of process loss in groups. Describe how group members handle unique information during discussion. Identify how groups could improve the sharing of information. Define transactive memory. (pp. 314-317)

8. Identify the antecedents, symptoms, and consequences of groupthink. Discuss historical examples of groupthink. Identify measures that can be taken to avoid groupthink. (pp. 317-319)

9. Describe the effects of group discussion on attitudes that are initially risky or initially cautious. Define group polarization. Describe the cognitive and motivational explanations of group polarization. Describe Brown's culture-value theory and discuss support for this theory. (pp. 319-321)

10. Describe the relationship between the great person theory and great leadership. Identify the personality traits and variables that are related to leadership. (pp. 321-323)

11. Contrast the great person theory with the contingency theory of leadership. Identify the two types of leaders according to the contingency theory. Discuss the situational conditions that lead to leadership effectiveness of each type of leader. (pp. 321-324)

12. Discuss the relationship between gender and leadership. Discuss research findings on this topic. (pp. 324-325)

13.   Discuss the history of conflict among humans and why it is important to study ways to foster peaceful conflict resolution. Define a social dilemma. Describe the prisoner's dilemma. Define the tit-for-tat strategy. Identify the most effective strategies when playing with a cooperative opponent versus a competitive one. (pp. 325-328)

14.   Define both a public goods dilemma and the commons dilemma. Give examples of public goods dilemmas and commons dilemmas. (pp. 328-329)

15.   Discuss the effects of using threats to resolve conflicts. Define negotiation. Identify effective negotiation strategies. Describe an integrative solution. Identify obstacles to finding integrative solutions. (pp. 329-333)

KEY TERMS

group (p. 301)

social roles (p. 302)

group cohesiveness (p. 305)

social facilitation (p. 307)

social loafing (p. 309)

deindividuation (p. 311)

process loss (p. 315)

transactive memory (p. 316)

groupthink (p. 317)

group polarization (p. 320)

great person theory (p. 321)

contingency theory of leadership (p. 322)

task-oriented leader (p. 322)

relationship-oriented leader (p. 322)

social dilemma (p. 326)

tit-for-tat strategy (p. 328)

public goods dilemma (p. 328)

commons dilemma (p. 328)

negotiation (p. 332)

integrative solution (p. 332)

STUDY QUESTIONS

1. What is the definition of a group? Why do people join groups?

2. What are social norms and social roles, including gender roles, and the functions they serve in groups? What are possible costs involved with social roles? What is the influence of group cohesiveness on group processes?

3. What are the conditions that facilitate social facilitation effects? What role does task difficulty play in social facilitation effects? How and why does arousal interact with task difficulty when people are performing a task in the presence of others?

4. What are the conditions that facilitate social loafing effects? What are effective ways to reduce social loafing? Who is more likely to engage in social loafing, men or women, Westerners or Asians?

5. What implications do social facilitation and social loafing have for organizing groups in work situations?

6. What is deindividuation? What behaviors does it help to explain? Why does deindividuation happen?

7. What is process loss in groups? How does it occur? How might it be avoided? What is transactive memory?

8. What is groupthink? What are its symptoms? How can it be avoided?

9. What is group polarization? How does it happen? What are cross-cultural differences in group decisionmaking according to the culture-value theory?

10.   What is the great person theory and what does it attempt to predict and explain?

11.   According to the contingency theory of leadership, what are two types of leaders? Under what conditions is each type of leader most effective?

12.   What do research findings tell us about gender differences in leadership effectiveness?

13.   What is a social dilemma? What is the tit-for-tat strategy? When is it best to use this strategy in the prisoner's dilemma game?

14.   What is a public goods dilemma? What is a commons dilemma?

15.   Are threats an effective means to reduce conflict? Why or why not? When can communication alleviate conflict?

16.   What strategies do people use when they negotiate? Which strategies are most successful for reducing conflict? What is an integrative solution and what are barriers to these solutions?

PRACTICE TEST 1

Fill in the Blank

1.   Two or more people who interact with each other and are interdependent comprise a
       _____.

2.   Arousal which results from other people's physical and evaluative presence and which enhances performance on simple tasks but impairs performance on complex tasks is called _____.

3.   Relaxation and the reduction of individual effort which results when the performance of group members cannot be evaluated is called _____.

4. The loosening of normal constraints on behavior, leading to an increase in impulsive and deviant acts, is called _____.

5. Shared expectations in a group about how certain people are supposed to behave are called _____.

6. Qualities of a group that foster liking and that tie members together are referred to as group _____.

7. The combined memory of two people that holds more information than either of their individual memories is called _____ memory.

8. Any aspect of group interaction that inhibits good problem solving is known as _____.

9. A kind of thinking in which maintaining group cohesiveness and solidarity is more important than considering the facts in a realistic manner is called _____.

10. The tendency for groups to make decisions that are more extreme than the initial inclinations of its members is called _____.

Multiple Choice

1. A group can be defined as ____ or more people who are ____, that is their needs and goals lead them to influence one another.
   a) one; dependent
   b) three; interdependent
   c) one; interdependent
   d) two; interdependent

2. If you are asked to perform in the presence of others, you are likely to feel aroused as a result of:
   a) anticipatory arousal.
   b) increased interpersonal conflict.
   c) increased alertness and evaluation apprehension.
   d) disinhibition.

3. Compared to individuals, members of social loafing groups perform ____ on simple tasks and ____ on complex tasks.
   a) better; worse
   b) worse; better
   c) worse; worse
   d) better; better

4. To maximize the performance of seasoned workers performing familiar tasks at your production plant, you should create groups that foster:
   a) social loafing.
   b) social facilitation.
   c) deindividuation.
   d) conflict.

5. What determines whether deindividuation will lead to positive or negative behaviors?
   a) whether deindividuation is caused by decreased accountability or decreased self-awareness
   b) whether we have committed more prosocial or antisocial acts in the past
   c) whether our inhibitions prevent us from performing positive or negative behaviors outside the group
   d) whether the situation encourages positive or negative behaviors

6. Shared expectations that a group has about how people are supposed to act are called social ____, while shared expectations about how certain people in a group should behave are called social ____.
   a) groups; norms
   b) norms; rules
   c) rules; norms
   d) norms; roles

7. Groups that strengthen the initial inclinations of their members, pushing their members' decisions to the extreme, exhibit:
   a) the risky shift.
   b) social facilitation.
   c) process loss.
   d) group polarization.

8. A type of social dilemma whereby individuals must contribute to a common pool of resources to ensure the benefit of all is a:
   a) process dilemma.
   b) public goods dilemma.
   c) common goods dilemma.
   d) commons dilemma.

9. Integrative solutions to conflicts are most likely to be reached if:
   a) opponents find out which issues being negotiated are most important to each party.
   b) opponents compromise on all issues being negotiated.
   c) negotiations are arbitrated by a neutral third party.
   d) communication between opponents is limited to a structured exchange of ideas.

10. Zajonc et al. (1969) observed that cockroaches took longer to reach a dark box at the end of a maze when other cockroaches were present if:
    a) the maze was a simple one.
    b) the maze was a complex one.
    c) the other cockroaches first modeled the escape behavior.
    d) the other cockroaches served as a source of evaluation.

11. In order to know whether the presence of others will improve a group member's performance or hinder it, you need to know:
    a) whether the individual can be evaluated and whether the task is simple or complex.
    b) whether group members interact and whether the goals of group members conflict.
    c) whether the members of the group are disposed to be lazy and whether the group will be tightly organized.
    d) how much communication among members is possible and how well members of the group get along.

12.   A social dilemma is a situation that may result in a conflict because:
        a)   people work harder in groups than they do when working alone.
        b)   individuals may seek to maximize personal gain at the expense of others.
        c)   process loss results when individuals are in a social situation.
        d)   individuals make better decisions than groups do.

13.   European soccer fans attacking each other and hysterical fans at rock concerts trampling one another to death
        demonstrate the horrendous consequences of:
        a)   social facilitation.
        b)   group polarization.
        c)   deindividuation.
        d)   interpersonal conflict.

14.   Parnell is a member of a group of people who feel very connected to each other. The characteristics of a group
        that tie members together and foster liking are high in his group. Parnell's group is most likely high in:
        a)   group cohesiveness.
        b)   social cohesion.
        c)   group coercion.
        d)   social facilitation.

15.   Having members of a group perform an interesting and complex task and making their outputs identifiable are
        ways to decrease:
        a)   social facilitation.
        b)   social loafing.
        c)   deindividuation.
        d)   group polarization.

Short Answer

1.   What is group polarization? Discuss the role of cognitive and motivational factors in producing group
        polarization.

2.   Riots and other instances of unruly mob behavior are the result of what group process? What characteristics of
        the group and situation combine to produce such negative behaviors?

PRACTICE TEST 2

Fill in the Blank

1.   The theory that leadership effectiveness depends on how task-oriented or relationship-oriented the leader is and
        on how much control over the group the leader has is called the _____ theory of leadership.

2.   A leader who is concerned mostly with how well workers are getting along is a _____
        leader.

3.   The theory that certain personality traits make a person an effective leader is called the
        _____ theory.

4.   A means of encouraging cooperation by acting cooperatively at first , and then by matching the (cooperative or
        competitive) responses of one's opponent on subsequent trials, is called the _____ strategy.

5.	A type of social dilemma whereby individuals must give resources to a public pool so that the good of all is perpetuated is a _____.

6.	A type of social dilemma whereby individuals can use common resources in moderation, but extreme overuse will result in resource depletion is called a _____.

7.	A form of communication between opposing sides in a conflict, in which offers and counteroffers are made and a solution occurs only when it is agreed on by both parties, is called _____.

8.	A solution to a conflict that finds outcomes favorable to both parties is called a(n) _____.

9.	A leader concerned more with getting the job completed than with workers' feelings and relationships is called a _____ leader.

10.	A conflict in which the best behavior for an individual will, if chosen by many people, have negative consequences for everyone is referred to as a _____.

Multiple Choice

1.	Which of the following proposes that leadership effectiveness can be predicted by traits that people may or may not possess?
	a)	the contingency theory of leadership
	b)	the integrative theory of leadership
	c)	the great person theory of leadership
	d)	the process theory of leadership

2.	In which situations are task-oriented leaders more effective than relationship-oriented leaders?
	a)	when situational control is moderate
	b)	when workers get along fairly well
	c)	when the task is somewhat structured
	d)	when situational control is high

3.	By making it clear that he favored the Bay of Pigs invasion and by asking his advisors to consider only how the invasion should be executed, Kennedy contributed to which of the following antecedents of groupthink?
	a)	group cohesiveness
	b)	directive leadership
	c)	group isolation
	d)	high stress

4.	According to Burnstein and Vinokur's (1977) persuasive arguments interpretation, group polarization results because:
	a)	individuals bring to the group strong and novel arguments supporting their initial inclinations.
	b)	group discussion reveals the position that the group values and individuals adopt this position in order to be liked.
	c)	individuals recognize that western culture values risk over caution.
	d)	groups actively censor opinions that deviate from those valued by our culture.

5. Initially choosing a cooperative response, and then matching your opponent's response on subsequent trials is an effective strategy in mixed-motive games called:
    a) dog-eat-dog.
    b) acquiescence.
    c) integrative solutions.
    d) tit-for-tat.

6. When groups don't try hard enough to discover who their most competent member is, when the most competent member finds it hard to voice disagreement, or when a group suffers from communication problems, the result may be:
    a) social facilitation.
    b) social dilemma.
    c) deindividuation.
    d) process loss.

7. Sue Ellen is in charge of remembering when to make doctor and dentist appointments for the family. Her partner is responsible for coordinating the family's social schedule. Each partner is obligated to remember certain information thereby increasing the total amount of information remembered. This is referred to as:
    a) process gain.
    b) relational memory.
    c) transactive memory.
    d) constructive memory.

8. How effective a leader is depends on being the right person in the appropriate situation according to the _____ theory of leadership.
    a) contingency
    b) great person
    c) relationship
    d) task

9. Eagly and her colleagues have found that _____ tend to be autocratic leaders and _____ tend to be democratic leaders.
    a) male leaders; female leaders
    b) female leaders; male leaders
    c) older leaders; younger leaders
    d) none of the above

10. Which of the following is FALSE regarding gender and leadership?
    a) Men are better leaders than women are in jobs that require the ability to control people.
    b) Women are better leaders than men are in jobs that require interpersonal skills.
    c) Women evaluate women leaders more negatively than men do when the women leaders adopt the same leadership techniques that men usually use.
    d) Men evaluate women leaders more negatively than women do when the women leaders adopt the same leadership techniques that men usually use.

11. Contemporary examples of the use of water and energy resources are _____ dilemmas.
    a) public goods
    b) commons
    c) ration
    d) societal

12. A form of communication between opposing sides in a conflict in which offers and counteroffers are made and a solution is not reached until both parties agree is called:
   a) collective bargaining.
   b) tit-for-tat strategy.
   c) bartering.
   d) negotiation.

13. Mrs. Perez, the owner of a small business, needs her employees to devise a plan to beat their competitors. Since she is aware of the groupthink phenomenon, she would most likely do which of the following to avoid groupthink?
   a) Keep the members of the group the same and not introduce anyone new into the group.
   b) Clearly express her views to the group at the beginning of the discussion.
   c) Have the group consider as many options as they can.
   d) Have the group discuss the problem quickly since last year was so successful.

14. Marcy studied a very long time for the final exam in her psychology class. She knows the material extremely well and can recall it easily. The final is a departmental exam and Marcy can choose in which classroom she takes the test. When she enters one classroom on the day of the test she finds it crowded. Another classroom across the hall has only a few students in it and is not crowded. Marcy should ____ to improve her performance on the test.
   a) take her test in a classroom where a noisy study group is practicing for an exam
   b) take her test in an empty classroom
   c) take her test in the crowded classroom
   d) take her test in the classroom that is not crowded

15. In a study of aggressive behavior, which of the following situations would increase deindividuation and thereby escalate aggression exhibited by research participants toward a confederate?
   a) having the participants introduce themselves to the confederate at the beginning of the study
   b) running participants individually
   c) having participants put on a mask or a special uniform
   d) running a large group of participants at once
   e) both c and d

Short Answer

1. Describe several causes, symptoms, and consequences of groupthink.

2. What is negotiation? Describe effective negotiation strategies. What strategies are likely to be helpful when negotiations break down?

WEB EXERCISE

Visit www.prenhall.com/aronson and click on the Links for Chapter 9. Click on Social Facilitation and participate in the online experimental simulation. Write up your findings. Or, visit sites on Social Dilemma Games link. Play the Prisoner Dilemma Game. What kinds of social dilemmas did you discover?

CHAPTER 10

Interpersonal Attraction: From First Impressions to Close Relationships

CHAPTER OVERVIEW

Chapter 10 examines the causes of liking and loving that have been studied. The factors which contribute to liking are revealed in the first section of this chapter. People like those who are familiar to them, physically attractive, similar to them, and who like them. These determinants of liking are accounted for by social exchange theory which considers each of them in terms of rewards.   In addition to rewards, equity theory asserts that perceived fairness is necessary for relationship satisfaction.

The next section of the chapter tackles the complexities of defining love. Two theories have conceptualized love by defining its types. For example, a distinction is made between passionate love and companionate love. A third conception of love states that people are guided in close relationships by their love styles. Six love styles have been identified as well as gender and cultural differences in the endorsement of these styles. Cultural differences in beliefs about romantic love and what is important in a marriage partner also are addressed.

The causes of love are examined next. Theories in the area of liking play a role in explaining the causes of loving relationships as well. In addition, evolutionary theory offers explanations of topics such as gender differences in mate selection. The influence of childhood relationships on adult relationship quality is discussed. Research on attachment styles is useful in understanding the dynamics of close relationships. Relational dialectics offers a conception of love as an interpersonal process that is always changing. Lastly, the negative aspects of close relationships and their dissolution are discussed. Strategies people use in response to relationship problems and the consequences of role in the dissolution process are explored.

CHAPTER OUTLINE

Major Antecedents of Attraction

> The Person Next Door: The Propinquity Effect

> Similarity

> Reciprocal Liking

> The Effects of Physical Attractiveness on Liking

> Recollections of Initial Attraction

> Theories of Interpersonal Attraction: Social Exchange and Equity

Close Relationships

> Defining Love

> The Role of Culture in Defining Love

Explanations of Love and Attraction

> Social Exchange in Long-Term Relationships

> Equity in Long-Term Relationships

Evolutionary Explanations of Love

Attachment Styles and Intimate Relationships

Relationships as an Interpersonal Process

Ending Intimate Relationships

LEARNING OBJECTIVES

After reading Chapter 10, you should be able to do the following:

1.   Describe the role of propinquity in attraction. Define the mere exposure effect. Distinguish between physical and functional distance. Explain why the propinquity effect works. (pp. 340-342)

2.   Discuss the importance of similarity in attraction. Explain why we like people whose characteristics, including interpersonal style and communication skill, and beliefs are similar to our own. (pp. 342-344)

3.   Discuss the importance of reciprocal liking in attraction and close relationships. Discuss the role of self-esteem in reciprocal liking. (pp. 344-345)

4.   Discuss the consequences of physical attractiveness for liking strangers and for maintaining relationships. Identify the facial features associated with high attractiveness in females and in males. Discuss cross-cultural findings on cultural standards of beauty. Explain how familiarity may play a role in the perception of attractiveness. (pp. 345-349)

5.   Describe the "what is beautiful is good" stereotype and explain how this stereotype might produce a self-fulfilling prophecy. Discuss cross-cultural research on this stereotype. (pp. 349-351)

6.   Discuss the findings from falling-in-love accounts and from opposite-sex friend accounts. Indicate how these data compare to data collected in the lab. (pp. 351-352)

7.   Describe social exchange theory. Identify the basic concepts of social exchange theory. Distinguish between comparison level and comparison level for alternatives. (pp. 352-354)

8.   Describe equity theory and indicate how partners in a relationship respond when they are over- or underbenefited in an inequitable relationship. Identify how equity theory differs from social exchange theory. (pp. 354-355)

9.   Identify obstacles to the study of long-term, close relationships. (p. 355)

10.   Distinguish between passionate and companionate types of love proposed by Hatfield and Walster. Describe cultural differences in the experience of companionate and passionate types of love. (pp. 355-357)

11.   Identify the combinations of intimacy, passion, and commitment that produce the various types of love outlined in Sternberg's triangular theory of love. (p. 358)

12.   Define the six styles of love according to Hendrick and Hendrick. Identify gender differences in love styles. (pp. 358-359)

13.	Discuss cultural differences in how people label the experiences of romantic love, in the emotions associated with romantic love, and in how people make decisions to marry. Identify cultural differences in love styles. (pp. 359-362)

14.	Discuss support for social exchange theory in long-term relationships. Describe the relationship between social exchange theory and Rusbult's investment model. Identify the three things we need to know in order to predict whether people will stay in an intimate relationship. (pp. 362-364)

15.	Describe how partners' concerns with equity differ depending on whether the partners are involved in an exchange or in a communal relationship. Identify the types of relationships that are likely to be communal. (pp. 364-366)

16.	Describe the evolutionary approach to romantic love. Identify the differences between men and women in the characteristics involved in mate selection and the different strategies of men and women in romantic relationships. Discuss support for evolutionary theory and discuss alternative explanations for the research findings. (pp. 366-368)

17.	Identify the key assumption of attachment theory and distinguish between the three attachment styles. Discuss support for attachment theory as it relates to intimate relationships. Describe the relationship between attribution and attachment styles. Identify a qualification of this research. (pp. 368-371)

18.	Define relational dialectics. Elaborate on how close relationships are characterized according to this approach. Distinguish between the types of tension-producing forces that are seen in close relationships. (pp. 371-373)

19.	Discuss research findings in the area of relationship termination. Identify the five basic categories people use to describe the ending of a relationship. Describe Duck's four-step process of relationship dissolution. (pp. 373-374)

20.	Identify and describe the four types of behaviors that indicate a troubled relationship. (p. 374)

21.	Describe why relationships end according to the relational dialectics approach. Discuss research on "fatal attractions." (p. 374-375)

22.	Identify the relationship between gender and who will end a relationship. Identify the most important determinant of how people feel after a romantic relationship is terminated. Identify individual and situational factors that determine whether ex-loved ones will want to remain friends. (pp. 375-377)

KEY TERMS

propinquity effect (p. 340)

mere exposure effect (p. 341)

social exchange theory (p. 353)

comparison level (p. 353)

comparison level for alternatives (p. 353)

equity theory (p. 354)

companionate love (p. 356)

passionate love (p. 356)

STUDY QUESTIONS

1.   What is the relationship between propinquity and attraction? What is the mere exposure effect?

2.   Why is similarity such an important factor in attraction?

3.   Why is reciprocal liking important in attraction? What role does self-esteem play in reciprocal liking?

4.   What are the effects of physical attractiveness on liking? What are facial features associated with high attractiveness in females and in males? What are cross-cultural findings on the perceptions of physical attractiveness?

5. Which stereotypes are associated with physical attractiveness? What role does the self-fulfilling prophecy play in the perpetuation of these assumptions? What are cross-cultural findings regarding the "what is beautiful is good" stereotype?

6. What are the predictors of initial attraction? Which factors have been mentioned most often in people's falling-in-love accounts? What are gender and cultural differences regarding predictors of attraction?

7. How does the social exchange theory explain how people feel about their relationships? What are comparisons that people make according to this theory?

8. What accounts for happy relationships according to equity theory?

9. Why is there little scientific data on close relationships?

10. What are differences between companionate love and passionate love?

11. What are the three basic ingredients of love according to the triangular theory of love? What are the types of love formed by varying degrees of these ingredients?

12. How do the six styles of love differ from each other? What roles do gender and culture play in the endorsement of the different love styles? What styles of love do men, women, people from Eastern cultures, and people from Western cultures typically have?

13. How does culture influence the definition of romantic love, the emotions associated with romantic love, and the behaviors that correspond with being in love?

14. What does the social exchange theory help explain regarding long-term relationships?

15.   What are the principles of the investment model? What is the definition of investments according to this
        model?

16.   How do exchange relationships differ from communal relationships?

17.   What are the major arguments of evolutionary theory as it relates to love? How does evolutionary theory
        explain people's choices regarding with whom they fall in love? What are other explanations for gender
        differences in mate selection?

18.   How do attachment styles develop and how do they manifest themselves in later relationships? What do people
        with each style report about their relationships? What role do attribution and attachment style play in
        relationship success?

19.   According to relational dialectics, what are the forces that cause tension and characterize close relationships?

20.   What are five basic categories of ending romantic relationships according to people's accounts of their
        breakups?

21.   What are the four stages of relationship dissolution according to Duck?

22.   What are the four types of behavior characteristic of troubled relationships?

23.   What is perhaps the most important predictor of psychological and physical effects of relationship dissolution?
        What is the best way to end a relationship? What determines whether people will remain friends after their
        relationship ends?

PRACTICE TEST 1

Fill in the Blank

1.   The finding that the more we see and interact with people, the more likely they are to become our friends is called the _____.

2.   The finding that the more exposure we have to a stimulus, the more apt we are to like it is called _____.

3.   The basic ideas people have about love that influence their behavior are called _____.

4.   An approach that studies long-term relationships and focuses on their dynamic interpersonal characteristics is _____.

5.   How people feel about a relationship depends on their perceptions of the rewards and costs of the relationship, the kind of relationship they deserve, and their chances for having a better relationship with someone else. This is the rationale of _____ theory.

6.   People's expectations about the level of rewards and punishments that they are likely to receive in a particular relationship comprise their _____.

7.   People's expectations about the level of rewards and punishments that they would receive in an alternative relationship comprise their _____.

8.   People are happiest with relationships in which the rewards, costs, and contributions of one person in a relationship roughly equal the rewards, costs, and contributions of the other person in the relationship. This is the rationale of _____ theory.

9.   The feelings of intimacy and affection we feel toward someone that are not accompanied by passion or physiological arousal are called _____.

10.   The feelings of intense longing for another person that are accompanied by physiological arousal are called _____.

11.   The theory that states different kinds of love consist of varying degrees intimacy, passion, and commitment is called the _____.

Multiple Choice

1.   When you were eight years old, chances are you were best friends with someone who lived on your block. Social psychologists would attribute this to:
        a)   the effects of attitude similarity.
        b)   your uniquely similar interests.
        c)   matched levels of physical attractiveness.
        d)   the propinquity effect.

2.   In their study of "blind dates," Elaine Hatfield and her colleagues (1966) found that an individual's desire to date his or her partner again was best predicted by the partner's:
        a)   physical attractiveness.
        b)   dominance and sensitivity.
        c)   complementary personality traits.
        d)   intelligence.

3.   Research has found all of the following facial features to be considered physically attractive EXCEPT:
     a)   large eyes.
     b)   wide cheeks.
     c)   big smile.
     d)   small nose.

4.   Perhaps the single most important determinant of whether we will like someone is whether:
     a)   that person is similar to us.
     b)   we believe that person likes us.
     c)   we believe that person is physically attractive.
     d)   that person is familiar to us.

5.   Social exchange theory maintains that people are happiest with relationships when:
     a)   the perceived rewards of the relationship are equal to the perceived costs of the relationship.
     b)   the rewards and costs a person experiences are roughly equal to the rewards and costs of the other person in a relationship.
     c)   the actual rewards and costs of the relationship exceed the expected rewards and costs.
     d)   the perceived rewards of the relationship outweigh the perceived costs of the relationship.

6.   When the rewards and costs a person experiences and the contributions he/she makes to the relationship are roughly equal to the rewards, costs, and contributions of the other person, the relationship is:
     a)   equitable.
     b)   communal.
     c)   intimate.
     d)   passionate.

7.   In Sternberg's triangular theory of love, consummate love is characterized by:
     a)   high levels of passion and low levels of commitment and intimacy.
     b)   high levels of passion, commitment, and intimacy.
     c)   high levels of commitment and passion and low levels of intimacy.
     d)   high levels of passion and intimacy and low levels of commitment.

8.   People are likely to remain committed to an intimate relationship even if they are dissatisfied with it and even if alternative relationships look promising if:
     a)   they suffer from low self-esteem.
     b)   they have a high comparison level.
     c)   they have benefited from the relationship in the past.
     d)   they have invested heavily in the relationship.

9.   In a happy communal relationship, partners believe that equity:
     a)   is of no importance.
     b)   should exist at any given time.
     c)   will be maintained in the long run.
     d)   requires close monitoring at all times.

10. The ludic love style is characterized by:
     a)   intense longing for one's partner.
     b)   beliefs that love requires a long-term commitment.
     c)   beliefs that love is a game to be played.
     d)   beliefs that love develops from friendship.

11. At the end of a romantic relationship, who is most likely to want to remain friends with his/her ex-lover?
    a) a female who has taken responsibility for the breakup
    b) a male who has taken responsibility for the breakup
    c) a male whose partner has taken responsibility for the breakup
    d) a female whose partner has taken responsibility for the breakup

12. The desire to be validated and the conclusions we draw about people's characters based on their attitudes lead us to prefer people whose attitudes:
    a) complement our own.
    b) are similar to our own.
    c) are generally positive.
    d) are well informed.

13. Which of the following is a behavior indicative of a troubled relationship?
    a) exit
    b) voice
    c) loyalty
    d) all of the above

14. The comparison level for alternatives is based on:
    a) perceptions of the level of rewards and punishments received from your primary caregiver during infancy.
    b) perceptions of the level of rewards and punishments others are receiving in their present relationships.
    c) expectations about the level of rewards and punishments others would receive if they were sharing a relationship with your partner.
    d) expectations about the level of rewards and punishments you would receive if you were in a different relationship.

15. Psychologists examining close intimate relationships from the perspective of social exchange theory have found that:
    a) rewards are always important to the outcome of intimate relationships while costs become increasingly important over time.
    b) costs are always important to the outcome of intimate relationships while rewards become increasingly important over time.
    c) both rewards and costs are equally important at the start of intimate relationships.
    d) social exchange theory does not adequately explain why intimate relationships endure.

16. A tit-for-tat equity norm governs _____ relationships.
    a) exchange
    b) communal
    c) familial
    d) romantic

17. Attachment styles are the expectations people develop about:
    a) the level of rewards and punishments they are likely to receive in a particular relationship.
    b) the level of rewards and punishments they would receive in an alternative relationship.
    c) the kinds of actions by their partners that constitute a threat to their self-worth and produce feelings of jealousy.
    d) relationships with others based on the relationship they had with their primary caregiver when they were infants.

18. An individual who has an anxious/ambivalent attachment style:
   a) finds it difficult to trust others and to develop close intimate relationships.
   b) is able to develop a mature, lasting relationship.
   c) wants to become very close to his/her partner but worries that his/her affections will not be returned.
   d) is not interested in developing a close relationship.

Short Answer

1. What factors have been demonstrated to increase interpersonal attraction among casual acquaintances?

2. Identify facial features associated with attractiveness in men and in women. Describe the assumptions we make about attractive people and a consequence of making such assumptions.

3. Describe the key assumption of attachment theory. Describe the formation of each of the attachment styles in infancy and the consequences of each of these for adult relationships.

4. Define the six styles of love and identify gender and cultural differences in the endorsement of each style.

PRACTICE TEST 2

Fill in the Blank

1. People's commitment to a relationship depends on their satisfaction with the relationship, their comparison level for alternatives, and their level of investment in the relationship. This is the rationale of the
_____.

2. Relationships governed by the need for equity are called _____ relationships.

3. Relationships in which people's primary concern is being responsive to the other person's needs are called _____ relationships.

4. The expectations people develop about relationships with others, based on the relationship they had with their primary caregiver when they were infants characterize their _____.

5. An attachment style characterized by trust, a lack of concern with being abandoned, and the view that one is worthy and well liked is called a(n) _____ attachment style.

6. An attachment style characterized by a suppression of attachment needs and by difficulty developing intimate relationships is known as a(n) _____ attachment style.

7. An attachment style characterized by a concern that others will not reciprocate one's desire for intimacy, resulting in higher-than-average levels of anxiety is called a (n) _____ attachment style.

8. A type of tension whereby people in a relationship want independence but also want emotional closeness is
_____.

9. A type of tension whereby people in a relationship want excitement but also want security is
_____.

10. A type of tension whereby people in a relationship want to self-disclose but also want to remain discrete is _____.

11. An approach to love that focuses on how men and women are motivated to ensure their reproductive success is known as the _____ approach to love.

Multiple Choice

1. Relationships are always in a state of change due to opposing forces of autonomy/connection, novelty/predictability, and openness/closedness according to:
   a) relational dialectics.
   b) social exchange theory.
   c) mere exposure.
   d) complementarity hypothesis.

2. Which of the following is the final step in Duck's (1982) process of relationship dissolution?
   a) Discussing the breakup with one's partner.
   b) Telling one's friends of the breakup.
   c) Forming an account of how and why the breakup occurred.
   d) Withdrawing emotionally from others.

3. An approach which states that men are attracted by women's appearance and that women are attracted by men's resources is the:
   a) communal exchange theory.
   b) investment model.
   c) propinquity effect.
   d) evolutionary approach to love.

4. Which of the following is a style of love according to Hendrick and Hendrick?
   a) mania
   b) ludus
   c) Eros
   e) all of the above

5. The more times we see someone, the more inclined we are to like the person. This is called the _____ effect.
   a) propinquity
   b) familiarity
   c) mere exposure
   d) social facilitation

6. Which of the following may explain why similarity is an important factor in becoming attracted to someone?
   a) People who are similar give each other social validation.
   b) Negative characteristics are given to people who are dissimilar.
   c) People who are similar are believed to like one another.
   d) All the above may explain why similarity is an important factor.

7. Which of the following is true regarding cultural standards that dictate which facial characteristics are considered beautiful?
   a) No cross-cultural agreement exists in what makes up a beautiful or a handsome face.
   b) Some cross-cultural agreement exists in what makes up a beautiful or a handsome face.
   c) Standards of beauty may reflect people's preferences for the familiar over the unfamiliar.
   d) Both b and c are true.

8. Which of the following is FALSE regarding assumptions people have about attractive people?
    a) The concern for physical attractiveness affects men's lives more than it does women's lives.
    b) The "what is beautiful is good" stereotype operates across cultures.
    c) Attractive people are higher in social competence than unattractive people.
    d) Attractive people are thought to be more popular and assertive than unattractive people.

9. Relationship satisfaction depends on people's comparison level or what they expect the outcome of their relationship to be in terms of:
    a) whether they can replace it with a better one.
    b) rewards and benefits.
    c) rewards and costs.
    d) time and money.

10. Intense longing and physiological arousal are to _____ love as intimacy and affection are to _____ love.
    a) fatuous; romantic
    b) companionate; romantic
    c) passionate; companionate
    d) romantic; empty

11. Men are more likely than women are to adopt the _____ love style while women are more likely than men are to adopt the _____ love style.
    a) ludic; agapic
    b) ludic; storgic
    c) ludic; pragmatic
    d) both a and b
    e) both b and c

12. According to Sternberg's triangular theory of love, sexual attraction is to _____ as self-disclosure is to _____.
    a) passion; commitment
    b) passion; intimacy
    c) intimacy; commitment
    d) intimacy; passion

13. According to Sternberg's triangular theory of love, intimacy plus passion equals _____ love while passion plus commitment equals _____ love.
    a) consummate; fatuous
    b) passionate; companionate
    c) fatuous; passionate
    d) romantic; fatuous

14. Which of the following is true regarding the role of culture in defining love?
    a) The Japanese have a term for love (amae) for which there is no equivalent word in the English language.
    b) Fixing someone's bicycle could be considered a romantic act in China.
    c) Research has found that love in Chinese songs is less erotic than love expressed in American songs.
    d) Both a and b are true.
    e) All the above are true.

15. Which of the following is FALSE regarding love in individualist versus collectivist societies?
    a) Romantic love is a more important basis for marriage in individualist compared to collectivist societies.
    b) Families often arrange the marriages of their children in collectivist societies.
    c) People in individualist societies are more likely to endorse the storgic love style than are people in collectivist societies.
    d) Culture determines how romantic love is experienced and expressed.

16. Individuals having which of the following attachment styles have the most short-lived romantic relationships?
    a) anxious/ambivalent
    b) avoidant
    c) secure
    d) detached

17. Individuals having which of the following attachment styles are the most likely to report never having been in love?
    a) anxious/ambivalent
    b) avoidant
    c) secure
    d) sincere

18. According to the study of attachment styles and relationship success (Kirkpatrick & Davis, 1994), which of the following relationship pairs had very stable relationships?
    a) anxious/ambivalent men involved with secure women
    b) anxious/ambivalent men involved with avoidant women
    c) secure women involved with avoidant men
    d) anxious/ambivalent women involved with avoidant men

Short Answer

1. Describe the effects of rewards, costs, and two kinds of comparison levels on the outcome of a relationship according to social exchange theory.

2. Compare and contrast social exchange theory with equity theory.

3. Rather than terminating a romance outright, people wanting to dissolve a relationship have been known to annoy their partners and deliberately cause problems in the relationship. Is this simply the act of a coward or could there be other motives underlying the use of such a strategy?

WEB EXERCISE

Visit the Social Psychology Network at www.socialpsychology.org. Click on Online Psychology Studies. Choose the Interpersonal Relations link and participate in an online study. What is the purpose of the study? What did you learn? What material in the text corresponds with the study's focus?

CHAPTER 11

Prosocial Behavior: Why Do People Help?

CHAPTER OVERVIEW

In the first section of this chapter, the three different motives that have been proposed to explain prosocial behavior are described. The theory of evolutionary psychology, social exchange theory, and the empathy-altruism hypothesis each help to understand why people help others. However, one of the difficulties of this research area is the complexity of distinguishing between behaviors motivated by self-interest and those that are truly altruistic.

The next section identifies the effects of individual differences such as personality, gender, culture, and mood on how likely people are to help in a variety of circumstances. Research topics on the altruistic personality, gender, and cultural differences in the propensity to help in certain situations are explored. Also, the conducive effects of both positive and negative moods on helping are examined. Situational determinants such as urban overload, the number of bystanders, and characteristics of the relationship, are discussed next. Latane and Darley's bystander intervention decision tree helps explain the several causes of the bystander effect. In the final section, strategies for increasing prosocial behavior and volunteerism are developed from lessons learned throughout this chapter.

CHAPTER OUTLINE

Basic Motives Underlying Prosocial Behavior: Why Do People Help?

>   Evolutionary Psychology: Instincts and Genes

>   Social Exchange: The Costs and Rewards of Helping

>   Empathy and Altruism: The Pure Motive for Helping

Personal Determinants of Prosocial Behavior: Why Do Some People Help More than Others?

>   Individual Differences: The Altruistic Personality

>   Gender Differences in Prosocial Behavior

>   Cultural Differences in Prosocial Behavior

>   The Effects of Mood on Prosocial Behavior

Situational Determinants of Prosocial Behavior: When Will People Help?

>   Environments: Rural versus Urban

>   The Number of Bystanders: The Bystander Effect

>   The Nature of the Relationship: Communal versus Exchange Relationships

How Can Helping Be Increased?

       Increasing the Likelihood that Bystanders Will Intervene

       Increasing Volunteerism

LEARNING OBJECTIVES

After reading Chapter 11, you should be able to do the following:

1.   Define prosocial behavior. Define altruism. (p. 382)

2.   Describe the approach of evolutionary psychology. Discuss the three factors that explain altruism according to evolutionary theory. (pp. 383-386)

3.   Describe social exchange theory. Indicate how this theory is different from evolutionary theory in its explanation of altruism. Provide examples of rewards and costs associated with helping behaviors. (pp. 386-387)

4.   Define empathy. Describe the empathy-altruism hypothesis. Describe the relationship between the empathy-altruism hypothesis and social exchange theory. Describe the debate that has arisen over whether empathy-driven helping is altruistic or egoistic. Describe research that attempts to provide evidence in support of the empathy-altruism hypothesis. (pp. 387-391)

5.   Indicate the limits to predicting helpfulness on the basis of personality and indicate what else we need to know in order to predict how helpful someone will be. Define altruistic personality. (pp. 391-393)

6.   Describe the relationship between gender and forms of prosocial behavior. Discuss reasons why males are more likely to help in some situations while females are more likely to help in others. (pp. 393-394)

7.   Discuss cultural differences in prosocial behavior. Define in-group and out-group. Discuss the importance of in-group membership in individualistic cultures compared to interdependent ones. Describe cultural differences in helping. (pp. 394-395)

8.   Describe the effects of mood on helping. Identify why a good mood and a bad mood can result in helping behavior. Define negative-state relief hypothesis. (pp. 395-397)

9.   Explain why, according to the urban-overload hypothesis, people in rural environments are more helpful than people in urban environments. (pp. 398-399)

10.   Describe the bystander effect. Identify and describe the step-by-step process by which people decide whether to intervene in an emergency. Describe the processes that may lead to nonintervention at each step in the decision tree. Define pluralistic ignorance. Define diffusion of responsibility. Discuss how bystanders influence pluralistic ignorance and the diffusion of responsibility and why these factors decrease helping behavior. (pp. 399-406)

11.   Describe the relationship between helping and type of relationship. Discuss the importance of rewards in an exchange versus a communal relationship. Identify when helping a friend can threaten one's self-esteem and reduce helping. (pp. 406-408)

12.   Describe how helping others can make them feel. Discuss ways to increase prosocial behavior by applying lessons learned about what increases and decreases prosocial behavior. Identify methods to increase volunteerism. (pp. 409-411)

KEY TERMS

prosocial behavior (p. 382)

altruism (p. 382)

evolutionary psychology (p. 383)

kin selection (p. 383)

norm of reciprocity (p. 385)

empathy (p. 387)

empathy-altruism hypothesis (p. 388)

altruistic personality (p. 391)

in-group (p. 394)

out-group (p. 394)

negative-state relief hypothesis (p. 397)

urban overload hypothesis (p. 398)

bystander effect (p. 401)

pluralistic ignorance (p. 403)

diffusion of responsibility (p. 405)

STUDY QUESTIONS

1. What is the difference between prosocial behavior and altruism?

2. How does the theory of evolutionary psychology explain altruism?

3. What is the basic assumption of social exchange theory as it relates to prosocial behavior? How is social exchange theory's explanation different from the evolutionary one? How is helping others rewarding? How is helping others costly?

4. How does the empathy-altruism hypothesis explain altruistic behavior? What are experimental strategies used to test the strength of this hypothesis? What other motives besides empathy could lead to helping?

5. What are three basic motives that could explain prosocial behavior?

6. What is the altruistic personality? Why is knowing a person's personality not enough information to predict whether this person will engage in prosocial behavior? What other factors are important for predicting prosocial behavior?

7. How do males and females differ in the area of prosocial behavior?

8. What are examples of cultural differences in prosocial behavior?

9. When and why do people in a good mood help others?

10. What is the negative-state relief hypothesis and what does it attempt to explain?

11. What aspects of the social situation are important for prosocial behavior to occur? What is the relationship between population size and prosocial behavior? How does the urban-overload hypothesis explain the greater likelihood of prosocial behavior in towns of certain population sizes?

12. What are the five steps that depict what people consider when deciding whether to intervene in an emergency? What influences whether people will continue through the steps and eventually help?

13. Why does the presence of others influence people's interpretation of an event as an emergency? How does informational social influence lead to the bystander effect? What are the consequences of the bystander effect?

14. How do motives to help differ in exchange versus communal relationships?

15. What are strategies to increase prosocial behavior? What factors are important to consider when attempting to make prosocial behavior more common? What are effective means to increase volunteerism?

PRACTICE TEST 1

Fill in the Blank

1. Any act that is performed with the goal of benefiting another person is called _____.

2. Helping another with no thoughts about oneself is called _____.

3. The notion that behaviors that help a genetic relative are favored by natural selection is called _____.

4. The assumption that others will treat us the way we treat them is called the _____.

5. The theory that attempts to explain social behavior by stressing the contributions of genetic factors and the principles of natural selection is called _____ psychology.

6. The ability to experience the events and emotions that another person is experiencing is called _____.

7. We will attempt to help a person regardless of what we have to gain if we feel empathy for that person. This is the rationale of the _____.

Multiple Choice

1. Prosocial behavior is:
   a) performed without any regard to self-interests.
   b) appreciated by everyone we help.
   c) performed with the goal of benefiting another person.
   d) all the above.

2. The notion of kin selection dictates that you are most likely to help someone who is:
   a) genetically similar to you.
   b) a potential mate.
   c) physically attractive.
   d) likely to return the favor.

3. According to social exchange theory, relationships are best understood by:
   a) assuming that others will treat us the way we treat them.
   b) realizing that people desire to maximize their benefits and minimize their costs.
   c) applying evolutionary theory to social behavior.
   d) examining people's use of information gleaned by observing others in the situation.

4. Batson's empathy-altruism hypotheses states that we will help a victim of misfortune regardless of whether helping is in our best interests if:
   a) we perceive that the victim is dissimilar to us.
   b) the costs of helping are minimal.
   c) the victim is unable to control his or her performance.
   d) we experience the victim's pain and suffering.

121

5.   Maria is more likely than John to help a(n):
    a)   child in a burning building.
    b)   pilot struggling from the wreckage of an airplane.
    c)   man drowning in a lake.
    d)   elderly neighbor do his weekly shopping.

6.   People in interdependent cultures are _____ likely to help members of the _____ than are people in individualistic cultures.
    a)   less; in-group
    b)   more; out-group
    c)   less; out-group
    d)   there are no cultural differences in prosocial behavior

7.   Which of the following best characterizes the effects of mood on helping behavior?
    a)   Good moods increase helping.
    b)   Bad moods increase helping.
    c)   Either good or bad moods can increase helping.
    d)   Neither good nor bad moods can increase helping.

8.   According to Cialdini's negative-state relief hypotheses, people help others in order to:
    a)   alleviate the sadness and distress of others.
    b)   alleviate their own sadness and distress.
    c)   prolong the good mood they're in.
    d)   reap the rewards of favors reciprocated in the future.

9.   The bystander effect can be defined as:
    a)   the attempt to help people regardless of what we have to gain.
    b)   the likelihood that any one person will help decreases as the number of witnesses to an emergency increases.
    c)   the assumption that others will treat us the way we treat them.
    d)   the likelihood that people will perform impulsive and deviant acts increases as group size increases.

10.   Having identified a situation as a clear emergency requiring help, helping may still be inhibited by:
    a)   pluralistic ignorance.
    b)   diffusion of responsibility.
    c)   distraction.
    d)   overjustification.

11.   Having read the chapter on prosocial behavior, you may be more likely to offer others help because:
    a)   you realize that people often need help to accomplish a task even when receiving help threatens their self-esteem.
    b)   you are now aware that the norm of reciprocity is universally accepted.
    c)   being aware of the barriers to helping can increase the likelihood that people can overcome these barriers.
    d)   viewing social exchanges as business exchanges makes it easier to recognize when helping is mutually beneficial to both you and a victim.

12.   Which of the following concepts have evolutionary psychologists used to explain prosocial behavior?
    a)   kin selection and norms of reciprocity
    b)   empathy and altruism
    c)   immediate rewards and punishments
    d)   urban overload and diffusion of responsibility

13. How does social exchange theory differ from the evolutionary approach to prosocial behavior?
   a) Only social exchange theory maintains that prosocial behavior is motivated by self-interest.
   b) Only social exchange theory maintains that prosocial behavior is truly altruistic.
   c) Only the evolutionary approach traces prosocial behavior back to evolutionary roots.
   d) Only the evolutionary approach maintains that people desire to maximize their rewards.

14. Parents who want to their children to grow up to exhibit prosocial behavior should:
   a) tell their children that their prosocial behavior results from their kind and helpful nature.
   b) emphasize to their children that instances of prosocial behavior will be rewarded.
   c) punish their children for failing to exhibit prosocial behaviors.
   d) all of the above

15. Why do researchers typically find that people who score high on personality tests of altruism are no more likely to help than those who score low?
   a) Because personality tests of altruism are invalid.
   b) Because situational influences also determine helping behavior.
   c) Because people's personalities change greatly over time.
   d) Because altruism can be instilled in children who might otherwise not score high on personality tests of altruism.

Short Answer

1. At a concert you see a person lying on the ground moaning and assume that this person is ill. Even though you are not a doctor, you decide to go and help this person. Describe this prosocial act from the perspective of social exchange theory.

2. Distinguish between prosocial and altruistic behavior. Why is it difficult for researchers to determine whether people ever help for purely altruistic reasons?

3. Having just slipped on a busy sidewalk, you feel a searing pain in your leg and fear that it is broken. Because you are familiar with Latane and Darley's bystander intervention decision tree, you realize that people may not help for a variety of reasons. What might you do to facilitate people's decision to help you at each stage in the decision tree?

PRACTICE TEST 2

Fill in the Blank

1. Those aspects of a person's make-up which are said to make him or her likely to help others in a wide variety of situations comprise a(n) _____.

2. The group with which one identifies and feels a sense of membership is called a(n) _____.

3. The hypothesis that states people help others in order to alleviate their own sadness and distress is called the _____.

4. The hypothesis that maintains city dwellers keep to themselves in order to avoid excessive stimulation is called the _____.

5. The greater number of bystanders who witness an emergency, the less likely anyone is to help. This finding has been termed the _____.

6. A phenomenon whereby everyone assumes that nothing is wrong in an emergency because no one else looks concerned is called _____.

7. A decrease in the obligation people feel to help someone as the number of other witnesses increases is called _____.

Multiple Choice

1. People experiencing guilt tend to be helpful because:
   a) they often act on the idea that good deeds cancel out bad deeds.
   b) they are more likely to interpret situations as emergencies.
   c) they are more likely to notice situations in which emergencies occur.
   d) gratitude from the victim will reassure them that they are still likable.

2. Milgram's (1970) urban-overload hypothesis states that people in cities are less likely to help than people in rural areas because city dwellers:
   a) are more aware of the negative consequences of helping.
   b) are less likely to know what form of assistance they should give.
   c) keep to themselves in order to avoid excess stimulation.
   d) are more likely to use confused bystanders as a source of misinformation.

3. Latane and Darley (1970) attributed the murder of Kitty Genovese in New York City to the:
   a) large number of bystanders who witnessed the emergency.
   b) small number of bystanders who witnessed the emergency.
   c) lessons that city dwellers learn about keeping to themselves.
   d) insufficient amount of stimulation experienced by the witnesses.

4. When may we be LESS helpful toward friends than toward strangers?
   a) when the task is not important to us
   b) when helping is not costly
   c) when the rewards are great
   d) when the task is very important to our self-esteem

5. In which type of relationship are people concerned less with equity and more with how much help is needed by the other person?
   a) exchange relationships
   b) social relationships
   c) romantic relationships
   d) communal relationships

6. Which of the following best illustrates the kind of thinking influenced by diffusion of responsibility throughout a group?
   a) "Everyone seems to be reacting calmly. Maybe there's no real problem."
   b) "I hope I don't make things worse than they already are by trying to help."
   c) "Why should I risk helping when others could as easily help?"
   d) "If no one else is offering help, I guess it's up to me."

124

7.   Altruism is:
      a)   the desire to help another person even if it involves a cost to the helper.
      b)   performed without any regard to self-interests.
      c)   helping another with hopes of getting something in return.
      d)   both a and b.
      e)   all of the above.

8.   If people help others with the expectation that the people they help will help them in the future, they are being guided by:
      a)   kin selection.
      b)   norm of reciprocity.
      c)   bystander effect.
      d)   empathy-altruism hypothesis.

9.   Which of the following is true regarding individual differences in helping behavior?
      a)   Characteristics of an altruistic personality have been identified and predict helping behavior.
      b)   Mood and situational pressures do not impact helping behavior.
      c)   People who score high on tests of altruism are much more likely to help others than are people who score low.
      d)   All the above are true.
      e)   None of the above are true.

10.   The group with which an individual identifies and of which an individual feels a part is called a(n):
      a)   kin group.
      b)   social group.
      c)   in-group.
      d)   common group.

11.   All of the following are situational determinants of prosocial behavior except which one?
      a)   type of environment
      b)   the number of people who are around
      c)   how much empathy people feel
      d)   being in a hurry

12.   Latane and Darley's (1970) study of the smoke-filled room experiment demonstrated which of the following?
      a)   pluralistic ignorance
      b)   negative-state relief hypothesis
      c)   bystander effect
      d)   both a and c

13.   To increase volunteerism, organizations should:
      a)   mandate volunteerism.
      b)   encourage volunteerism.
      c)   provide people with a sense they freely chose to volunteer.
      d)   do both b and c.
      e)   do all the above.

14.   Suppose a group of individuals witness a painter fall off a ladder and groan. Because it is not clear whether the painter is seriously hurt or not, they all look to each other to see what everyone else is doing. Because no one is offering to help, each individual fails to do anything at all. This is an example of failure to help due to:
      a)   shock.
      b)   informational social influence.
      c)   normative social influence.
      d)   reciprocity.

15. According to Latane and Darley's (1970) step-by-step description of how people decide whether to help in an emergency, noticing the event is followed by:
   a) assuming responsibility.
   b) interpreting the event as an emergency.
   c) implementing a decision.
   d) knowing how to help.

Short Answer

1. By considering the situational determinants of prosocial behavior, describe the steps you can take to increase helping among others.

2. Describe the basic motives underlying prosocial behavior according to the evolutionary approach, social exchange theory, and the empathy-altruism hypothesis.

3. Imagine that you have just taken a drug which, your doctor tells you, has the side effect of prolonging whatever mood you are in. This, unfortunately, is bad news because you are presently experiencing some sadness and distress. As you leave the doctor's office, a man falls down in front of you. How does the negative-state relief hypothesis predict you will behave and why?

WEB EXERCISE

Go to www.prenhall.com/aronson. Click on the Links for Chapter 11 and go to What Makes Kids Care? Summarize the information you read and compare it to what the authors of the text say about increasing prosocial behavior in children.

CHAPTER 12

Aggression: Why We Hurt Other People

CHAPTER OVERVIEW

Aggression is a complicated concept that is defined and elaborated upon in the first section of this chapter. The study of human aggression has led philosophers and scientists to wonder about basic human nature. A common question concerns the degree to which aggression is innate or learned. To help answer this question, cross-cultural research findings are discussed.

The next section focuses on the biological and situational causes of aggression. The contributing factors of the brain and hormones, alcohol, pain and discomfort, and viewing media violence, on the exhibition of aggressive behavior are examined. Gender and cultural differences regarding the influences of some of these factors are explored. Situations that cause pain, discomfort, or frustration facilitate aggression. Since aggression is largely a learned response that is more likely to be made after observing aggressive models, television violence and violent pornography have been found to be related to increases in aggression.

In the final section, strategies to reduce aggressive behaviors are reviewed. Aggression can be reduced by punishment only under certain conditions. These situations are outlined. Although intuitively appealing, the catharsis hypothesis, which states that venting anger reduces future aggressive tendencies, has not been validated in research. Other options to deal with aggressive feelings and reduce another's aggression are proposed.

CHAPTER OUTLINE

What Is Aggression?

      Is Aggression Inborn or Learned?

      Is Aggression Instinctual? Situational? Optional?

      Aggressiveness Across Cultures

Neural and Chemical Causes of Aggression

      Serotonin and Testosterone

      Alcohol and Aggression

Situational Causes of Aggression

      Pain and Discomfort as Causes of Aggression

      Social Situations Leading to Aggression

      Aggressive Objects and Cues

      Exposure to Violence in the Media

      Violent Pornography and Violence Against Women

How to Reduce Aggression

    Does Punishing Aggression Reduce Aggressive Behavior?

    Catharsis and Aggression

    What Are We Supposed to Do with Our Anger?

    Could the Columbine Massacre Have Been Prevented?

LEARNING OBJECTIVES

After reading Chapter 12, you should be able to do the following:

1.   Identify the critical feature that distinguishes aggressive from nonaggressive behavior. Explain why behavior that causes no physical harm to anyone can still be considered aggressive behavior. Distinguish between hostile and instrumental aggression. (p. 417)

2.   Contrast the philosophy of Rousseau with the philosophies of Hobbes and Freud concerning people's natural inclinations to aggress. Define Freud's concepts of Eros and Thanatos, and describe his hydraulic theory. (pp. 417-418)

3.   Discuss animal studies which support the role of instinct and those which support the role of learning in the production of aggressive behavior. Discuss why aggression can be considered an optional strategy. (pp. 418-419)

4.   Identify the importance of culture and social change in the degree of human aggression that exists using the examples of the Iroquois and regional differences in the U.S. (pp. 419-421)

5.   Identify the relationship between the body and aggressive responses. Describe conditions when stimulation of the amygdala produces aggression and when it produces escape behavior. Identify the effects that serotonin has on impulsive aggression. Describe evidence that suggests the male sex hormone, testosterone, produces aggression. (pp. 421-422)

6.   Discuss the relationship between gender, culture, and aggressive behavior. Describe the relationship between gender and overt versus covert aggression. Describe the relationship between gender and aggressive behavior as a result of direct provocation. Contrast the large gender differences in lethal violence committed against intimate partners. (pp. 422-423)

7.   Discuss the relationship between alcohol use and aggression. (p. 423)

8.   Describe anecdotal and experimental evidence that suggests people are more likely to behave aggressively when they experience pain or discomfort. Identify the environmental factor that has been linked to riots and violent crime. (pp. 423-425)

9.   Describe the frustration-aggression theory. Identify factors that accentuate frustration and thereby increase the probability of aggressive behavior. Discuss the mediating role of anger or annoyance in the frustration-aggression theory. Identify situational factors which might inhibit aggression even by somebody who has been angered. (pp. 425-427)

10.   Define relative deprivation and discuss its impact on frustration and subsequent aggression. (p. 427)

11.   Identify conditions when direct provocation is likely to evoke aggressive retaliation. (pp. 427-428)

12. Discuss the cognitive and behavioral effects of aggressive stimuli (e.g., guns) in the presence of angry individuals. Discuss evidence that the presence of guns increases the aggressive behavior of people in the real world. (pp. 428-430)

13. Describe social learning theory and the basic procedure used by Bandura and his colleagues to demonstrate social learning in the laboratory. Discuss the consequences of exposing children to an aggressive model. (pp. 430-431)

14. Discuss the effects of watching violence in the media. Identify the conclusions that can be drawn from correlational and experimental research on media violence and aggressive behavior in children and adults. Describe evidence that suggests repeated exposure to TV violence has a numbing effect on people. Identify the effects of watching a lot of television on people's views of the world. State five reasons why media violence produces aggression. (pp. 431-435)

15. Define scripts and describe the role they play in sexual relationships. Discuss the effects of viewing sexually explicit material compared to viewing materials that combine sex and violence on the acceptance of sexual violence toward women and on aggressive behavior toward women. (pp. 435-437)

16. Identify the conditions under which punishing aggression reduces aggressive behavior in children and adults. (pp. 438-441)

17. Define catharsis. Describe evidence that "blowing off steam" by engaging in physical activities, by watching others engage in aggressive behavior, or by behaving aggressively increases rather than decreases hostile feelings. Explain how cognitive dissonance theory accounts for findings that aggression breeds subsequent aggression toward victims of one's aggression. Discuss the effects of war on the aggressive behavior of people. (pp. 441-445)

18. Identify the most effective means of dealing with pent-up anger. Contrast the effects of venting versus self-awareness on subsequent aggression. Identify the benefits and underlying process of expressing feelings in a nonviolent manner. (pp. 445-446)

19. Identify the most effective means of defusing anger that someone is experiencing as a consequence of your behavior. (pp. 446-447)

20. Discuss the effects of training, reinforcing, and of modeling nonaggressive behaviors on aggression in children. Discuss the effects of empathy and empathy training on reducing aggression. (pp. 447-449)

21. Identify the benefits of teaching empathy in school. Discuss the possible effects of empathy training on preventing school shootings. Identify why it is important to look to the social situation when trying to understand why these tragic events happened. (pp. 449-452)

KEY TERMS

aggressive action (p. 417)

hostile aggression (p. 417)

instrumental aggression (p. 417)

Eros (p. 418)

Thanatos (p. 418)

hydraulic theory (p. 418)

amygdala (p. 421)

serotonin (p. 421)

testosterone (p. 421)

frustration-aggression theory (p. 426)

relative deprivation (p. 427)

aggressive stimulus (p. 428)

social learning theory (p. 430)

scripts (p. 436)

catharsis (p. 441)

STUDY QUESTIONS

1.   What is an aggressive action? Why is aggression difficult to define?

2.   What is the difference between hostile and instrumental aggression?

3.   How do Freud's Eros, Thanatos, and hydraulic theory explain human aggression?

4.   What factors besides instinct determine if an animal will behave aggressively?

5.   What are cultural and regional differences in human aggressive behavior that have been documented throughout history? What do these findings tell us about the importance of instinct in driving human aggression?

6.   What roles do the amygdala and testosterone play in aggressive behavior? What effect does serotonin have on aggressive behavior? What research findings support the influence of testosterone on aggressive behavior?

7. What is the relationship between gender, culture, and aggressive behavior? What are examples of overt versus covert aggression? Are males more or less likely to engage in either type of aggression? Are females more or less likely to engage in either type of aggression? What is the extent of gender differences in aggressive behavior as a result of direct provocation? What gender differences exist in lethal violence committed against intimate partners?

8. Under what conditions is the consumption of alcohol related to aggressive behavior?

9. How are pain and heat related to aggressive behavior?

10. How does the frustration-aggression theory explain aggressive behavior? What situations produce frustration? Why is relative deprivation more likely to lead to frustration and aggression than simply deprivation?

11. How do aggressive stimuli increase the probability of aggressive behavior? What are data that support the relationship between aggressive stimuli and aggressive behavior?

12. How does social learning theory explain aggressive behavior? What is evidence that supports the explanations provided by this theory?

13. What are the effects on children and adults of watching media violence? What are the effects of constant exposure to media violence? How does watching a lot of television affect people's view of the world? Why might media violence increase aggressive behavior?

14. What are the consequences of viewing sexually explicit material versus violent pornography on aggressive behavior in general and toward women in particular?

15. What type of punishment is most likely to deter aggressiveness? Why is the threat of punishment not always an effective deterrent?

16. What are the assumptions of the catharsis hypothesis? Does engaging in aggressive or physical behavior reduce future aggressive behavior? What are the cognitive implications of behaving aggressively toward another? How does acting aggressively toward someone affect one's feelings toward this individual? How does cognitive dissonance theory explain these findings?

17. What effects does wartime have on a nation's aggressive behavior at home and on attitudes toward victims abroad?

18. What are more effective strategies to reduce aggressive tendencies besides venting them? Why does self-awareness and "opening up" reduce aggression? How can individuals who cause frustration reduce aggression in those they have frustrated?

19. How effective are modeling and communication training at reducing aggression? What can empathy do to aggressive tendencies and the ill treatment of victims?

20. What are the advantages of teaching empathy in school? What effects could empathy training have on the prevention of school shootings? Why it is important to look to the social situation when trying to understand why these tragic events happened?

PRACTICE TEST 1

Fill in the Blank

1. A behavior aimed at causing either physical or psychological pain is called a(n) _____.

2. An act of aggression stemming from feelings of anger and aimed at inflicting pain is called _____.

3. Aggression as a means to some goal other than causing pain is called _____.

4. The instinct toward life that Freud theorized all humans are born with is called _____.

5. The instinctual drive toward death that Freud said leads to aggressive actions is called _____.

6. The theory that unexpressed emotions build up pressure and must be expressed to relieve that pressure is called the _____.

7. An area in the core of the brain that is associated with aggressive behavior is called the _____.

8. A chemical in the brain that may inhibit aggressive behavior is called _____.

Multiple Choice

1. Which of the following behaviors best demonstrates instrumental aggression?
   a) shooting clay pigeons with a shotgun
   b) intentionally tripping a classmate during recess
   c) running a stop sign, thereby causing an accident
   d) holding up a clerk while robbing a convenience store

2. The hydraulic theory of aggression maintains that:
   a) aggression will leak if the individual is not emotionally strong enough to restrain his/her aggressive urges.
   b) heated, frustrating situations heighten aggressive energy to the boiling point.
   c) people who pour out their aggressive energies are likely to flood others with aggressive urges.
   d) aggressive energy must be released to avoid build-up and an explosion resulting in illness.

3. There is much evidence to support the general contention held by most social psychologists that, for humans, innate patterns of behavior:
   a) are rigidly preprogrammed.
   b) are nonexistent.
   c) are modifiable by situational and social events.
   d) are incompatible with a social existence.

4. Research reveals that naturally occurring testosterone levels are higher among prisoners:
   a) with neurological disorders.
   b) convicted of violent crimes.
   c) with personality disorders.
   d) convicted of embezzlement.

5. Carlsmith and Anderson (1979) found that riots between 1967 and 1971 were far more likely to occur on:
   a) hot days than on cool days.
   b) rainy days than on sunny days.
   c) weekends than on weekdays.
   d) odd-numbered years than on even-numbered years.

6. Findings by Berkowitz and LePage (1967) that angry participants were more likely to deliver shocks to a fellow student when a gun was present in the room indicate that:
   a) the presence of weapons increases the probability that frustration will occur.
   b) the presence of weapons in and of itself is sufficient to trigger aggressive actions.
   c) the presence of weapons increases the probability an aggressive response will occur.
   d) all the above.

7. At recess, a boy can choose to play with one of four classmates. Which classmate should he AVOID if he wants to play a nonviolent game of basketball?
   a) Johnny, who tends to be aggressive and has just watched Mr. Rogers on television.
   b) Rich, who is generally not aggressive and has just watched a violent G.I. Joe cartoon on television.
   c) Sam, who tends to be aggressive and has just watched a violent G.I. Joe cartoon on television.
   d) Tim, who is generally not aggressive and has just watched Mr. Rogers on television.

8. Physical punishment may not curb aggressive actions by children because such punishment:
   a) is difficult for children to understand.
   b) is not supported by social norms.
   c) models aggressive behavior.
   d) provides insufficient justification for behaving nonaggressively.

9. Research shows that "blowing off steam" by engaging in competitive and aggressive games or by watching others do so:
   a) increases aggressive feelings.
   b) decreases aggressive feelings.
   c) evokes people's primary tendencies.
   d) inhibits aggressive behavior.

10. Dissonance arises when we aggress toward someone who is deserving of our retaliation because:
    a) our retaliations are often more hurtful than the act for which we are retaliating.
    b) we often fail to perceive that people are deserving of retaliation.
    c) we often underestimate the impact retaliation has on deserving victims.
    d) we do not like to think of ourselves as aggressive even when aggression is warranted.

11. If you are feeling angry with someone, what is the most effective way to deal with your anger?
    a) Keep your feelings to yourself.
    b) Express your anger in an aggressive manner.
    c) Observe violence among others.
    d) Calmly indicate that you are feeling angry and explain why.

12. Ohbuchi et al. (1989) found that participants liked a blundering experimental assistant better and were less likely to aggress toward him if:
    a) the experimenter insisted that the blunder had caused no harm.
    b) the assistant blamed his blunder on the experimenter.
    c) the assistant apologized for his blunder.
    d) the assistant allowed the participants to be in the experiment a second time.

13. According to Freud, "Thanatos" is the:
    a) life instinct that humans are born with.
    b) death instinct that drives aggressive actions.
    c) process by which memories are pushed into the unconscious.
    d) subconscious reenactment of the human evolutionary process.

14. Kuo's (1961) finding that a cat raised with a rat from birth refrained from attacking the rat or other rats suggests that:
    a)   instincts may be inhibited by experience.
    b)   aggressive behavior is not instinctive.
    c)   raising different species of animals together lowers the animals' levels of testosterone.
    d)   frustration is necessary to produce an aggressive response.

15. When the amygdala of a less-dominant monkey is stimulated in the presence of dominant monkeys, the less-dominant monkey exhibits:
    a)   attack behavior.
    b)   escape/avoidance behavior.
    c)   no noticeable change in behavior.
    d)   confusion and inconsistent behavior.

16. The theory that predicts you will act with the intention to hurt others when you are thwarted from attaining a goal is called:
    a)   social learning theory.
    b)   cathartic aggression theory.
    c)   frustration-aggression theory.
    d)   deprivation theory.

17. When the Iron Curtain in Eastern Europe crumbled, people expected the quality of their lives to dramatically improve. When economic reforms stalled, aggressive behavior resulted from:
    a)   deprivation.
    b)   social learning.
    c)   dehumanization.
    d)   relative deprivation.

18. Findings that children were more likely to beat up a Bobo doll after watching an adult do so led Bandura (1961, 1963) to conclude that:
    a)   aggression may be learned by imitating aggressive models.
    b)   there are striking differences in instinctive aggressive drives among children.
    c)   watching aggressive behavior is intrinsically rewarding.
    d)   observing aggression by adults unleashes children's inherent aggressiveness.

Short Answer

1. What evidence suggests that, among humans, innate patterns of aggression are modified by the surrounding culture?

2. Imagine that you are on a debate team opposing a team from the National Rifle Association, which maintains that "Gun's don't kill, people do." Based on what you know about the effects of "aggressive stimuli," defend your position that guns do kill people.

3. What are the effects on children and adults of long-term exposure to television violence?

PRACTICE TEST 2

Fill in the Blank

1. A hormone associated with aggression is called _____.

2. The theory that frustration will increase the probability of an aggressive response is called _____.

3. The perception that you (or your group) have less than what you deserve, what you have been led to expect, or what people similar to you have, is known as _____.

4. An object that is associated with aggressive responses and whose mere presence can increase the probability of aggression is called a(n) _____.

5. The theory that people learn social behavior by observing others and imitating them is called _____.

6. The notion that "blowing off steam" relieves built-up aggressive energies and hence reduces the likelihood of further aggressive behavior is called _____.

7. Patterns of social behaviors learned implicitly from one's culture are called _____.

Multiple Choice

1. Which of the following best summarizes the effects of viewing sexually explicit material on aggression toward women?
    a) Viewing sexually explicit material, in and of itself, increases the likelihood of aggressive behavior toward women.
    b) Viewing materials that combine sex with violence increases the likelihood of aggressive behavior toward women.
    c) Viewing materials that combine sex with violence appears to be harmless.
    d) Viewing nonviolent material that depict women as objects increases the likelihood of aggression toward women.

2. Geen et al. (1975) found that participants were most likely to shock an experimental accomplice who had angered them if:
    a) they had shocked the accomplice on a previous occasion.
    b) they had been unable to shock the accomplice on a previous occasion.
    c) they expected the accomplice to shock them later in the experiment.
    d) the experimenter had informed them that the shocks would facilitate learning by the accomplice.

3. Pennebaker (1990) suggests that the beneficial effects of "opening up" and talking about one's feelings are the result of:
    a) blowing off steam.
    b) increased insight and self-awareness.
    c) revealing one's dependency on others.
    d) increased empathy with others.

4.   Evidence that people find it easier to aggress toward those they have dehumanized suggests that people will find it difficult to aggress toward people who:
   a)   they feel empathy toward.
   b)   are dissimilar to them.
   c)   have not provoked them.
   d)   model aggressive behavior.

5.   According to social psychologists, voluntary behavior geared to cause either psychological or physical pain is called a(n):
   a)   hostile action.
   b)   aggressive action.
   c)   violent action.
   d)   antisocial action.

6.   An act of aggression arising from feelings of anger and intended to cause pain or injury is called _____ aggression.
   a)   violent
   b)   antisocial
   c)   hostile
   d)   instrumental

7.   The aggression exhibited by the Iroquois in the past and the regional differences in aggressive behavior in the U. S. today support the hypothesis that aggression can be:
   a)   innate.
   b)   instinctual.
   c)   learned.
   d)   universal.

8.   The chemical substance produced in the midbrain that seems to inhibit aggression is:
   a)   dopamine.
   b)   testosterone.
   c)   norepinephrine.
   d)   serotonin.

9.   Which of the following best characterizes the relationship between gender differences and aggression?
   a)   There are no gender differences in aggression.
   b)   Boys engage in all types of aggression more than girls do.
   c)   Girls engage in covert acts of aggression while boys engage in overt acts of aggression.
   d)   Girls engage in overt acts of aggression while boys engage in covert acts of aggression.

10.   Which of the following is FALSE regarding the relationship between gender differences and aggression?
   a)   Women are less likely than men are to perceive an ambiguous situation as requiring aggression.
   b)   Even when provoked, women continue to display significantly less aggression than men do.
   c)   Women feel guiltier after committing overt acts of aggression than men do.
   d)   In the last few decades, the number of nonviolent crimes committed by women has increased more than it has for men.

11.   In 1998, of the women killed in the U. S., about _____ of them were killed by their husbands, boyfriends, former husbands, or former boyfriends while about _____ of the men who were killed were killed by their current or former intimate partner.
   a)   10%; 20%
   b)   5%; 15%
   c)   50%; 50%
   d)   30%; 5%

12. The presence of which stimulus has been found to increase aggression?
    a) alcohol
    b) pain
    c) heat
    d) a gun
    e) all the above

13. Which of the following can increase frustration and therefore increase the likelihood of aggression?
    a) being close to a goal and being thwarted
    b) experiencing unexpected frustration
    c) experiencing legitimate frustration
    d) both a and b
    e) all the above

14. According to social psychologist Leonard Eron, how many murders and other acts of violence have U. S. children seen by the time they finish elementary school?
    a) 1,000 murders and 25, 000 other violent acts
    b) 3,000 murders and 50,000 other violent acts
    c) 5,000 murders and 75,000 other violent acts
    d) 8,000 murders and 100,000 other violent acts

15. Which of the following is true about children viewing media violence?
    a) The more violence children watch on television, the more violence they show in their later years.
    b) Children who watch violent programs engage in more acts of violence than do children who watch nonviolent programs.
    c) Watching television violence increases violent behavior only in children who are violent already.
    d) Both a and b are true.
    e) All the above are true.

16. Which of the following is FALSE about adults and viewing media violence?
    a) There exists a consistent relationship between viewing television violence and the viewer's antisocial behavior.
    b) Men who watch more television show more physiological arousal when watching violence than do men who watch less television.
    c) College students exposed to a lot of television violence give others more powerful shocks than do students who are exposed to nonviolent television.
    d) People who watch more than four hours of television a day have a greater fear of being assaulted than do people who watch less than two hours a day.

17. Which of the following is a reason why exposure to media violence can increase aggression?
    a) It weakens inhibitions against violent behavior.
    b) It might trigger imitation and give people ideas about how to engage in violent acts.
    c) It increases angry feelings and primes aggressive responses to those feelings.
    d) It make people think the world is a dangerous place.
    e) All the above are reasons.

18. Josh is very angry because he just found out that his girlfriend has cheated on him. He hears about Freud's catharsis theory and decides to break some dishes to see if this will help reduce his anger. Research indicates that this dish-breaking behavior:
    a) may lead him to perform future violent acts.
    b) will decrease the prevalence of violent acts in his life.
    c) will have no effect on his anger and violent behavior.
    d) will lead him to break less dishes in the future.

Short Answer

1.   Describe the frustration-aggression theory. What produces frustration? What is the role played by anger in this theory? According to this theory, what factors determine the likelihood that aggression will result from frustration?

2.   Outline steps you can take to reduce aggressive behavior in yourself and others.

WEB EXERCISE

Go to www.prenhall.com/aronson. Click on the Links for Chapter 12. Click on Stability of Aggression. What did you learn regarding the consistency of aggressive behavior from early childhood to young adulthood? Is there stability in aggression for males and for females? Or, click on the Aggressive Horn Honking link. Summarize the field study that looked at whether or not the visibility of the target makes a difference as to how long it takes to act aggressively against the target. Write your reactions to the findings.

CHAPTER 13

Prejudice: Causes and Cures

CHAPTER OVERVIEW

The causes of and the remedies for the worldwide social phenomenon of prejudice are the focus of this chapter. The ubiquitous nature of prejudice is described in the first section. The definitions of prejudice, stereotyping, and discrimination are given. Distinctions between the emotional, cognitive, and behavioral components of prejudice are made. Stereotyping, as it relates to gender, is a focus here.

The causes of prejudice are detailed next. The way people think about and categorize the world is one cause of prejudice that is examined. How stereotypes become activated and possibly revised are topics discussed. How people explain the behavior of others also has been linked to prejudice. People may make dispositional attributions about an entire group, thus perpetuating stereotypes, prejudice, and discrimination. The consequences related to such attribution formation, blaming the victim and the self-fulfilling prophecy, are explored. The allocation of resources and the competition that may result has been shown to cause prejudice, as well. The role of normative social influence is another cause of prejudice that is considered.

Finally, strategies for reducing prejudice are described. Intergroup contact has been shown to reduce prejudice in certain situations. Lessons learned about the conditions necessary to make contact effective at reducing prejudice are outlined. These conditions have been used among school children via the use of jigsaw classrooms. The many benefits of this approach are discussed.

CHAPTER OUTLINE

Prejudice: The Ubiquitous Social Phenomenon

    Prejudice and Self-Esteem

    A Progress Report

Prejudice, Stereotyping, and Discrimination

    Prejudice: The Affective Component

    Stereotypes: The Cognitive Component

    Discrimination: The Behavioral Component

What Causes Prejudice?

    The Way We Think: Social Cognition

    The Way We Assign Meaning: Attributional Biases

    The Way We Allocate Resources: Realistic Conflict Theory

    The Way We Conform: Normative Rules

How Can Prejudice Be Reduced?

    The Contact Hypothesis

    When Contact Reduces Prejudice: Six Conditions

    Cooperation and Interdependence: The Jigsaw Classroom

LEARNING OBJECTIVES

After reading Chapter 13, you should be able to do the following:

1.   Describe the ubiquitous nature of prejudice. Identify what aspects of people's identities are targeted for prejudice. Discuss the consequences of prejudice for the self-esteem of the targets of prejudice. Describe the nature of prejudice today. Describe indications that prejudice has been reduced since the 1950s. (pp. 457-460)

2.   Define prejudice. Describe the affective component of prejudice. (p. 460)

3.   Describe the cognitive component of prejudice. Identify why we develop stereotypes and what functions they serve. Discuss the effects of stereotypes on the relationship between sports, race, and attribution. Discuss the effects of gender stereotypes on attributions for achievement of men and women. Identify the effects of gender stereotypes on young girls' performance in math and state the important influence on girls' perceptions of their math ability. (pp. 461-465)

4.   Describe the behavioral component of prejudice and discuss findings that discrimination is unwittingly practiced today even among trained professionals. (p. 465)

5.   Discuss conclusions drawn by social psychologists and evolutionary psychologists regarding the role of biology and learning in causing prejudice. Identify when parents and children are most likely to hold the same attitudes and values. Describe the classroom study conducted by Jane Elliot (1977) and the purpose it served. (pp. 466-467)

6.   Describe the social cognition approach to the study of the causes of prejudice. Identify important consequences of social categorization that facilitate prejudice. Discuss the findings of research on minimal groups and the motives underlying in-group bias. Define out-group homogeneity. Describe how in-group bias and out-group homogeneity contribute to the formation and perpetuation of prejudice. (pp. 467-470)

7.   Identify how affective and cognitive components of prejudice make prejudice resistant to change. Explain why logical arguments may not be effective at reducing prejudice. (pp. 470-472)

8.   Identify why stereotypes are difficult to change. Explain why unwanted stereotypes persist. Describe Devine's two-step model of cognitive processing as it relates to stereotypes and prejudice. Describe the role of automatic processes in the activation of stereotypes and of controlled processes in disregarding the stereotype and reducing its effect on behavior. (pp. 472-476)

9.   Describe research regarding the variability of people's automatic prejudice. Discuss the work of Fazio and others on the automatic nature of prejudice. According to the research of Fazio and colleagues, identify the three kinds of people that exist. Discuss the work of Bargh and his colleagues that shows the effects of certain triggers on stereotype activation. (pp. 476-477)

10.   Describe how illusory correlations perpetuate stereotypic thinking. Identify why we are likely to perceive illusory correlations among minorities and unrelated events. Discuss how other cognitive factors such as the out-group homogeneity effect and stereotypes increase the negative effects of illusory correlations. (pp. 477-479)

11. Discuss models for revising stereotypic beliefs with disconfirming information. Identify the kinds of disconfirming information necessary to result in stereotype revision by "bookkeeping," "subtyping," and "conversion". Describe the exact nature of stereotype revision that is proposed according to each model, and identify which models have received support. (pp. 479-480)

12. Define the ultimate attribution error and discuss the influence of stereotyping in the committance of this error. (pp. 480-481)

13. Discuss the revisiting of *The Bell Curve* debate. Identify alternative explanations for the differences in academic test scores that are found between groups. Discuss the role of stereotype threat in producing these differences. Identify when stereotype threat applies to gender as well as ethnicity. (pp. 481-483)

14. Describe how expectations and distortions can strengthen stereotypes. Explain how the belief in a just world leads us to "blame the victim" for his or her misfortune. Identify the role of dispositional attributions in laying such blame. (pp. 483-484)

15. Describe the relevance of the self-fulfilling prophecy to stereotyping and discrimination both at the individual level and at the societal level. (pp. 484-486)

16. Describe realistic conflict theory as well as correlational and experimental support for this theory. Discuss scapegoat theory. Explain how frustration leads to the creation of a scapegoat. Identify characteristics of some groups that make them likely targets of scapegoating. (pp. 486-490)

17. Describe how stereotypes and prejudiced attitudes are propagated according to social learning theory and identify the types of discrimination that result from such a process. Define institutionalized racism and institutionalized sexism. Discuss evidence that supports the role of normative conformity in prejudice. (pp. 490-492)

18. Describe modern racism. Identify the conditions that reveal modern racism and the consequences of these in the study of discrimination. Discuss research techniques necessary to reveal modern racist attitudes. Discuss the types of prejudice found in Western Europe. (pp. 492-494)

19. Contrast the success of desegregation in housing projects studied by Deutsch and Collins (1951) with the initial failure of desegregation in schools nationwide. Define the contact hypothesis as stated by Allport (1954) and identify the six conditions necessary to reduce prejudice when there is contact between groups. Define mutual interdependence. (pp. 494-497)

20. Define jigsaw classroom. Describe how contact between students in the jigsaw classroom differs from contact in traditional classroom settings. Identify the advantages that have been gained by students learning in jigsaw classrooms. (pp. 497-500)

21. Discuss why the jigsaw classroom is effective. Identify what this and other cooperative learning environments encourage and its importance for interpersonal relations. (pp. 500-501)

KEY TERMS

prejudice (p. 460)

stereotype (p. 461)

discrimination (p. 465)

out-group homogeneity (p. 469)

illusory correlation (p. 477)

bookkeeping model (p. 479)

conversion model (p. 479)

subtyping model (p. 479)

ultimate attribution error (p. 481)

stereotype threat (p. 482)

blaming the victim (p. 483)

self-fulfilling prophecy (p. 484)

realistic conflict theory (p. 486)

scapegoating (p. 490)

institutionalized racism (p. 491)

institutionalized sexism (p. 491)

normative conformity (p. 491)

modern racism (p. 492)

mutual interdependence (p. 496)

jigsaw classroom (p. 498)

STUDY QUESTIONS

1.   What are the consequences of prejudice?

2.   How is prejudice different from discrimination? What are the three components of a prejudiced attitude?

3.   How do gender stereotypes affect achievement attributions of men's and women's successes and failures? What type of attributions are made by individuals and society for the successes of men compared to those of women?

4.   What is an example of discrimination?

5.   What role does human thinking have in the causes of prejudice? How does social categorization increase prejudice? What are motives behind the in-group bias?

6.   What is the out-group homogeneity effect and how does it contribute to prejudice?

7.   Focusing on the affective and cognitive components of prejudice, why is it difficult to change prejudice?

8.   What does Devine's (1989) two-step model of cognitive processing explain about prejudice? What has research by Fazio and Bargh and their respective colleagues discovered about the variability in people's automatic prejudice?

9.   What is an illusory correlation? What factors lead to the formation of this type of correlation and how does this process promote prejudice?

10.   What are the three models of stereotype revision? How does each model operate in the face of information that is stereotype inconsistent? Which models have received research support? Why is the conversion model rarely supported?

11.   What is the ultimate attribution error? What are the consequences of committing this error?

12.   What is stereotype threat and what does it help to explain?

13.   What is the relationship between the belief in a just world and blaming the victim?

14.   How does the self-fulfilling prophecy perpetuate prejudice and discrimination?

15.   According to the realistic conflict theory, what are the causes of prejudice and discrimination?

16.   What is the scapegoat theory and why do people need scapegoats?

17.   According to social learning theory, what maintains and perpetuates prejudice and discrimination at the societal level? What forms do societal prejudice and discrimination take? What evidence exists that supports the explanations provided by social learning theory?

18.   How is the expression of racism in today's society different from its expression fifty years ago? What are findings that support modern racism theory? How have research techniques adapted to study this "new" racism?

19.   What are effective strategies to reduce prejudice? What characteristics of intergroup contact are necessary for the contact hypothesis to reduce prejudice and discrimination? What is mutual interdependence?

20.   What are the characteristics of the jigsaw classroom? What are the benefits of the jigsaw classroom?

21.   Why is the jigsaw classroom effective? What does this learning environment encourage?

PRACTICE TEST 1

Fill in the Blank

1.   A hostile or negative attitude toward a distinguishable group of people, based solely on their membership in that group is called _____.

2.   A generalization about a group of people in which identical characteristics are assigned to virtually all members of the group, regardless of the actual variation among the members is called a(n) _____.

3.   Unjustified negative or harmful action toward a member of a group, simply because of his or her membership in that group, is called _____.

4. The perception that members of the out-group are more similar to one another than they really are, and more similar to one another than are the members of one's in-group, is called the perception of

    _____.

5. The belief that variables are correlated when they actually are not is called a(n)

    _____.

6. A model for modifying stereotypic beliefs when information inconsistent with the stereotype is encountered among many members of the categorized group is called the _____ model.

7. A model for radically changing stereotypic beliefs when confronted with a fact that very strongly disconfirms the stereotype is called the _____ model.

8. A model for creating a subcategory of a stereotype when information inconsistent with the stereotype is concentrated among only a few individuals in the categorized group is called the _____ model.

9. The tendency to make dispositional attributions about an entire group of people is called the

    _____.

10. The tendency to blame individuals for their victimization is known as _____.

Multiple Choice

1. Once formed, stereotypes:
    a) easily change when contradictory information is encountered.
    b) develop into more elaborate and complex categories.
    c) deteriorate unless challenged by contradictory information.
    d) are resistant to change on the basis of new information.

2. According to Stipek and Galinski (1991), young girls attribute success in math to ____ and boys attribute success in math to ____.
    a) luck; hard work
    b) hard work; luck
    c) luck; ability
    d) ability; luck

3. According to the social cognition approach, stereotypes result:
    a) as the inevitable by-product of the way we process and categorize information.
    b) from the breakdown of once normal cognitive processes.
    c) from conflicts that exist between groups when resources are limited.
    d) when individuals adhere to norms which foster prejudice.

4. Individuals emotionally involved in their beliefs about a target group are not likely to be persuaded by opposing arguments because:
    a) such individuals have amassed a large number of arguments to defend their position.
    b) attitudes based on emotions are not affected by logical arguments.
    c) arousal caused by emotional involvement interferes with normal cognitive processing.
    d) they are unable to process arguments and must rely on less persuasive peripheral cues.

5. According to Devine's (1989) two-step model of cognitive processing, simply knowing stereotypes that you do not believe affects your cognitive processing because:
   a) we are constantly aware of the stereotypes.
   b) we can recall the stereotypes at will.
   c) the stereotypes are inconsistent with our beliefs.
   d) the stereotypes are automatically activated.

6. According to Weber and Crocker's (1983) subtyping model, information that is inconsistent with a stereotype leads to the creation of a subtype of a stereotype when:
   a) the inconsistent information is found among many members of the stereotyped group.
   b) the inconsistent information is concentrated among only a few members of the stereotyped group.
   c) a fact that very strongly disconfirms the stereotype is encountered.
   d) a fact that very strongly confirms the stereotype is ignored.

7. When students read that a prisoner had committed a crime that matched the common stereotype of the offender, Bodenhausen and Wyer (1985) found that the students:
   a) ignored other information that was inconsistent with the stereotype and were harsher in their recommendations for parole.
   b) were puzzled by other information that was inconsistent with the stereotype and refrained from making any recommendations.
   c) dismissed the information that was consistent with the stereotype and were harsher in their recommendations for parole.
   d) made situational attributions for the crime and were more lenient in their recommendations for parole.

8. Defense attorneys who focus the jury's attention on the sexual histories of sexual assault victims are exploiting people's tendency to:
   a) make situational attributions.
   b) perceive out-group heterogeneity.
   c) blame the victim.
   d) convict rather than to acquit the accused.

9. Realistic conflict theory maintains that:
   a) abundant resources produces greed and negative feelings toward out-groups.
   b) conflict experienced within a group is likely to be attributed to members of an out-group.
   c) mutual interdependence among groups produces competition and negative feelings toward competing groups.
   d) limited resources produce competition and negative feelings toward competing groups.

10. Institutional racism and sexism arise when:
    a) people are angered or frustrated by social institutions.
    b) two or more groups must depend on each other in order to accomplish a common goal.
    c) negative stereotypes become the fundamental categories people use to organize their experiences.
    d) people live in a society where stereotypes and discrimination are normative.

147

11. Friendly, informal interactions with a single member of the out-group are likely to:
    a)   foster the perception that the out-group member is typical of his or her out-group.
    b)   foster the perception that the out-group member is an exception to one's stereotype of outgroup members.
    c)   promote and support equality between the in-group and out-group.
    d)   promote and support mutual interdependence between the in-group and outgroup.

12. Prejudice is:
    a)   any behavior aimed at physically or emotionally harming people who are members of a discernible group.
    b)   a generalization about a group of people in which identical characteristics are assigned to virtually all members of the group.
    c)   a hostile or negative attitude toward a distinguishable group of people, based solely on their membership in that group.
    d)   the tendency to categorize people into groups based on some specific characterization.

13. Attributing a higher level of motivation to successful females than to successful males may be one way of:
    a)   implying that the successful female has less actual skill than her male counterpart.
    b)   rationalizing the presence of the obstacles society imposes on women's endeavors to be successful.
    c)   implying that the successful female is more emotional than her male counterpart.
    d)   rationalizing the prejudice toward women that exists in our society.

14. The bigot's cry, "They all look alike to me," illustrates one consequence of social categorization called the:
    a)   perception of out-group homogeneity.
    b)   in-group bias.
    c)   illusory correlation.
    d)   ultimate attribution error.

15. Which of the following best describes the relationship between knowing and believing stereotypes?
    a)   To know a stereotype is to believe the stereotype.
    b)   You can know a stereotype without believing the stereotype.
    c)   You can believe a stereotype without knowing the stereotype.
    d)   Stereotypes have no impact unless they are both known and believed.

16. Illusory correlations are especially likely to be found between minorities and unrelated events because minorities are:
    a)   powerless.
    b)   outspoken.
    c)   distinctive.
    d)   victimized.

17. Furnham and Gunter (1984) have found that negative attitudes toward the poor and homeless are more prevalent among individuals who:
    a)   score high on measures of self-esteem.
    b)   tend to be high in self-awareness.
    c)   believe we live in a "dog-eat-dog" world.
    d)   have a strong belief in a "just world."

18.   To demoralized and frustrated Germans who blamed Jews for troubles in Germany following World War I, the Jews provided a convenient:
        a)   minimal group.
        b)   scapegoat.
        c)   out-group.
        d)   stereotype.

Short Answer

1.   Why, according to Devine's two-step model of cognitive processing, are people who are high in prejudice more likely to express stereotypic thinking than people who are low in prejudice?

2.   How does the self-fulfilling prophecy serve to perpetuate biased expectations produced by the ultimate attribution error?

3.   Provide examples of modern racism.

PRACTICE TEST 2

Fill in the Blank

1.   The theory that maintains limited resources lead to conflict between groups and result in increased prejudice and discrimination is called _____.

2.   The tendency for individuals, when frustrated or unhappy, to displace aggression onto groups that are disliked, visible, and relatively powerless is known as _____.

3.   Racist attitudes that are held by the vast majority of us because we are living in a society in which stereotypes and discrimination are the norm are called _____.

4.   Sexist attitudes that are held by the vast majority of us because we are living in a society in which stereotypes and discrimination are the norm are called _____.

5.   The tendency to go along with the group in order to fulfill members' expectations and gain their acceptance is called _____.

6.   Prejudice revealed in subtle, indirect ways because people have learned to hide prejudiced attitudes in order to avoid being labeled as racist is called _____.

7.   When two or more groups need each other and must depend on each other in order to accomplish a goal that is important to each of them, the groups are _____.

8.   A technique for structuring the classroom designed to reduce prejudice and raise the self-esteem of children by placing them in small, desegregated groups and making each child dependent on the other children for his or her group to learn the material is called the _____.

9.   Fear of confirming a negative evaluation of a group that impairs the performance of a member of that group is called _____.

10.   A _____ prophecy is an attribution process by which people confirm their stereotypes of others by creating the stereotypical behavior through their treatment of others.

Multiple Choice

1. Findings that people's prejudices change when they move to areas where norms are more or less prejudicial support the notion that prejudice is largely the result of:
    a)   social cognition processes.
    b)   an inheritable factor.
    c)   competition.
    d)   conformity.

2. According to Allport (1954), contact between majority and minority groups will reduce prejudice when members of the groups:
    a)   interact voluntarily in an unstructured setting.
    b)   have low expectations for increased intergroup harmony.
    c)   compete for limited available resources.
    d)   are of equal status and in pursuit of common goals.

3. The action or behavioral aspect of prejudice is:
    a)   generalization.
    b)   discrimination.
    c)   stereotyping.
    d)   none of the above.

4. A stereotype revision model (Webber & Crocker, 1983) in which each item of information that disconfirms the stereotype, changes the stereotype is called the _____ model.
    a)   bookkeeping
    b)   conversion
    c)   subtyping
    d)   modification

5. Which of the following stereotype revision models proposed by Webber and Crocker (1983) is the least effective at weakening people's stereotypes?
    a)   subtyping
    b)   conversion
    c)   bookkeeping
    d)   All are equally ineffective.

6. Randall believes that the homeless man he sees everyday when he goes to work is lazy and just does not want to work. In fact, Randall thinks all homeless people are lazy. When Randall makes dispositional attributions about an entire group of people he is committing the:
    a)   fundamental attribution error.
    b)   ultimate attribution bias.
    c)   universal attribution error.
    d)   ultimate attribution error.

7. Feeling apprehensive about confirming a negative cultural stereotype when working on a task can lead people to feel _____, which can result in _____ performance on the task.
    a)   stereotype anxiety; poor
    b)   stereotype threat; poor
    c)   stereotype anxiety; improved
    d)   stereotype threat; improved

8. Steele and Aronson (1995) found that when African American students are given a test that they are told measures their intellectual ability they perform _____ the white students do. When they are told that the test does not measure their intellectual ability they perform _____ the white students do.
    a) worse than; better than
    b) better than; worse than
    c) worse than; as well as
    d) as well as; as well as

9. Word, Zanna, and Cooper (1974) found that when African Americans are interviewed by whites, they are likely to perform less well than white interviewees. This is explained best by:
    a) the ultimate attribution error.
    b) scapegoating.
    c) blaming the victim.
    d) the self-fulfilling prophecy.

10. The study by Ayers and his colleagues (1991) of 90 auto dealers found that higher final prices were quoted to African American men and African American women compared to white men and women. The results of this study offer an example of:
    a) scapegoating.
    b) stereotype threat.
    c) modern racism.
    d) belief in a just world.

11. A situation where two or more groups need and depend on each other to accomplish a goal important to each of them defines:
    a) common dependence.
    b) common interdependence.
    c) mutual dependence.
    d) mutual interdependence.

12. All of the following are conditions of contact necessary to decrease stereotyping, prejudice, and discrimination except which one?
    a) equal status
    b) social norms of equality
    c) formal contact
    d) a common goal
    e) all the above

13. Which of the following is true about the jigsaw classroom and its effects?
    a) Students are placed in diverse learning groups.
    b) Students depend on each other for the class material.
    c) Students in jigsaw classrooms show a decrease in prejudice and stereotyping compared to students in traditional classrooms.
    d) Students in jigsaw classrooms show an increase in self-esteem compared to students in traditional classrooms.
    e) All the above are true.

14. Which of the following explains why the jigsaw classroom works to reduce prejudice, stereotyping, and discrimination?
    a) It breaks down in-group versus out-group delineations.
    b) It increases competitive strategies.
    c) It encourages the development of empathy.
    d) both a and c
    e) all the above

15. In the jigsaw classroom, if one student in a group is having difficulty mastering his or her material, other members will benefit most if they:
    a) pay more attention to students who have mastered the material already.
    b) compete with the student for the teacher's praise.
    c) encourage the student and ask friendly, probing questions.
    d) complete the student's assignment for him/her.

16. The phenomenon of modern prejudice refers to the finding that over the past 50 years:
    a) the economic gap between minority and white Americans has become greater than ever.
    b) radical hate groups have become more prevalent.
    c) people have learned to hide their prejudice when it is socially unacceptable to express it.
    d) the popularity of ultraconservative political groups has increased.

17. Rochelle is walking across campus one night. As two males walk by, she feels her heart race. Her reaction demonstrates the _____ component of her prejudice.
    a) stereotypical
    b) affective
    c) cognitive
    d) behavioral

18. Stereotypes result from our tendency to:
    a) present ourselves favorably.
    b) categorize people and events.
    c) reduce cognitive dissonance.
    d) maintain our self-esteem.

Short Answer

1. During the past couple of months, you have become increasingly aware and concerned that a friend of yours is prejudiced against a particular ethnic group on campus. Explain why you anticipate having a difficult time eliminating your friend's prejudice by presenting evidence that disconfirms his stereotype. Propose a model for modifying stereotypic beliefs with disconfirming evidence that may work under these difficult conditions.

2. Describe the process by which institutional racism and sexism is taught to members of society and is sustained within the society.

3. In what ways have children in jigsaw classrooms benefited from learning in this environment compared to children in traditional classrooms?

WEB EXERCISE

Visit the Social Psychology Network at www.socialpsychology.org. Click on the link to the Jigsaw Classroom. Read Chapter 1 of Aronson's book, No One Left To Hate. Find out about the jigsaw classroom technique. Summarize the overview of the technique, the history behind its use, and the steps involved with the implementation of this cooperative learning procedure.

SOCIAL PSYCHOLOGY IN ACTION 1

Social Psychology and Health

OVERVIEW

People's awareness of health-related issues has increased tremendously in the past decade. Research has revealed that physical health is affected by people's interpretation of events as stressful, by the amount of control people feel over such events, and by the way people explain negative outcomes. How humans cope with stress is another important health concern. Gender differences in coping with stress are identified. The benefits of social support are described. The module discusses two main personality types and their relationship with health. Also, the effective coping style of "opening up" is discussed. Understanding these issues from the perspective of a social psychologist suggests some ways to change unhealthy behavior. The final section reviews how the use of social psychological principles, for example dissonance theory, can improve health habits.

OUTLINE

Stress and Human Health

> Effects of Negative Life Events

> Perceived Stress and Health

> Feeling in Charge: The Importance of Perceived Control

> Knowing You Can Do It: Self-Efficacy

> Explaining Negative Events: Learned Helplessness

Coping with Stress

> Gender Differences in Coping with Stress

> Social Support: Getting Help From Others

> Personality and Coping Styles

> Opening Up: Confiding to Others

Prevention: Improving Health Habits

> Message Framing: Stressing Gains versus Losses

> Changing Health-Relevant Behaviors Using Dissonance Theory

LEARNING OBJECTIVES

After reading Social Psychology in Action 1, you should be able to do the following:

1. Explain the connection between stress and health. Describe attempts to show this connection using the Social Readjustment Rating Scale which measures major life events. Identify problems associated with this approach. Identify solutions to these problems and the importance of studying subjective rather than objective stress. Define stress. Describe recent research that suggests stress lowers people's resistance to infectious disease. (pp. 507-512)

2. Describe correlational and experimental research that suggests perceived control is associated with better adjustment to chronic diseases, with greater immunity to disease, and with better health and adjustment. Define perceived control. Distinguish between the effects of a temporary and an enduring sense of control. (pp. 512-515)

3. Identify a potential risk of feeling in control of an illness that persists despite perceived control. Discuss what can be done in this situation so that perceived control is not lost. Describe cultural differences in the relationship between perceived control and health. (p. 515)

4. Define self-efficacy. Discuss the role that self-efficacy plays in one's health. Describe how self-efficacy can be increased. (pp. 515-517)

5. Define learned helplessness. Describe the attributions for negative events that result in learned helplessness and depression. Identify and define each component of a pessimistic attribution style. Describe the link between learned helplessness and academic performance. Discuss the association between a pessimistic attribution style and health. Identify the factors, including stereotype threat, that contribute to the development of a pessimistic or an optimistic style. (pp. 517-522)

6. Discuss research on coping styles. Identify and explain gender differences in coping with stress. Define the stress responses of fight-or-flight and tend-and-befriend. Identify the problem with oversimplifying gender differences in coping with stress. (pp. 522-524)

7. Define social support. Identify the health benefits of social support. Discuss cultural differences in the existence of social support and the consequences of these differences. Define the buffering hypothesis and describe its relationship with stress and health. (pp. 524-525)

8. Discuss how personality can affect health. Identify the characteristics of the Type A and of the Type B personalities. Identify the characteristic of a Type A that can lead to health problems. Discuss how the Type A and the Type B may develop. Discuss cultural differences in the incidence of coronary disease and how this may be linked to individualism versus collectivism. Identify the positive aspect of collectivism that is related to better health. (pp. 526-528)

9. Discuss the effectiveness of "opening up" as a coping style. Explain why "opening up" can lead to better health. (pp. 528-529

10. Discuss how social psychological principles can be applied to improve health by reducing stress and by getting people to change their health habits. Describe how message framing can affect people's adherence to a persuasive communication. (pp. 530-532)

11. Identify a basic principle important to consider when attempting to change human behavior. Describe the role of hypocrisy and dissonance in inducing change. Discuss the effectiveness of changing health-relevant behaviors using dissonance theory. (pp. 532-534)

KEY TERMS

stress (p. 510)

perceived control (p. 512)

self-efficacy (p. 516)

learned helplessness (p. 517)

stable attribution (p. 517)

internal attribution (p. 517)

global attribution (p. 517)

coping styles (p. 522)

fight-or-flight response (p. 522)

tend-and-befriend response (p. 523)

social support (p. 524)

buffering hypothesis (p. 525)

Type A versus B personality (p. 527)

STUDY QUESTIONS

1.   What are definitions of stress? What are the Social Readjustment Rating Scale and "life change units" and their relationship to stress? What factor has been found to be important in determining what is stressful for people?

2.   What are the consequences of subjective stress for one's health?

3.   What role does perceived control play in reducing the perception of stress and its detrimental effects? What is learned helplessness, how does it develop, and what are its consequences?

4.   What is self-efficacy? How does the perception of it affect one's health?

5.	How do findings from studies conducted in nursing homes confirm the importance of perceived control for reducing stress? Why is it better never to have had control than to have had it and have it taken away? When is the perception of control problematic for one's psychological and physical health?

6.	How and why are attributions an important determinant of stress? What are the three aspects of a pessimistic attribution? What are the consequences of making pessimistic attributions?

7.	How are learned helplessness, attribution style, and achievement related? What can be done to reduce learned helplessness in first-year college students? What influences the development of attribution styles?

8.	What are gender differences in coping styles? What is the stress response fight-or-flight? What is the stress response tend-and-befriend? Which one may men use more than women? Which one may apply to women more than men? Why?

9.	Why is the availability and use of social support a successful way to deal with stress? What benefits exist in collectivist cultures regarding the availability of social support? What does the buffering hypothesis propose regarding the necessity of social support?

10.	What is the relationship between coping styles, personality, and health? What are the characteristics of a Type A and a Type B personality? What factors determine if people have a Type A or a Type B personality? What is the main aspect of a Type A personality that research shows is related to health problems?

11.	Why is "opening up" a successful coping style? What are the long-term benefits of "opening up" in response to a negative life event?

12.	How can we help people engage in healthy behaviors? What important social psychological techniques would be helpful in getting people to live healthier lives? What may be one of the best ways to change people's behavior and solve applied problems?

PRACTICE TEST 1

Fill in the Blank

1.   The negative feelings and beliefs that occur whenever people feel that they cannot cope with demands from their environment are called _____.

2.   The belief that we can influence our environment in ways that determine whether we experience positive or negative outcomes is called _____.

3.   The belief that one can perform a given behavior that produces desired results is called _____.

4.   The state of pessimism that results from explaining a negative event as due to stable, internal, and global causes is called _____.

5.   The belief that the cause of an event is due to factors that will not change over time is called a(n) _____.

6.   The belief that the cause of an event is due to things about you, such as your ability or effort, is called a(n) _____.

7.   The belief that the cause of an event is due to factors that apply in a large number of situations is called a(n) _____.

Multiple Choice

1.   Social psychologists in applied areas such as health psychology try to understand the relationship between how _____ and people's health.
     a)   people interpret their social world
     b)   personality traits change as people age
     c)   genetic influences affect people's health habits
     d)   situations themselves determine people's behavior

2.   Stress is the:
     a)   state of pessimism that results from attributing a negative event to stable, internal, and global causes.
     b)   inability to control the outcomes of one's efforts.
     c)   awareness of heightened physiological arousal.
     d)   negative feelings and beliefs that occur whenever people feel they cannot cope with demands from their environment.

3.   Americans have begun to reject aspects of the traditional medical model, especially the submissive role expected of patients by many doctors. One reason why this new approach to medicine may be catching on is that patients:
     a)   gain a more objective conceptualization of health issues.
     b)   benefit from greater perceived control over their illness.
     c)   enjoy the status that is usually reserved for medical doctors.
     d)   pay lower insurance costs when they make use of nontraditional medical approaches.

4. Langer and Rodin (1976) found that nursing home residents were happier, more active, and lived longer when:
   a) they were provided with interesting movies to watch.
   b) their surroundings were beautified with plants.
   c) they were given responsibility and control over decisions.
   d) the staff made potentially stressful choices for them.

5. An individual who exaggerates the role of perceived control in alleviating physical illness runs the risk of:
   a) experiencing self-blame and failure if the illness persists.
   b) experiencing stress by maintaining a perception that the course of the disease is unpredictable.
   c) making unstable, external, and specific attributions if the illness persists.
   d) all of the above

6. If Ken believes that he flunked his English test because he's lazy and lacks intelligence, he is attributing his failure to _____ causes.
   a) external, unstable, and specific
   b) internal, stable, and global
   c) external, stable, and specific
   d) internal, unstable, and global

7. Research by Aronson and colleagues found that individuals were more likely to practice safe sex when they were:
   a) informed of the consequences of practicing unsafe sex.
   b) induced to publicly advocate safe sex.
   c) made mindful of their own failure to practice safe sex.
   d) made aware of their own hypocrisy.

8. High positive correlations between scores on Holmes and Rahe's (1967) Social Readjustment Rating Scale and the likelihood of physical illness indicate that health problems are associated with:
   a) people's interpretations of their social world.
   b) a pessimistic attribution style.
   c) learned helplessness.
   d) changes in a person's life.

9. Participants in a study by Cohen et al. (1991) who experienced low or high amounts of stress were exposed to a virus that causes the common cold. Results indicated that:
   a) increasing participants' awareness of the virus made them more susceptible to catching a cold.
   b) exposure to the virus is sufficient to trigger illness, regardless of the amount of stress experienced by participants.
   c) participants who experienced high amounts of stress were more likely to catch a cold.
   d) extraneous factors such as age, weight, and gender masked the relationship between stress and immunological response.

10. According to Lazarus (1966), what is the most important influence on how stressful a person considers an event?
    a) the objective event itself
    b) the person's interpretation of the event
    c) the culture's interpretation of the event
    d) whether the event was positive or negative

11. The unforeseen tragic results of the Schulz (1976) nursing home study suggest that institutions that strive to give their patients a sense of control should ensure that:
   a) patients are not overwhelmed by responsibilities.
   b) patients will not have to relinquish that control.
   c) certain restrictions on the amount of control are enforced.
   d) decisions are made for patients who do not want control.

12. If you believe that the cause of an event is due to things about you, such as your ability or effort, you are making a(n) _____ attribution.
   a) specific
   b) internal
   c) stable
   d) global

13. Which of the following factors is the most important determinant of learned helplessness?
   a) the individual's perceptions of the causes of events
   b) the accuracy of the individual's causal attributions
   c) the actual causes of events
   d) the individual's attributions for events that did not, but could have, occurred

14. Cultures that stress _____ suffer less from stress-related diseases.
   a) collectivism
   b) independence
   c) individualism
   d) competition

15. Who is most likely to suffer from stress-related diseases?
   a) Joe, who is competitive, hostile, and impatient
   b) John, who is competitive, patient, and caring
   c) James, who is easygoing, relaxed, and ambitious
   d) Jerry, who is calm, noncompetitive, and reserved

Short Answer

1. Describe means of improving people's health that have been suggested by social psychologists.

2. Imagine that you have just become the director of a home for the elderly. Describe the conditions that you would implement at the home to make residents happier and healthier.

PRACTICE TEST 2

Fill in the Blank

1. The ways in which people react to stressful events are called _____.

2. A person who is typically competitive, impatient, and hostile is called a(n) _____ and a person who is typically more patient, relaxed, and noncompetitive is called a(n) _____.

3. The perception that others are responsive and receptive to one's needs is called _____.

4. The _____ stresses the importance of social support when we are facing the effects of negative life events.

5. The response to stress characterized by either attacking the source of the stress or by running away from it is called _____.

6. The stress response characterized by engaging in nurturing behaviors and creating social networks to protect oneself and one's loved ones from the stress is called _____.

Multiple Choice

1. Which of the following are successful coping styles?
    a) "opening up"
    b) becoming hostile and confrontational
    c) engaging social support
    d) both a and c

2. Which of the following is true regarding perceived control and failing health?
    a) It is important for people to feel in control of something.
    b) People's perceptions of control over the consequences of the disease influence psychological adjustment.
    c) Maintaining a sense of control can improve one's psychological well-being.
    d) All the above are true.

3. Sondra and her family want her to quit smoking. If Sondra believes she can quit smoking, she has a sense of _____ regarding quitting smoking.
    a) perceived control
    b) self-efficacy
    c) learned helplessness
    d) perceived efficiency

4. Which of the following is FALSE regarding self-efficacy?
    a) People's sense of self-efficacy can predict the likelihood that they will quit smoking and exercise regularly.
    b) A person high in self-efficacy in one area, say losing weight, will be high in other health-related domains, say quitting smoking.
    c) People with high self-efficacy experience less anxiety while working on a difficult task compared to people with low self-efficacy.
    d) People can instill a sense of self-efficacy in others.

5. According to learned helplessness theory, when people make stable, internal, and _____ attributions for negative events they run the risk of hopelessness, _____, reduced effort, and difficulty learning new tasks.
    a) specific; schizophrenia
    b) specific; depression
    c) global; depression
    d) external; heart disease

6. People who explain negative events in optimistic rather than pessimistic ways:
    a) are more depressed.
    b) suffer from more short-term illnesses.
    c) do better than others in school and in their careers.
    d) experience all the above.
    e) experience none of the above.

7. When we are feeling threatened, the body releases hormones such as norepinephrine and epinephrine that allow people to attack or to flee. This describes the ____ response to stress.
   a) tend-or-flight
   b) befriend-or-fight
   c) tend-and-befriend
   d) fight-or-flight

8. Women may be more likely than males are to exhibit the ____ response to stress while males may be more likely than women are to exhibit the ____ response to stress.
   a) flight-and-tend; fight-or-flight
   b) fight-or-befriend; tend-and-befriend
   c) tend-and-befriend; fight-or-flight
   d) fight-or-flight; tend-and-befriend

9. Spencer feels that people in his life are receptive and responsive to his needs. Spencer perceives ____ in his life.
   a) perceived control
   b) stress
   c) social support
   d) buffering

10. According to the ____, people need social support only when they are experiencing stress.
   a) buffering hypothesis
   b) learned helplessness hypothesis
   c) self-efficacy hypothesis
   d) social support hypothesis

11. Type A personality is to ____ as Type B personality is to ____.
   a) competitive; control-oriented
   b) impatient; relaxed
   c) hostile; aggressive
   d) relaxed; noncompetitive

12. Rothman and his colleagues (1993) found that framing a message in terms of ____ increases people's detection behaviors whereas framing a message in terms of ____ increases people's prevention behaviors.
   a) rewards; costs
   b) costs; losses
   c) gains; losses
   d) losses; gains

13. Based on research in health psychology, what advice is appropriate for someone whose family member just entered a nursing home?
   a) Give her a pet or plant for which she must provide care.
   b) Let her decide when she wants you to visit her.
   c) Sign her up to watch a movie every Friday night.
   d) Tell her to relax and let people take care of her.
   e) Both a and b are appropriate.

14. Tomas is a fourth grader who recently failed his test on multiplication. Since this is not the first test he has failed in math, he begins to believe that he is stupid and will not do well on any other math tests or even on tests in other subjects. Tomas may be experiencing ____.
   a) learned helplessness
   b) the actor observer bias
   c) self-serving bias
   d) self-efficacy

15.   Why does the coping strategy of "opening up" lead to improved health?
       a)   It may help people suppress negative thoughts.
       b)   It may help people explain a negative event.
       c)   It may help people understand a negative event.
       d)   both b and c
       e)   all the above

Short Answer

1.   A researcher who is interested in the effects of relationship dissolution on people's self-esteem is surprised to
      find no correlation between the recency of people's romantic breakups and measures of self-esteem. As a social
      psychologist, what explanation for these apparently shocking findings might you offer?

2.   Imagine that you are a clinical psychologist and a client comes to you complaining about persistent though not
      severe depression. Using what you know about learned helplessness theory, suggest changes in the way your
      client explains events that will alleviate the melancholia.

WEB EXERCISE

Go to www.prenhall.com/aronson. Click on the Links for the Health Chapter. Go to Self-efficacy Across
Cultures which is a study of self-efficacy in fourteen cultures. Summarize what you learned. Or, click on the
link to the Biology of Stress. Summarize the paper on the physiological aspects of stress.

SOCIAL PSYCHOLOGY IN ACTION 2

Social Psychology and the Environment

OVERVIEW

People's reactions to environmental stimuli (e.g., noise, crowds) are largely a consequence of how stressful they perceive them to be. This module discusses how both noise and crowding can be stressful. The harmful effects of these environmental factors are reviewed. Social psychology offers assistance in changing environmentally damaging behaviors. However, obstacles to engaging in energy-conscious behaviors are social dilemmas. How people can resolve these dilemmas is examined in this module as are the successes of social psychologists at getting people to conserve water and energy. The influences of injunctive and descriptive norms on reducing littering are discussed. Also covered are ways to get people to recycle. Finally, two strategies to increase environmental consciousness and environmentally sound behaviors are detailed.

OUTLINE

The Environment as a Source of Stress

      Noise as a Source of Stress

      Crowding as a Source of Stress

Using Social Psychology to Change Environmentally Damaging Behaviors

      Resolving Social Dilemmas

      Conserving Water

      Conserving Energy

      Reducing Litter

      Getting People to Recycle

LEARNING OBJECTIVES

After reading Social Psychology in Action 2, you should be able to do the following:

1.   Identify stressors that have been eliminated and others that have been created as civilization has progressed. (pp. 538-539)

2.   Describe the conditions under which noise is psychologically stressful. Identify the effects of uncontrollable noise on blood pressure, distraction, perseverance, and task performance. Discuss when noise leads to learned helplessness and has detrimental future effects. Discuss the research findings on the effects of noise on children's academic performance. Identify ways to decrease noise in schools. (pp. 539-542)

3.　Describe the effects of crowding on animal and human behavior. Distinguish between density and crowding and identify factors that turn density into crowding. Discuss what norms other cultures have developed to avoid crowding even in a very dense environment. Describe the relationship between the effects of crowding and attribution. Define sensory overload and its relationship to crowding. (pp. 542-545)

4.　Identify conditions that decrease selfish behaviors and foster trust in response to social dilemmas in small groups and in large communities. (pp. 545-548)

5.　Explain how cognitive dissonance and hypocrisy techniques have been used to increase water conservation. (pp. 549-550)

6.　Explain why most American consumers have not taken steps to conserve energy even when doing so would save them a great deal of money. Discuss how social psychologists persuade homeowners to conserve energy. Identify successful strategies aimed at increasing energy conservation behavior. (pp. 550-552)

7.　Distinguish between injunctive and descriptive norms. Describe how Cialdini and colleagues have reduced littering by reminding people of these norms. Identify how descriptive norms are most effectively communicated. Identify the limitation of using descriptive norms to communicate appropriate behavior. (pp. 552-554)

8.　Discuss ways to get people to recycle. Identify the strategy that may yield the best results. (pp. 554-557)

KEY TERMS

density (p. 543)

crowding (p. 543)

sensory overload (p. 544)

injunctive norms (p. 552)

descriptive norms (p. 552)

STUDY QUESTIONS

1.　When is an environment stressful? What are relatively recent environmental stressors that our civilization has to face?

2.　When is noise psychologically stressful? What conditions are necessary to reduce the ill effects of loud noise? What are detrimental effects of uncontrollable noise? How has environmental noise affected the performance of school children?

3.   What are findings from studies of crowding in animals and humans? What psychological effects do crowded dorms have on students? Why is crowding aversive? What factors are linked with perceptions of crowding?

4.   How are the effects of noise and crowding similar?

5.   What is sensory overload and what are its consequences?

6.   According to research, how can we resolve social dilemmas?

7.   What is the role of cognitive dissonance and hypocrisy in increasing environmentally sound behaviors? Why is the hypocrisy technique successful at increasing water conservation? What type of information do we need to give people so that they will conserve?

8.   How can we get people to stop littering? What roles do injunctive and descriptive norms play in decreasing littering? Why are injunctive norms more effective than descriptive norms?

9.   What strategies have been successful at increasing energy conservation behaviors such as recycling?

PRACTICE TEST 1

Fill in the blank

1.   The number of people who occupy a given space is called _____.

2.   The subjective feeling of unpleasantness due to the presence of other people is called _____.

3.   Receiving more stimulation from the environment than we can pay attention to or process leads to _____.

Multiple Choice

1.   People who go to rock concerts do not find the extremely loud noise to be stressful because:
     a)   many other people are also present.
     b)   they chose to go to the concert.
     c)   norms dictate that anxiety is inappropriate for leisure activities.
     d)   they cannot pay attention to all the stimulation that is encountered.

2.   Participants who solved problems while being exposed to uncontrollable and loud noise performed more poorly on subsequent problems that were solved under quiet conditions because:
     a)   they had adapted to the noise and were uncomfortable in its absence.
     b)   they naturally lost the ability to concentrate over time.
     c)   they succumbed to learned helplessness after initially fighting the noxious effects of the noise.
     d)   the tasks presented during the second session were more difficult.

3.   Paulus et al. (1981) found that at crowded prisons:
     a)   friendships are more likely to be formed.
     b)   overall death rates increase.
     c)   escapes are more common.
     d)   released prisoners are less likely to return.

4.   Density turns into crowding when:
     a)   the presence of others lowers our feelings of control.
     b)   the number of people per square foot exceed the density ratio.
     c)   we are unable to determine the social structure of the situation.
     d)   external stimulation becomes more than we can process.

5.   Though driving affords you greater personal freedom, the pollution created by millions of drivers represents a global problem. This situation is a classic example of a problem known as a(n):
     a)   high-density situation.
     b)   paradoxical affair.
     c)   social dilemma.
     d)   attributional spiral.

6.   Aronson and his students increased the energy-conserving behavior of homeowners by:
     a)   reminding people of the need to make certain repairs.
     b)   publicizing problems to the neighborhood homeowner's association.
     c)   increasing people's perceived control over making such changes.
     d)   having energy auditors present their findings in a more dramatic way.

7.   People's perceptions of how others are actually behaving in a given situation, regardless of what they ought to be doing are _____ norms.
     a)   injunctive
     b)   conjunctive
     c)   descriptive
     d)   global

8.   Littering is LEAST likely to occur in which of the following situations?
     a)   an immaculately clean room
     b)   a badly littered room
     c)   a badly littered room with a sign prohibiting litter
     d)   an otherwise clean room with a single piece of litter

9.   Rosen and his colleagues (1962) found that, compared to people living in the industrialized world, the Mabaans:
a)   were more susceptible to physical illness.
b)   were more likely to exhibit psychological disorders.
c)   had less per capita violence in their culture.
d)   had less hypertension and obesity.

10.   Though you enjoy blasting your favorite tunes on your car stereo, you find it annoying when someone pulls up to you at a stoplight with the stereo blaring. A social psychologist would attribute your different reactions to loud music to:
a)   the perceived control that you have over the volume of the music.
b)   different tastes that people acquired for music in various subcultures.
c)   attributional biases in explaining the behavior of others.
d)   tension produced by dissonant thoughts about liking music and obeying social norms.

11.   Compared to children who attended quiet schools, children who attended schools in the air corridor of Los Angeles Airport:
a)   had higher blood pressure.
b)   were more easily distracted.
c)   were less likely to persevere on difficult problems.
d)   experienced all the above.

12.   Students will feel crowded in a classroom if:
a)   there are more than twenty people in the classroom.
b)   they feel that there are too many people in the classroom.
c)   the class is very highly structured.
d)   they receive too much stimulation in the classroom.

13.   Differences in people's reactions to crowding may be explained, in part, by:
a)   the attributions they make for their physiological arousal.
b)   their ability to resolve cognitive dissonance.
c)   their overall level of self-esteem.
d)   their overall level of physical fitness.

14.   Orbell et al. (1988) found that participants were most likely to donate money to a community pot, and thereby benefit everyone in the group, if they:
a)   were made to feel dissonance between being a nice person and being selfish.
b)   first heard a sermon about the Good Samaritan.
c)   interacted with other participants for ten minutes before having to decide whether or not to donate.
d)   all of the above interventions increased donations.

15.   The difficulty of getting people to conserve water and energy and to recycle their waste goods demonstrates the difficulty of resolving:
a)   attributional biases.
b)   disjunctive tasks.
c)   social dilemmas.
d)   self-serving biases.

16.   Which of the following is true about norms and reducing littering?
        a)   Focusing people's attention on descriptive norms is the most effective way to reduce littering.
        b)   Focusing people's attention on social norms is the most effective way to reduce littering.
        c)   Focusing people's attention on gender norms is the most effective way to reduce littering.
        d)   Focusing people's attention on injunctive norms is the most effective way to reduce littering.

Short Answer

1.   Describe a social dilemma that you face every day. Why is it a dilemma? How have you responded to the dilemma?

2.   If you were a member of a local water conservation committee, how might you go about inducing community members to save water when they know that it is in their own immediate best interests to use all the water that they want?

3.   At a local park, littering has become a serious problem. Describe techniques you could employ to evoke injunctive and descriptive norms against littering. Which kind of norm is most likely to be effective in the long run? Why?

PRACTICE TEST 2

Fill in the Blank

1.   People's perceptions of what behaviors are approved of by others are called _____.

2.   People's perceptions of how other people are actually behaving in a given situation, regardless of what they ought to be doing, are called _____.

Multiple Choice

1.   You are most likely to feel social pressure to conform if you are exposed to a(n) _____ norm.
        a)   injunctive
        b)   descriptive
        c)   peripheral
        d)   elaborative

2.   Which types of norms depend upon everyone's cooperation in order to be effective?
        a)   injunctive norms
        b)   descriptive norms
        c)   nonsalient norms
        d)   generosity norms

3. To find out the effects of noise on test performance, researchers disrupt students by playing loud bursts of noise randomly while the students are taking an exam. According to research, the noise most likely will impede performance:
   a) when the students take the first section of the test without any noise and the second section of the test with the random noise.
   b) when students are told to anticipate random noise throughout the exam, but none actually occurs.
   c) when the students are told that they can control the level of noise throughout the exam.
   d) when students take the first section of the test with the random noise and the second section of the test without any noise.
   e) when students are told that they can control the noise while taking the first section of the test and take the second section without any noise.

4. Sharla and Bobby are having a big picnic at their house and they do not want people to throw litter on their lawn. According to research on descriptive norms, what should they do?
   a) Clean their lawn carefully and make sure it is spotless.
   b) Plant one or two pieces of distinctive looking trash on their lawn before guests arrive.
   c) Plant a lot of trash on their lawn before the guests arrive.
   d) Put some extra garbage cans in their yard.

5. A term that refers to the number of people who occupy a given space is _____ and the unpleasant feeling that may be experienced when the presence of others is stressful is _____.
   a) crowding; social facilitation
   b) density; social anxiety
   c) density; crowding
   d) density; sensory overload

6. When we receive more stimulation from the environment than we can attend to or process, we experience _____ overload.
   a) cognitive
   b) sensory
   c) mental
   d) physical
   e) stress

7. Which of the following is a strategy to decrease the negative effects of social dilemmas?
   a) Allow people to communicate with each other.
   b) Allow people to monitor their own behaviors or rate of consumption.
   c) Make people's behaviors as public as possible.
   d) All the above are strategies.

8. All of the following can increase recycling in a community except which one?
   a) having residents sort the materials
   b) instituting curbside recycling
   c) adding more recycling bins in a community
   d) implementing a media campaign that targets people's attitudes toward recycling

9. Which of the following is important to consider when judging whether or not people consider loud noise stressful?
   a) how much perceived control people have over the noise
   b) how well people can predict when the noise will occur
   c) how people interpret the noise
   d) Both a and b are important.
   e) All the above are important.

169

10. Which of the following was a finding in the Glass and Singer (1972) experiment on the effects of noise on task performance?
    a) Participants who could control the noise heard less noise than did participants who could not control the noise.
    b) The noise did not affect task performance in any group during the initial 25-minute experimental session.
    c) The participants who could control the noise did significantly worse in the second session than did the participants in the no-noise condition.
    d) The participants who could control the noise made the same number of errors during the second session as did the participants who could not control the noise.

11. In their study of children living in a high-rise apartment building located next to a busy highway, Cohen et al. (1973) found that children who lived on the lower floors:
    a) were more aggressive than were children living on the higher floors.
    b) were more likely to get in trouble with the law than were children living on the higher floors.
    c) did poorer on reading tests than did children who lived on the higher floors.
    d) All the above were found.

12. All of the following happen when animals are crowded together except which one?
    a) they take longer to reproduce
    b) they become less susceptible to disease
    c) they take poor care of their young
    d) none of the above

13. Glass and Singer's (1972) study on the effects of noise on task performance were mirrored in Sherrod's (1974) study of the effects of _____ on task performance.
    a) predictable noise
    b) density
    c) crowding
    d) heat

14. Which of the following is NOT true regarding cultural norms that protect people's privacy?
    a) Eastern cultures do not have norms to protect people's privacy.
    b) A norm in Mexico prohibits people from going to someone's house without an invitation.
    c) The Japanese entertain in their homes more often than Americans do.
    d) The norm to have control over crowding seems to be universal.
    e) Both a and c are not true.

15. The outbreak of pfiesteria, a bacteria that may cause nerve damage, memory loss, and confusion, in Maryland in 1997, appears to be an example of:
    a) a commons dilemma.
    b) a public goods dilemma.
    c) corporate welfare.
    d) crowding.

16. Aronson and his colleagues' hypocrisy technique, having people preach behaviors that they are not practicing, has been found to increase:
    a) water conservation
    b) social dilemmas
    c) recycling
    d) both a and c
    e) none of the above

Short Answer

1.	You and other members of your community are fighting to decrease noise pollution caused by jets taking off and landing at a nearby airport. What arguments might you present to officials at the FAA in order to convince them that the noise is having detrimental effects on community members?

2.	Describe conditions that have been used successfully to resolve social dilemmas.

3.	Describe research that suggests one of the best ways to solve health and environmental problems is often to change people's interpretations of the situation.

WEB EXERCISE

Go to www.prenhall.com/aronson. Click on the Links for the Environmental Chapter. Click on the link to Environmental Psychology. Write an overview of this subfield of psychology. Or, read at least two studies on the effects of noise on children's health by clicking on Aircraft Noise and Kids. Write a summary of what you learned.

SOCIAL PSYCHOLOGY IN ACTION 3

Social Psychology and the Law

OVERVIEW

In this module, topics include how social psychologists apply principles, which by now are familiar, to initiate change in our legal system and promote justice for everyone involved. The application of social psychological principles to law is detailed. Although jurors are influenced heavily by eyewitness testimony, distortions in social cognition and attribution introduce unintentional errors into such testimony. When a witness purposely lies, there is an even greater likelihood that testimony will distort the opinions of jurors who, like most people, are not very skilled at detecting deception. Finally, jurors can be biased by publicity before the trial, by the way they process information during the trial, and by social influences that operate while the jury deliberates. Also covered in this module is the question of why people obey laws. One theory focuses on the deterrent effect of severe penalties. In addition, the importance of people's conception of a fair legal system is addressed.

OUTLINE

Eyewitness Testimony

      Why Are Eyewitnesses Often Wrong?

      Judging Whether Eyewitnesses Are Mistaken

      Judging Whether Witnesses Are Lying

      Can Eyewitness Testimony Be Improved?

      The Recovered Memory Debate

Juries: Group Processes in Action

      Effects of Pretrial Publicity

      How Jurors Process Information during the Trial

      Deliberations in the Jury Room

      Jury Size: Are Twelve Heads Better Than Six?

Why Do People Obey the Law?

      Do Severe Penalties Deter Crime?

      Procedural Justice: People's Sense of Fairness

LEARNING OBJECTIVES

After reading Social Psychology in Action 3, you should be able to do the following:

1.   Describe the social psychological aspects of the legal system. (p. 560-561)

2.   Discuss jurors' reliance on eyewitness testimony and their tendency to overestimate the accuracy of eyewitnesses. Identify why the accuracy of such testimony is overestimated. (pp. 561-562)

3.   Identify biases in memory processing that lead to inaccurate eyewitness testimony. Distinguish between acquisition, storage, and retrieval. (pp. 562-563)

4.   Identify situational factors that influence acquisition. Discuss the effect of previous expectancies on the acquisition of information. (pp. 563-565)

5.   Discuss the influence of familiarity on memory. Define own-race bias and discuss its significance in eyewitness testimony. (p. 565)

6.   Contrast the notion that memories are stored in our minds as static photographs with the notion that memories are actively reconstructed. Define reconstructive memory. Identify the role of misleading questions in reconstructive memory. Discuss how misleading questions alter what is stored in witnesses' memories. Define source monitoring and discuss its importance. (pp. 565-568)

7.   Identify the role of retrieval in identifying a suspect from a police lineup. List the seven steps that social psychologists recommend to reduce the likelihood that witnesses will mistakenly pick an innocent individual out of a lineup when that person resembles the suspect. (pp. 568-570)

8.   Discuss why the confidence of a witness does not necessarily equal the accuracy of his/her testimony. Describe the problem with verbalization. Identify ways to assess the accuracy of a witness's testimony. (pp. 570-572)

9.   Contrast the ability of novices and experts to detect deception. (pp. 572-574)

10.   Describe the controversy over the use of the polygraph. Discuss the results of research on the accuracy of polygraph tests. Discuss why social psychologists doubt that a foolproof method of lie detection will ever be developed. (pp. 574-575)

11.   Identify ways to improve the accuracy of eyewitness testimony. Define the cognitive interview technique. Discuss the effectiveness of these strategies. (pp. 576-577)

12.   Define recovered memories and the false memory syndrome and discuss the controversy surrounding these topics. (pp. 577-578)

13.   Discuss why the use of the jury system in legal proceedings is relevant to social psychology. Describe the effects of emotional pretrial publicity on jurors' verdicts. Identify ways in which pretrial publicity biases jurors' verdicts. Identify legal procedures aimed at eliminating these biases and indicate their effectiveness. (pp. 578-580)

14.   Describe the strategy jurors use to process information during a trial. Identify the implications for such a strategy on how lawyers present their cases. Distinguish between story order and witness order presentations of evidence. State the consequences of using each type of presentation both for prosecutors and defense lawyers. (pp. 581-582)

15.   Identify the role of group processes and social interactions in the way juries reach verdicts. Discuss the role of conformity in the process of jury deliberation. Identify the effects minorities are likely to have on the process of jury deliberation and on the sentence rendered. Explain why social psychologists believe that juries should consist of twelve people. (pp. 582-584)

16.   Discuss why people generally obey laws. Examine the theory that severe penalties prevent crime. Define deterrence theory and identify its assumptions and limitations. (pp. 584-587)

17.   Define procedural justice and discuss its role in people's adherence to laws and attitudes toward the legal system. (pp. 587-588)

KEY TERMS

acquisition (p. 562)

storage (p. 563)

retrieval (p. 563)

own-race bias (p. 565)

reconstructive memory (p. 566)

source monitoring (p. 567)

polygraph (p. 574)

cognitive interview (p. 576)

recovered memories (p. 577)

false memory syndrome (p. 578)

deterrence theory (p. 584)

procedural justice (p. 588)

STUDY QUESTIONS

1.   What can social psychologists offer to the study of the legal system?

2.   Why do jurors overestimate the accuracy of eyewitness testimony?

3.   What are the three stages of memory processing? What can interfere with processing at each stage of memory? What conditions are present at most crime scenes and how does this affect acquisition? How do expectancies affect the acquisition of information?

4. Why is familiarity an important factor in memory processing? What is the own-race bias? What consequences does this bias have on eyewitness testimony?

5. What are the characteristics of our memory storage? What is reconstructive memory? What has been discovered about the accuracy of our memory? What is source monitoring? What effects do misleading questions have on source monitoring? Why is incorrect source monitoring a problem for eyewitness accuracy?

6. What consequences does retrieval have for the correct identification of a suspect from a police lineup? What are five steps to follow when conducting a police lineup? What is the rationale behind each step?

7. How can we tell if a witness' testimony is accurate? Why is confidence of one's testimony not always a good estimate of the accuracy of one's testimony? What are the consequences of trying to put a face into words for the accuracy of identifying the face?

8. How well can people detect deception? Do those working in the field of law enforcement do better than others at detecting deception?

9. What is a polygraph machine designed to do and how does it do it? What is the assumption behind the use of the polygraph? How accurate, on average, are polygraphs at detecting when someone is lying? Does failing a polygraph test always mean that one is lying? Why is a machine intended to tell if a human is lying not ever likely to be completely accurate?

10. What methods have been used in the attempt to improve the accuracy of eyewitness testimony? What is a cognitive interview?

11. What are recovered memories? What is the false memory syndrome? How are they relevant to the issue of eyewitness testimony?

12.   What are three phases of a jury trial in which problems can occur? What are the effects of pretrial publicity on jurors' perceptions of suspects? How can judges and lawyers attempt to remedy the problem of pretrial publicity bias?

13.   How do individual jurors process evidence during a trial? In which two orders can lawyers present evidence? Which order is more effective? Given these findings, why may the felony conviction rate in America be as high as it is?

14.   What are the benefits of jury deliberations? How are minorities influential in jury deliberation?

15.   Why do people obey laws? What explanation does deterrence theory offer? What does this theory fail to explain? Why?

16.   What is procedural justice? How important do people consider it to be?

PRACTICE TEST 1

Fill in the Blank

1.   The process by which people notice and pay attention to a subset of information available in the environment is called _____.

2.   The process by which people store in memory information they have acquired from the environment is called _____.

3.   The process by which people recall information stored in their memories is called _____.

4.   The process in which memory for an event becomes distorted by information that is encountered after the event has occurred is called _____.

5.   The process whereby people try to identify the sources of their memories is called _____.

6.   A machine used in lie detection that measures people's physiological responses while they answer questions is called a(n) _____.

Multiple Choice

1. The process whereby people notice and attend to information in the environment is called ____ and the process of keeping that information in memory is called ____.
   a) acquisition; storage
   b) learning; acquisition
   c) learning; storage
   d) attention; retrieval

2. It is very likely that witnesses to real crimes will give inaccurate testimony because:
   a) eyewitnesses feel that criminals will seek revenge for testimony that convicts them.
   b) emotions experienced while witnessing the crime will be evoked during testimony and interfere with recall.
   c) crimes usually occur under the very conditions that make acquisition difficult.
   d) arousal interferes with the storage of memories.

3. A cognitive process where memory for an event becomes distorted by information that is encountered after the event occurs is called:
   a) acquisition.
   b) storage.
   c) retrieval.
   d) reconstructive memory.

4. Lindsay and Wells (1985) found that witnesses were less likely to identify an innocent individual as a criminal when they viewed pictures of people presented:
   a) simultaneously.
   b) sequentially.
   c) repeatedly.
   d) on a single occasion.

5. Someone who is motivated to tell a lie:
   a) is likely to be caught by anyone.
   b) will be unable to conceal the lie as well as someone who lies casually.
   c) can usually get away with it.
   d) is likely to be caught only by experts in lie detection.

6. Which of the following influences are likely to lead juries to reach unfair verdicts?
   a) biased pretrial publicity
   b) faulty information processing during the trial
   c) normative influence during deliberation
   d) all of the above

7. Which of the following is the most effective means of avoiding the effects of pretrial publicity?
   a) a change of venue
   b) instructions by the judge to disregard such publicity
   c) the voir dire process
   d) a strong defense attorney

8. Since jurors decide upon a "best story" to explain the evidence, a good lawyer would present her witnesses:
   a) in order of ascending credibility.
   b) in order of descending credibility.
   c) in an manner which reveals the order of the events as they occurred.
   d) in a manner which leads to a startling and dramatic revelation.

9. Jurors tend to put a lot of faith in eyewitness testimony because:
    a) eyewitnesses are in a position of high status in the courtroom.
    b) jurors have a natural bias toward conviction.
    c) normative pressures to side with the eyewitness are high in the courtroom.
    d) they assume that the witness's confidence is a good indicator of accuracy.

10. Retrieval is the process by which people:
    a) notice and pay attention to a subset of information available in the environment.
    b) store information in memory that they have acquired from the environment.
    c) rehearse information so that it will not be immediately forgotten.
    d) recall information that is stored in their memories.

11. Which of the following coincides with the own-race bias?
    a) Sheila, an African American woman, is better at recognizing white faces than Black or Asian faces.
    b) Juan, an African American man, is better at recognizing Asian faces than white or Black faces.
    c) Steve, a white man, is better at recognizing white faces than Black or Asian faces.
    d) Lily, an Asian woman, is better at recognizing Asian faces than Black or white faces.
    e) Both c and d coincide.

12. Why are people likely to give inaccurate accounts of events when asked misleading questions?
    a) The questions change what people are willing to report.
    b) People assume that the misinformation presented in the question came from their own memories.
    c) The misinformation presented in the question conflicts with stored information and produces dissonance.
    d) The questions bias acquisition.

13. Joe believes that he has nothing to lose by taking a polygraph test in order to be considered for a part-time sales job at a local pharmaceutical company. In fact, the probability that Joe will be mistakenly identified as a liar even though he tells the truth is:
    a) 2%.
    b) 5%.
    c) 15%.
    d) 35%.

14. Pretrial publicity tends to bias jurors in favor of "guilty" verdicts if the publicity:
    a) arouses public passions.
    b) evokes counterargumentation by prospective jurors.
    c) is presented in a factual manner.
    d) frustrates prospective jurors trying to form an unbiased opinion.

15. Though the media qualifies incriminating statements with words like "allegedly," such statements bias readers because:
    a) mere exposure to the name of the accused increases liking for the individual.
    b) readers envy the status given to people whose name appears in the paper.
    c) readers associate the name of the accused with the crime.
    d) people have a difficult time processing qualifiers while they read.

Short Answer

1. As a social psychologist, you have been contracted by a defense attorney to give your expert opinion on eyewitness accuracy following testimony by a woman who swears that she saw the defendant murder someone. What would you tell the court?

2. If juries usually stick with the verdict favored by the initial majority of jurors, why should we insist that juries deliberate until they reach consensus on that verdict?

3. Describe the three stages of memory processing that an eyewitness must successfully complete in order to give accurate testimony.

PRACTICE TEST 2

Fill in the Blank

1. The finding that people are better at recognizing faces within their own race than of other races is called _____.

2. A technique which attempts to increase the accuracy of eyewitness testimony by directing attention to details of the crime is called the _____.

3. The belief that harsh penalties keep people from breaking laws is the major tenet of _____.

4. People's judgments as to the fairness of the legal system constitute _____.

5. Remembrances of past events that had been forgotten or repressed are called _____ memories.

6. The _____ syndrome is characterized by people remembering past trauma that they believed happened when, in fact, it never did.

Multiple Choice

1. The presence of minority opposition in a jury increases the likelihood that:
   a) a guilty verdict will be rendered.
   b) the facts in the case will be carefully considered.
   c) self-awareness among jurors will be high.
   d) a not guilty verdict will be rendered.

2. According to your text, which of the following has been used to increase the accuracy of eyewitness testimony?
   a) the cognitive interview
   b) exposure to pretrial publicity
   c) memory enhancing drugs
   d) inducing belief in the just world hypothesis

3. Regarding jury size, most social psychologists recommend that all juries consist of _____ people so that _____ will be likely to occur.
   a) 6; groupthink
   b) 5; group polarization
   c) 12; minority representation
   a) 6; minority influence

4. A memory of a past trauma that is objectively false but is believed to have occurred defines the:
   a) recovered memory syndrome.
   b) deception memory syndrome.
   c) implicit memory syndrome.
   d) false memory syndrome.

5. Since people pay less attention to features that characterize the individual in cross-race people and instead focus on facial characteristics of the entire group, they are likely to commit _____ when trying to recognize these faces.
   a) the ultimate attribution error
   b) the fundamental attribution error
   c) source monitoring
   d) the own-race bias

6. When people get confused about where and when they heard or saw something, they are having problems with:
   a) source monitoring.
   b) recall.
   c) acquisition.
   d) cognitive monitoring.

7. All of the following are social psychologists' recommendations to police regarding lineups except which one?
   a) The person conducting the lineup should not know which person in the lineup is the suspect.
   b) Ask witnesses how confident they are that they can identify the suspect before they are given feedback about their lineup performance.
   c) Present witnesses with either photos of people or sound recordings of people suspected of the crime.
   d) Conduct lineups both with and without the suspect in the lineup.

8. Regarding judging whether eyewitnesses are accurate, which of the following is correct?
   a) The confidence level of the eyewitness is a good indication of how accurate an eyewitness is.
   b) Eyewitnesses who take less time identifying the defendant are correct more often than are eyewitnesses who take more time.
   c) Eyewitnesses who put a face of a suspect into words are more accurate than are those who do not verbalize the suspect's facial features.
   d) Eyewitnesses may lie deliberately when on the witness stand.
   e) Both b and d are correct.

9. According to Ekman et al. (1999), which of the following groups was the best at detecting deception?
   a) a group of law enforcement officers
   b) a group of clinical psychologists
   c) a group of sheriffs
   d) a group of federal officers (mostly CIA employees)
   e) a group of social psychologists

10. According to Ekman et al. (1999), which of the following groups was the worst at detecting deception?
   a) a group of law enforcement officers
   b) a group of clinical psychologists
   c) a group of sheriffs
   d) a group of federal officers (mostly CIA employees)
   e) a group of social psychologists

11. In the _____ version of the polygraph, the operator asks people both relevant questions about the crime and questions that people typically answer truthfully.
   a) control question test
   b) control knowledge test
   c) guilty knowledge test
   d) guilty question test

12. A technique to improve eyewitnesses' memories that has them focus their attention on the details and context of the event by asking them to recall the event several times and by asking them to create a mental picture of the scene is called:
   a) source retrieval.
   b) retrieval.
   c) cognitive interview.
   d) constructive interview.

13. Which of the following is true regarding how lawyers present information to the jury in a trial and its effects?
   a) Prosecutors usually present evidence in the witness order.
   b) Defense attorneys usually present evidence in the witness order.
   c) Juries are more likely to convict the defendant when the prosecutor uses the story order.
   d) Both b and c are true.
   e) None of the above are true.

14. Deterrence theory proposes that people obey the law because of the threat of legal punishment, as long as the punishment is perceived as:
   a) severe.
   b) certain.
   c) swift.
   d) all the above.

15. Which of the following is true about why people obey the law?
   a) People who perceive that the procedures used to determine outcomes in court are fair will be more likely to obey the law than people who do not.
   b) Perceived procedural justice is a better explanation for why people obey the law than is deterrence theory.
   c) The death penalty prevents murders.
   d) Both a and b are true.
   e) All the above are true.

Short Answer

1. Describe legal procedures aimed at eliminating biases created by pretrial publicity. Why are some of these procedures less than perfect remedies?

2. What reasons exist to explain why people obey the law? What are aspects of the legal system that help keep people from committing crimes?

WEB EXERCISE

Visit www.prenhall.com/aronson. Click on the Try It! for the Chapter on Law. Take the quiz on the death penalty. What are your reactions to the quiz and your score on the quiz? Or, click on the link to the Recovered Memory Debate and summarize what you learned. Or, go to www.socialpsychology.org, click on Social Topics, click on Disciplines Related to Social Psychology, and click on Psychology and Law. What three things did you learn from this site?

ANSWER SECTION

CHAPTER 1: INTRODUCTION TO SOCIAL PSYCHOLOGY

Answer Key

Practice Test 1

Fill in the Blank

1. social psychology (p. 6)
2. social influence (p. 6)
3. construal (p. 6)
4. sociology (p. 10)
5. individual differences (p. 11)
6. personality psychology (p. 11)

Multiple Choice

1. A (p. 6)
2. C (p. 9)
3. A (p. 11)
4. C (p. 13)
5. D (p. 14)
6. A (p. 15)
7. A (p. 19)
8. D (p. 21)
9. A (p. 7)
10. A (p. 11)
11. A (p. 13)
12. D (p. 16)
13. D (pp. 18, 21)
14. B (p. 21)
15. D (p. 22)

Short Answer

1. Linda is most likely to identify psychological processes, like frustration, that produce aggression. Mark is likely to identify broad societal factors, like social class, that may affect aggression. (pp. 10-11)

2. The self-esteem approach assumes that behavior is motivated by the desire to perceive ourselves favorably and that we may place a slightly different spin on reality to achieve this end. The social cognition approach assumes that we want to perceive the world accurately but that several obstacles may block this goal. (pp. 17-22)

3. Social psychology takes a scientific approach to the study of human behavior which allows it to explain the causes of behavior and demonstrate the conditions under which (sometimes opposite) behaviors will occur. (pp. 8-9)

Practice Test 2

Fill in the Blank

1. the fundamental attribution error (p. 13)
2. Behaviorism (p. 15)
3. Gestalt psychology (p. 16)
4. self-esteem (p. 18)
5. self-justification (p. 19)
6. social cognition (p. 21)
7. self-fulfilling prophecy (p. 22)

Multiple Choice

1. C (p. 24)
2. D (p. 6)
3. B (pp. 8-9)
4. B (p. 11)
5. A (p. 11)
6. B (p. 16)
7. C (p. 17)
8. B (p. 23)
9. C (p. 6)
10. B (p. 12)
11. C (p. 15)
12. B (p. 16)
13. A (p. 19)
14. C (p. 13)
15. D (p. 17)

Short Answer

1. Your example should reflect how an expectancy actually caused a change in your social environment so that your expectancy was confirmed. Expecting it to rain and finding that it does rain, for instance, is not an example of the self-fulfilling prophesy because you did not cause it to rain. (p. 22)

2. Your essay should include instances of how pervasive social influence is and how we are not always aware of how it changes our behavior. (pp. 13-15)

CHAPTER 2: METHODOLOGY: HOW SOCIAL PSYCHOLOGISTS DO RESEARCH

Answer Key

Practice Test 1

Fill in the Blank

1.   ethnography (p. 33)
2.   participant observation (p. 33)
3.   archival analysis (p. 33)
4.   interjudge reliability (p. 33)
5.   correlational method (p. 36)
6.   correlation coefficient (p. 36)
7.   random selection (p. 38)
8.   experimental method (p. 41)
9.   independent variable (p. 43)
10.   dependent variable (p. 43)
11.   internal validity (p. 45)
12.   random assignment to condition (p. 45)
13.   surveys (p. 37)

Multiple Choice

1.   B (p. 31)
2.   D (pp. 33-35)
3.   B (p. 37)
4.   A (p. 38)
5.   D (pp. 39-42)
6.   B (p. 50)
7.   A (pp. 50-51)
8.   D (p. 32)
9.   C (p. 48)
10.   A (p. 33)
11.   B (p. 37)
12.   B (p. 43)
13.   A (p. 45)
14.   D (pp. 46-48)
15.   B (p. 46)

Short Answer

1.   Anything in addition to the independent variable that varies could also have caused your results to turn out the way they did. Therefore, the exact cause of your results cannot be known. (pp. 44-45)

2.   The setting of highly controlled experiments is often artificial. Results from such experiments may not generalize to everyday life. By replicating the experiment in the field, this limitation can be overcome. (pp. 46-47)

3.   The APA guidelines tell us deception may be used only if no other means of testing the hypothesis is available and only if an Institutional Review Board rules that the experiment does not put participants at undo risk. Following the deception experiment, participants must be provided with a full description and explanation of all procedures including the necessity of deception. (pp. 52-53)

Practice Test 2

Fill in the Blank

1.   probability level (p. 45)
2.   external validity (p. 46)
3.   psychological realism (p. 46)
4.   replication (p. 48)
5.   meta analysis (p. 48)
6.   field experiment (p. 50)
7.   applied research (p. 53)
8.   informed consent (p. 52)
9.   deception (p. 52)
10.   debriefing (p. 52)
11.   observational (p. 32)
12.   mundane (p. 46)
13.   cover (p. 46)

Multiple Choice

1.   A (pp. 50-51)
2.   B (pp. 53-54)
3.   C (p. 53)
4.   C (p. 41)
5.   D (p. 41)
6.   C (p. 45)
7.   C (p. 33)
8.   B (p. 46)
9.   B (p. 46)
10.   C (p. 52)
11.   C (p. 31)
12.   C (p. 46)
13.   D (p. 43)
14.   E (p. 46)
15.   C (pp. 36-37)

Short Answer

1.   Common public behaviors are assessed by unobtrusive systematic observation. Behaviors not observable to "outsiders" are assessed by participant observation. Behaviors that change over time or across different cultures are assessed by archival analysis. (pp. 32-35)

2.   You cannot generalize survey results to a population that is not represented by your sample. Members of the community who watch other local news programs, who were not home on this particular night, or who were unwilling to call the station are not represented here. (pp. 37-38)

CHAPTER 3: SOCIAL COGNITION: HOW WE THINK ABOUT THE SOCIAL WORLD

Answer Key

Practice Test 1

Fill in the Blank

1.   schemas (p. 59)
2.   counterfactual thinking (p. 87)
3.   automatic (p. 59)
4.   accessibility (p. 63)
5.   suppression (p. 85)
6.   perseverance effect (p. 66)
7.   self-fulfilling prophecy (p. 67)
8.   judgmental heuristic (p. 74)

Multiple Choice

1.   D (p. 58)
2.   A (p. 62)
3.   C (p. 60)
4.   A (pp. 61-62)
5.   D (pp. 63, 64)
6.   B (p. 66)
7.   B (p. 67)
8.   A (p. 75)
9.   D (p. 77)
10.   B (p. 82)
11.   D (p. 89)
12.   D (pp. 60-61)
13.   B (pp. 66)
14.   B (p. 64)
15.   B (p. 67)

Short Answer

1.   Judgments are based on the ease with which something can be brought to mind when the availability heuristic is used. Things are classified according to how similar they are to a "typical" case when the representativeness heuristic is used. When the anchoring/adjustment heuristic is used, judgments are made by adjusting an answer away from an initial value. (pp. 74-81)

2.   Asking people to consider the opposite point of view to their own makes people realize that there are other ways to construe the world. The effectiveness of this approach suggests that overconfidence results from people noticing, interpreting, and remembering only information that is consistent with their particular schemas. (pp. 89-91)

3.   Cultures determine what schemas we learn and remember. What is valued in a particular culture is more likely to be a part of a well-developed schema. (pp. 71-74)

Practice Test 2

Fill in the Blank

1. availability heuristic (p. 74)
2. representativeness heuristic (p. 77)
3. base rate information (p. 77)
4. anchoring/adjustment heuristic (p. 78)
5. biased sampling (p. 79)
6. overconfidence barrier (p. 89)
7. priming (p. 64)
8. controlled (p. 82)
9. social cognition (p. 58)

Multiple Choice

1. B (p. 77)
2. A (pp. 87-88)
3. A (p. 83)
4. D (p. 79)
5. A (pp. 59, 82)
6. D (pp. 59-63)
7. C (p. 85)
8. C (pp. 85-87)
9. C (p. 67)
10. D (p. 64)
11. D (pp. 87-88)
12. C (p. 78)
13. D (p. 74)
14. D (pp. 89-91)
15. A (p. 63)

Short Answer

1. Automatic thinking requires less mental effort than does controlled thinking. Automatic thinking is nonconscious while controlled thinking requires conscious awareness. Thought suppression requires the cooperation of both automatic and controlled thinking. Automatic thinking searches for the unwanted thought and controlled thinking is used to think about something else when the thought is present. (pp. 59, 82, 85-87)

2. Amy's counting on people's tendency to insufficiently adjust their estimates away from an anchor when they use the adjustment/anchoring heuristic to decide how much they'll offer for the car. (pp. 78-80)

3. Your attempts at correcting your friend's errors of inference should be aimed at reducing his/her overconfidence (first by overcoming the overconfidence barrier), by asking him/her to consider the opposite point of view, and by recommending college statistics courses, one-time lessons in reasoning, or training in research design. (pp. 89-91)

CHAPTER 4: SOCIAL PERCEPTION: HOW WE COME TO UNDERSTAND OTHER PEOPLE

Answer Key

Practice Test 1

Fill in the Blank

1.   social perception (p.97)
2.   nonverbal communication (p. 97)
3.   encode, decode (p. 99)
4.   display rules (p. 102)
5.   affect blends (p. 101)
6.   emblems   (p. 103)
7.   social role theory (p. 106)
8.   implicit personality theories (p. 107)
9.   attribution theory (p. 110)
10.   internal attribution (p. 110)
11.   external attribution (p. 110)
12.   spotlight effect (p. 119)
13.   correspondence bias (p. 129)

Multiple Choice

1.   A (pp. 103, 105)
2.   C (p. 110)
3.   C (p. 119)
4.   A (p. 126)
5.   D (p. 97)
6.   A (p. 102)
7.   C (p. 103)
8.   C (p. 106)
9.   D (p. 101)
10.   B (p. 110)
11.   B (p. 97)
12.   D (p. 111)
13.   B (p. 128)
14.   D (p. 116)
15.   C (p. 132)

Short Answer

1.   Social role theory states that division of labor produces gender-role expectations as well as skills and attitudes based on gender roles. In many societies the gender roles of women dictate that they learn to be more polite. To be polite, women may turn off their ability to detect deception in others' nonverbal cues. Hall (1979) found that in oppressive societies, where prescriptions for women to be polite are especially strong, women were less likely to key into nonverbal communications that "leaked" true feelings that were being covered up. (p. 106)

2.   Kelley focused on the information (consensus, distinctiveness, and consistency) that we use to decide whether to make an internal or an external attribution for multiple instances of behaviors. (pp. 111-113)

3.   Your impression of John is wrong because you've relied on fallible mental shortcuts. The fundamental attribution error and your implicit personality theories are among these. While your impression may be inaccurate, you can accurately predict John's behavior if: (1) You observe John across limited situations. In these cases situational variability won't affect behavior and the fundamental attribution error won't lead to poor predictions. (2) You cause John's behavior to confirm your predictions (self-fulfilling prophesy). (pp. 132-135)

Practice Test 2

Fill in the Blank

1.   covariation model (p. 111)
2.   consensus information (p. 112)
3.   distinctiveness information (p. 112)
4.   consistency information (p. 112)
5.   fundamental attribution error (p. 114)
6.   actor/observer difference (p. 119)
7.   self-serving attributions (p. 122)
8.   unrealistic optimism (p. 125)
9.   belief in a just world (p. 126)
10.   perceptual salience (p. 115)
11.   two-step (p. 116)
12.   defensive (p. 125)

Multiple Choice

1.   A (pp. 134)
2.   C (p. 99)
3.   C (p. 106)
4.   D (pp. 107-109)
5.   B (pp. 109-111)
6.   A (p. 112)
7.   B (p. 112)
8.   C (p. 100)
9.   D (pp. 101-102)
10.   D (pp. 115-116)
11.   B (p. 119)
12.   C (p. 122)
13.   D (pp. 122-125)
14.   B (p. 125)
15.   D (pp. 129-131)

Short Answer

1.   People go through two steps in making attributions. They initially assume that the perceptually salient actor caused the behavior and so make an internal attribution. Using this initial estimate as an anchor, they make an adjustment to take the situation into account. As often happens using the anchoring/adjustment heuristic (see Chapter 3), this adjustment is insufficient. (pp. 115-116)

2.   Your example should depict an internal attribution for a recent success and an external attribution for a recent failure. (p. 122-124)

CHAPTER 5: SELF-KNOWLEDGE: HOW WE COME TO UNDERSTAND OURSELVES

Answer Key

Practice Test 1

Fill in the Blank

1. self-concept (p. 141)
2. introspection (p. 146)
3. self-awareness theory (p. 148)
4. causal theory (p. 152)
5. self-perception theory (p. 154)
6. performance-contingent (p. 157)
7. intrinsic motivation (p. 155)
8. overjustification effect (p. 156)
9. two-factor theory of emotion (p. 159)
10. misattribution of arousal (p. 161)
11. cognitive appraisal (p. 163)
12. social comparison theory (p. 164)

Multiple Choice:

1. A (p. 141)
2. C (p. 144)
3. D (pp. 152-153)
4. D (p. 154)
5. D (p. 141)
6. B (pp. 156-158)
7. B (p. 157)
8. C (p. 159)
9. B (pp. 161-162)
10. D (p. 163)
11. D (pp. 142-143)
12. A (pp. 142-143)
13. C (p. 154)
14. D (p. 168)
15. D (pp. 146-147)

Short Answer

1. According to self-perception theory, when the causes of our behavior are ambiguous, we are in functionally the same role as an outside observer attributing our own behavior to our attitudes and traits (note that these are therefore internal attributions). (pp. 154-155)

2. As you introspect about the reasons why you are attracted to your recent dating partner, you are likely to bring to mind reasons that sound plausible and are available but which may not be the actual reasons. A negative consequence of identifying the wrong reasons is that you may change your mind about how you feel to match those reasons. For instance, if you decide that you are attracted to someone because the two of you share a common hobby, you may decide that such a reason is not justification for pursuing a relationship and lose interest. (pp. 150-154)

3.   When we're self-aware, we form more accurate judgments of ourselves and may behave in a manner more consistent with our internal values and standards. However, self-awareness is uncomfortable and may cause us to engage in deleterious behaviors such as drinking alcohol, etc., to avoid self-awareness when we cannot change our behaviors. (pp. 148-150)

Practice Test 2

Fill in the Blank

1.   upward social comparison (p. 165)
2.   self-presentation (p. 166)
3.   impression management (p. 166)
4.   ingratiation (p. 168)
5.   self-handicapping (p. 168)
6.   interdependent (p. 144)
7.   independent (p. 144)
8.   extrinsic motivation (p. 155)
9.   reasons-generated (p. 154)
10. task-contingent (p. 157)
11. downward (p. 166)

Multiple Choice

1.   B (p. 152)
2.   D (p. 156)
3.   B (pp. 159-161)
4.   B (p. 148)
5.   B (p. 154)
6.   D (p. 141)
7.   A (pp. 164-166)
8.   C (pp. 168-169)
9.   A (p. 155)
10. B (pp. 165-166)
11. C (p. 166)
12. D (pp. 164-165)
13. B (p. 154)
14. D (p. 152)
15. C (p. 156)

Short Answer

1.   Both theories maintain that we come to understand ourselves by observing our own behavior and finding an appropriate explanation. The theories differ in two ways. First, each explains how we come to know a different feature of ourselves. Self-perception theory explains how we know what we think and what kind of person we are. The two-factor theory explains how we know how we feel. Second, each theory claims we use a different type of behavior to achieve self-understanding. Self-perception theory says we make internal attributions from observing overt behavior. The two factor theory states we label behavior that is associated with physiological arousal. (pp. 154-155, 159-162)

2.   Before your pay raise there were no large extrinsic rewards for working at the library. When asked, therefore, you are more likely to conclude that you work there because you like it. If you overjustify your reason for working there after your pay raise, the conspicuous external reward will grab your attention, cause you to discount the role of your intrinsic interest in the job, and lead you to conclude that you like the job less. (pp. 155-158)

CHAPTER 6: SELF-JUSTIFICATION AND THE NEED TO MAINTAIN SELF-ESTEEM

Answer Key

Practice Test 1

Fill in the Blank

1. cognitive dissonance (p. 174)
2. post-decision dissonance (p. 178)
3. lowballing (p. 179)
4. justification of effort (p. 182)
5. external justification (p. 184)
6. internal justification (p. 185)
7. counterattitudinal advocacy (p. 185)
8. self-discrepancy theory (p. 198)

Multiple Choice:

1. B (p. 175)
2. D (p. 178)
3. A (p. 179)
4. C (p. 181)
5. C (p. 185)
6. B (p. 195)
7. C (p. 201)
8. A (pp. 201-203)
9. C (pp. 206-208)
10. D (pp. 209-210)
11. B (p. 181)
12. D (pp. 178-179)
13. A (pp. 184-186)
14. C (p. 189)
15. B (pp. 192-194)

Short Answer

1. Members will justify their efforts to join the group and will find the group attractive even if the group turns out to have little to offer. (pp. 182-184)

2. According to self-discrepancy theory, sources of dissonance are inconsistencies between our ideal, ought, and actual selves. According to self-completion theory, sources of dissonance are threats to an important aspect of one's self-concept. (pp. 198-201)

3. A prize of $100 is sufficient external justification for claiming loyalty to any radio station. A T-shirt is insufficient justification that will motivate a search for internal justification and will result in a more favorable evaluation of the radio station. (pp. 185-186)

Practice Test 2

Fill in the Blank

1. insufficient punishment (p. 189)
2. self-persuasion (p. 190)
3. self-evaluation maintenance theory (p. 201)
4. self-affirmation theory (p. 204)
5. self-verification theory (p. 207)
6. rationalization trap (p. 209)
7. self-justification (p. 207)
8. self-completion theory (p. 200)

Multiple Choice

1. B (pp. 186-187)
2. A (p. 204)
3. C (pp. 174, 201, 204)
4. B (p. 209)
5. A (p. 182)
6. D (p. 179)
7. C (p. 207)
8. B (p. 198)
9. D (pp. 184-185)
10. D (pp. 198-200)
11. A (pp. 200-201)
12. D (pp. 208-209)
13. E (p. 175)
14. D (pp. 184-185)
15. C (p. 174)

Short Answer

1. If writing the essay caused physiological arousal then participants who believed they should be feeling relaxed felt this arousal and assumed that it would have been greater still had they not taken the drug. If arousal motivates attitude change then   participants believing that they are highly aroused should have been especially motivated to change their attitudes. Greater attitude change among subjects who'd taken the relaxing placebo supports these claims. (pp. 196-198)

2. Cognitive dissonance theory maintains that we reduce dissonance by changing behaviors or by adding or changing cognitions to justify behaviors. Self-evaluation maintenance theory states that we reduce dissonance by improving our performance relative to our friend's, distancing ourselves from the individual, or by reducing how relevant the task is to our self-image. Self-affirmation theory asserts that we reduce dissonance by affirming our competence and integrity in an unrelated area where our esteem is not threatened. (pp. 174, 201, 204)

CHAPTER 7: ATTITUDES AND ATTITUDE CHANGE: INFLUENCING THOUGHTS AND FEELINGS

Answer Key

Practice Test 1

Fill in the Blank

1.   attitude (p. 217)
2.   affective (p. 217)
3.   cognitive (p. 217)
4.   behavioral (p. 217)
5.   persuasive communication (p. 223)
6.   Yale Attitude Change Approach (p. 224)
7.   elaboration likelihood model (p. 225)
8.   central (p. 225)
9.   peripheral (p. 225)
10.   personal relevance (p. 225)
11.   fear-arousing communication (p. 231)
12.   cognitively based attitudes (p. 218)

Multiple Choice

1.   C (p. 217)
2.   A (p. 224)
3.   B (p. 228)
4.   D (pp. 231-232)
5.   C (p. 219)
6.   E (pp. 238-239)
7.   D (p. 227)
8.   C (p. 230)
9.   B (p. 243)
10.   D (p. 239)
11.   B (p. 225)
12.   D (pp. 230, 235)
13.   C (pp. 233-234)
14.   B (p. 221)
15.   C (p. 237)

Short Answer

1.   Your example should indicate that a cognitively based attitude is founded on people's beliefs about the properties of the attitude object, that an affectively based attitude is founded on people's emotions and values that are evoked by the attitude object, and that a behaviorally based attitude is derived from people's observations of how they behave toward the attitude object. (pp. 218-220)

2. Persuasive attempts "boomerang," or cause an increased interest in the activity your persuasive attempt is aimed at discouraging, when strong prohibitions for engaging in the activity are used. In part, this occurs because, according to reactance theory, we are motivated to restore a sense of freedom when we perceive that we are not free to engage in the activity. One means of restoring a sense of freedom is to perform the behavior. The boomerang effect also occurs because strong prohibitions provide ample and conspicuous external justification for not engaging in the behavior. Under such conditions, overjustification is likely to occur. That is, people will underestimate the intrinsic reasons for avoiding the behavior and come to believe that they enjoy the activity
more. (p. 237)

3. People's attitudes toward greeting cards are clearly affectively based. Your approach should therefore be to play on these emotions. You would recommend presenting ads that depict joyous birthdays and weddings, proud moments like graduation etc. (pp. 218, 241-243)

Practice Test 2

Fill in the Blank

1. affectively based attitudes (p. 218)
2. classical conditioning (p. 219)
3. operant conditioning (p. 219)
4. behaviorally based attitudes (p. 220)
5. attitude accessibility (p. 221)
6. attitude inoculation (p. 235)
7. reactance theory (p. 237)
8. theory of planned behavior (p. 239)
9. subjective norms (p. 240)
10. subliminal messages (p. 243)
11. cognition (p. 227)
12. heuristic-systematic (p. 232)

Multiple Choice

1. D (p. 240)
2. C (p. 223)
3. B (pp. 222-223)
4. D (pp. 231-232)
5. C (pp. 225, 232)
6. A (p. 235)
7. A (p. 240)
8. C (p. 241)
9. A (pp. 243-248)
10. B (pp. 225-227)
11. D (pp. 223-224)
12. B (p. 217)
13. A (pp. 222-223)
14. A (pp. 225-227)
15. D (pp. 222-223)

Short Answer

1.   According to the Elaboration Likelihood Model, people take the central route to persuasion when they are both motivated and able to attend to arguments presented. Subsequent attitude change will persist, be consistent with behaviors, and resist counterpersuasion. If people are either unmotivated or unable to attend to the arguments, they will attend to cues, which are peripheral to the message, and take the peripheral route to persuasion. Subsequent attitude change will be short-lived, be inconsistent with behaviors, and will change again in the face of counterpersuasion. (pp. 225-230)

2.   Attitude inoculation makes people immune to attempts to change cognitively based attitudes by initially exposing them to small doses of the arguments against their position. Peer pressure is likely to play on adolescents' feelings of autonomy and social rejection. That is, it is directed at changing affectively, rather than cognitively based attitudes. The attitude inoculation technique can be modified by exposing adolescents to small doses of peer pressure during role-playing interventions. (pp. 235-237)

CHAPTER 8: CONFORMITY: INFLUENCING BEHAVIOR

Answer Key

Practice Test 1

Fill in the Blank

1.   conformity (p. 253)
2.   informational social influence (p. 255)
3.   private acceptance (p. 256)
4.   public compliance   (p. 257)
5.   contagion (p. 259)
6.   mass psychogenic illness (p. 260)
7.   social norms (p. 263)
8.   normative social influence (p. 264)
9.   mindless conformity (p. 281)

Multiple Choice:

1.   A (pp. 255-257)
2.   A (pp. 262-263)
3.   B (pp. 255-257, 264-267)
4.   C (p. 267)
5.   D (p. 286)
6.   D (p. 275)
7.   C (pp. 278-279)
8.   B (pp. 257-258)
9.   D (pp. 280-281)
10.   D (pp. 289-291)
11.   C (pp. 291-293)
12.   D (p. 253)
13.   B (p. 267)
14.   B (p. 260)
15.   C (pp. 264-266)
16.   A (p. 275)
17.   A (p. 279)
18.   D (pp. 279-280)

Short Answer

1.   You'd capitalize on people's tendency to mindlessly conform to the reciprocity norm, which dictates that if people do something nice for you, you should reciprocate by doing something nice for them. You'd recommend that the client offer free samples of the pizza to customers at grocery stores. Even if they do not like anchovies on their pizzas, they will feel obligated to buy the product. (pp. 284-286)

2.   Participants complied to normative pressures to please the experimenter, used the experimenter as an expert source of information in an ambiguous situation, and got caught in a web of conflicting social norms that led them to follow an inappropriate "obey authority" norm. (pp. 289-295)

3.   Informational Social Influence   Normative Social Influence
         Sherif   Asch
         Milgram   Schachter
         minority influence   Milgram
         contagion   "mindless" conformity
         (pp. 255, 259, 264, 268, 281, 284, 289)

4.   Both forms of influence produce conformity to the behaviors of others. Informational social influence, which
         produces private acceptance, is motivated by the need to be right while normative social influence, which
         produces public compliance, is motivated by the need to be liked. (pp. 255, 264)

Practice Test 2

Fill in the Blank

1.   door-in-the-face technique (p. 285)
2.   reciprocity norm (p. 286)
3.   social impact theory (p. 275)
4.   idiosyncrasy credits (p. 280)
5.   minority influence (p. 281)
6.   foot in the door technique (p. 287)
7.   descriptive (p. 282)
8.   injunctive (p. 282)
9.   compliance (p. 284)

Multiple Choice

1.   B (pp. 280-281)
2.   C (p. 284)
3.   B (p. 286)
4.   C (p. 291)
5.   A (pp. 293-295)
6.   D (p. 260)
7.   D (pp. 262-263)
8.   D (p. 263)
9.   A (pp. 267-268)
10.   B (pp. 271-275)
11.   D (p. 280)
12.   C (p. 282)
13.   A (p. 284)
14.   D (p. 284)
15.   B (p. 287)
16.   D (p. 253)
17.   D (pp. 255-257)
18.   D (p. 287)

Short Answer

1.   The unambiguous nature of Asch's line matching task required that participants blindly conform in order to go
         along. The demonstration is all the more dramatic because participants conformed in order to be liked by a
         group of strangers. (pp. 264-267)

2. According to social impact theory, the impact that a group will have on an individual is a function of the group's strength, or how important the group is to the individual, its immediacy, or how close the group is to the individual in space and time during the influence attempt, and the size of the group. (pp. 275-277)

3. Informational social influence is resisted by realizing that resistance is possible and by ascertaining the validity of the potentially influencing information. Information from an expert is more likely to be valid than information from other sources. Becoming mindful about what you are doing prevents normative social influence as does taking whatever actions you can to make resistance easier. For instance, finding an ally makes it easier to resist a majority. (pp. 262-263, 280-281)

CHAPTER 9: GROUP PROCESSES: INFLUENCE IN SOCIAL GROUPS

Answer Key

Practice Test 1

Fill in the Blank

1.   group (p. 301)
2.   social facilitation   (p. 307)
3.   social loafing (p. 308)
4.   deindividuation (p. 311)
5.   social roles (p. 302)
6.   cohesiveness (p. 305)
7.   transactive (p. 316)
8.   process loss (p. 315)
9.   groupthink (p. 317)
10.   group polarization (p. 320)

Multiple Choice

1.   D (p. 301)
2.   C (pp. 307-308)
3.   B (pp. 308-310)
4.   B (p. 307)
5.   D (p. 314)
6.   B (pp. 302-304)
7.   D (p. 320)
8.   B (p. 328)
9.   A (p. 332)
10.   B (p. 306)
11.   A (pp. 305-308)
12.   B (p. 326)
13.   C (p. 311)
14.   A (p. 305)
15.   B (pp. 308-310)

Short Answer

1.   Group polarization is the tendency for a group to make decisions that are more extreme than the initial inclinations of its members. According to a persuasive arguments interpretation of group polarization, the phenomenon results because members present strong and novel arguments in support of their initial recommendation to the group during discussion. According to a motivational interpretation, discussion serves to reveal the recommendation that is favored by the group. In order to be liked by the group, members then adopt a recommendation similar to everyone else's but a little more extreme. (pp. 319-321)

2.   Deindividuation loosens constraints on behaviors when crowds make members less accountable for their actions and foster anonymity. Add to this a situation that presents negative cues, and inhibitions against negative behaviors will be decreased. Negative behavior will ensue. (pp. 311-314)

Practice Test 2

Fill in the Blank

1. contingency theory of leadership (p. 322)
2. relationship-oriented leader (p. 322)
3. great person theory (p. 321)
4. tit-for-tat (p. 328)
5. public goods dilemma (p. 328)
6. commons dilemma (p. 328)
7. negotiation (p. 332)
8. integrative solution (p. 332)
9. task-oriented (p. 322)
10. social dilemma (p. 326

Multiple Choice

1. C (p. 321)
2. D (pp. 322, 324)
3. B (pp. 317-319)
4. A (pp. 320-321)
5. D (p. 328)
6. D (p. 315)
7. C (p. 316)
8. A (p. 322)
9. A (pp. 324-325)
10. C (p. 324-325)
11. B (p. 328)
12. D (p. 332)
13. C (pp. 317-319)
14. C (pp. 305-308)
15. E (pp. 311-314)

Short Answer

1. Groupthink occurs when certain preconditions are met, such as when the group is highly cohesive, is isolated from contrary opinion, and is ruled by a directive leader. Symptoms of groupthink include feelings of invulnerability, self-censorship, direct pressures on dissenters to conform, and an illusion of unanimity. Groupthink prevents groups from considering the full range of alternatives available to them, from developing contingency plans, and from considering the risks of the preferred choice. (pp. 317-319)

2. Negotiation is a form of communication between opposing sides in a conflict in which the parties make offers and counteroffers, and where a solution occurs only when both parties agree. Two strategies that groups communicating with one another can use are to make concessions and to look for integrative solutions, solutions to a conflict that find outcomes favorable to both sides. When negotiations break down because the two sides refuse to communicate, a neutral third party may be called on to mediate or arbitrate. Mediators allow the opposing parties to resolve their conflict by making suggestions and by searching for agreeable solutions. Arbitrators impose a decision on the parties after hearing arguments on both sides. (pp. 331-333)

CHAPTER 10: INTERPERSONAL ATTRACTION: FROM FIRST IMPRESSIONS TO CLOSE RELATIONSHIPS

Answer Key

Practice Test 1

Fill in the Blank

1.   propinquity effect (p. 340)
2.   mere exposure effect (p. 341)
3.   love styles (p. 358)
4.   relational dialectics (p. 372)
5.   social exchange (p. 353)
6.   comparison level (p. 353)
7.   comparison level for alternatives (p. 353)
8.   equity (p. 354)
9.   companionate love (p. 356)
10.   passionate love (p. 356)
11.   triangular theory of love (p. 358)

Multiple Choice

1.   D (p. 340)
2.   A (p. 345)
3.   B (p. 347)
4.   B (p. 344)
5.   D (p. 353)
6.   A (p. 354)
7.   B (p. 358)
8.   D (pp. 362-364)
9.   C (p. 365)
10.   C (p. 358)
11.   D (pp. 376-377)
12.   B (pp. 342-343)
13.   D (p. 374)
14.   D (p. 353)
15.   A (p. 353)
16.   A (p. 364)
17.   D (p. 368)
18.   C (p. 369)

Short Answer

1.   We develop favorable impressions of individuals when repeated exposure owing to propinquity makes the person familiar. We like individuals whose characteristics and beliefs are similar to our own. We like people who offer praise so long as it seems sincere. We like people who like us, especially if we have gained in their positive estimation of us. Finally, good looks can increase interpersonal attraction. (pp. 340-342, 344-345)

2.   The facial features associated with the attractiveness of females include: large eyes, a small nose, a small chin, prominent cheekbones, and a big smile. The features associated with attractiveness in males include: large eyes, prominent cheekbones, a large chin, and a big smile. Assumptions people make about attractive versus less attractive people include: they are more successful, intelligent, adjusted, exciting, and socially competent. A consequence of making such assumptions is that due to the self-fulfilling prophecy, we may behave in ways that confirm our expectations about attractive people. (pp. 346-351)

3.   Attachment theory assumes that attachment styles that we learn as infants and young children generalize to all of our relationships with others. Infants with responsive caregivers develop a secure attachment style and are able to develop mature, stable relationships later in life. Infants with aloof and distant caregivers develop an avoidant style are untrusting and find it difficult to develop intimacy. Infants whose caregivers are inconsistent and overbearing in their affections develop an anxious/ambivalent style. These individuals desire intimacy but fear that their affections will not be returned. (pp. 368-371)

4.   The six styles of love are ludus (love is a game), Eros (passionate love), storge (friendship love), mania (emotional love), agape (selfless love), and pragma (pragmatic love). Men tend to report a ludic style more than women. Women tend to report a storgic style more than men. People from Eastern cultures are more likely to endorse storgic styles than are Westerners. (pp. 358-359, 361)

Practice Test 2

Fill in the Blank

1.   investment model (p. 362)
2.   exchange (p. 364)
3.   communal (p. 365)
4.   attachment styles (p. 368)
5.   secure (p. 368)
6.   avoidant (p. 369)
7.   anxious/ambivalent (p. 369)
8.   autonomy/closeness (p. 372)
9.   novelty/predictability (p. 372)
10.   openness/closedness (p. 372)
11.   evolutionary (p. 366)

Multiple Choice

1.   A (p. 372)
2.   C (p. 374)
3.   D (p. 366)
4.   D (pp. 358-359)
5.   C (p. 341)
6.   D (pp. 342-344)
7.   D (pp. 347-349)
8.   A (pp. 349-351)
9.   C (p. 353)
10.   C (p. 356)
11.   E (p. 359)
12.   B (p. 358)
13.   D (p. 358)
14.   D (pp. 359-360)
15.   C (pp. 360-362)
16.   A (p. 370)

17.   B (p. 370)
18.   D (pp. 370-371)

Short Answer

1.   The outcome is defined as rewards minus costs. The greater the rewards relative to the costs, the better the individual will feel about the relationship and remain in it. The expectations one has about the level of rewards and punishments that one is likely to receive in a particular relationship, and in an alternative relationship, define the comparison level and comparison level of alternatives respectively. These affect one's subjective interpretation of rewards and costs and so affect the outcome as well. (pp. 352-354)

2.   Both theories claim that perceived rewards and punishments in a relationship determine relationship satisfaction. Equity theory claims that the notion of fairness or equity is additionally important. According to equity theory, even if the rewards of both partners outweigh the costs, the relationship will be unsatisfying if it is inequitable. (pp. 352-354)

3.   Research suggests that the less responsible an individual is for the breakup, the worse that person is likely to feel after the romantic relationship is terminated. By causing problems in a relationship and by annoying one's partner, an individual who desires to terminate the relationship may be allowing his/her partner to take some responsibility for the breakup in order to relieve some of the pain his/her ex-lover will experience. (pp. 376-377)

CHAPTER 11: PROSOCIAL BEHAVIOR: WHY DO PEOPLE HELP?

Answer Key

Practice Test 1

Fill in the Blank

1.   prosocial behavior (p. 382)
2.   altruism (p. 382)
3.   kin selection (p. 383)
4.   norm of reciprocity (p. 385)
5.   evolutionary psychology (p. 383)
6.   empathy (p. 387)
7.   empathy-altruism hypothesis (p. 388)

Multiple Choice

1.   C (p. 382)
2.   A (p. 383)
3.   B (pp. 386-387)
4.   D (p. 388)
5.   D (pp. 393-394)
6.   C (p. 394)
7.   C (pp. 396-397)
8.   B (p. 397)
9.   B (p. 401)
10.   B (pp. 404-405)
11.   C (p. 410)
12.   A (pp. 383-385)
13.   C (pp. 383, 386-387)
14.   A (p. 411)
15.   B (pp. 392-393)

Short Answer

1.   According to social exchange theory, we will help others when the rewards of helping outweigh the costs. In this situation, the rewards, such as the esteem of others at the concert and self-esteem, must have outweighed the costs. Costs include the potential embarrassment of attempting to help someone who, in fact, was not ill and the possibility that you yourself might get hurt. (pp. 386-387)

2.   Prosocial behavior is performed with the goal of benefiting another. It may or may not be performed without any regard to self-interests. Altruistic behavior is performed with the goal of benefiting others without any regard to self-interests. Hence, all altruistic acts are prosocial, but not all prosocial acts may be altruistic. (pp. 382-383)

3.   1) Get people's attention so that they will notice that there is a potential problem, 2) indicate that you are indeed hurt and need assistance, 3) single someone out by making eye contact and addressing the person so that he or she feels that the responsibility is his or hers alone, 4) suggest an appropriate form of assistance, and 5) ensure that the person implements the assistance by reassuring the person that you would be greatly appreciative of his or her help. (pp. 401-406)

Practice Test 2

Fill in the Blank

1. altruistic personality (p. 391)
2. in-group (p. 394)
3. negative-state relief hypothesis (p. 397)
4. urban overload hypothesis (p. 398)
5. bystander effect (p. 401)
6. pluralistic ignorance (p. 403)
7. diffusion of responsibility (p. 405)

Multiple Choice

1. A (p. 397)
2. C (p. 398)
3. A (pp. 400-401)
4. D (p. 408)
5. D (p. 408)
6. C (p. 405)
7. D (p. 382)
8. B (p. 385)
9. E (pp. 391-393, 396)
10. C (p. 394)
11. C (pp. 398-399, 401)
12. D (pp. 403-404)
13. D (pp. 410-411)
14. B (p. 403)
15. B (p. 402)

Short Answer

1. By reducing the stimulation people encounter, helping can be increased. You may not be able to reduce the population of a city but as an architect you might be able to design buildings that limit the amount of unwanted contact people experience. Likewise, though you might not be able to reduce the number of bystanders present in emergency situations, you can instruct people on the causes of bystander intervention. Research has shown that such instruction increases prosocial behavior. (pp. 398-399, 410)

2. According to the sociobiological approach, we are motivated to help others when helping increases the likelihood that our genes will live on in subsequent generations. Social exchange theory maintains that we help when the rewards of doing so outweigh the costs. The empathy-altruism hypothesis states that when we feel empathy for another person, altruistic concerns for that person motivate helping without any concern for ourselves. (pp. 383, 386, 388)

3. According to the negative-state relief hypothesis, we help people in order to relieve our own sadness and distress. Given that you believe that your negative state will be prolonged by the drug you have just taken, helping in this situation will not make you feel any better. The negative-state relief hypothesis therefore predicts that you will not help. (p. 397)

CHAPTER 12: AGGRESSION: WHY WE HURT OTHER PEOPLE

Answer Key

Practice Test 1

Fill in the Blank

1. aggressive action (p. 417)
2. hostile aggression (p. 417)
3. instrumental aggression (p. 417)
4. Eros (p. 418)
5. Thanatos (p. 418)
6. hydraulic theory (p. 418)
7. amygdala (p. 421)
8. serotonin (p. 421)

Multiple Choice

1. D (p. 417)
2. D (p. 418)
3. C (p. 421)
4. B (p. 421)
5. A (p. 424)
6. C (pp. 428-429)
7. C (pp. 432-433)
8. C (p. 438)
9. A (p. 442)
10. A (p. 443)
11. D (pp. 445)
12. C (p. 447)
13. B (p. 418)
14. A (p. 418)
15. B (p. 421)
16. C (p. 426)
17. D (p. 427)
18. A (pp. 430-431)

Short Answer

1. Cultures vary widely in their degree of aggressiveness. For instance, "primitive" tribes in Central Africa and New Guinea are far less aggressive than our "civilized" United States. Moreover, there is evidence of changes in the aggression within a culture over time. The Iroquois Indians were peaceful until the European influence brought them into economic competition with neighboring tribes. (pp. 419-421)

2. Berkowitz and LePage (1967) have demonstrated increased aggression by angered individuals in the presence of an aggressive stimulus (a gun) and concluded that the "trigger can also pull the finger" of individuals ready to aggress and who have no strong inhibitions against doing so. (pp. 428-430)

3. Children exposed to a steady diet of violent television are more likely to behave aggressively even if they are not disposed to such behavior. Additionally, children who watch a lot of violence on TV are less sensitive to subsequent violence they observe. The effects of viewing television violence on aggressive behavior are similar for adults. (pp. 431-435)

Practice Test 2

Fill in the Blank

1. testosterone (p. 421)
2. frustration-aggression theory (p.426)
3. relative deprivation (p. 427)
4. aggressive stimulus (p. 428)
5. social learning theory (p. 430)
6. catharsis (p. 441)
7. scripts (p. 436)

Multiple Choice

1. B (p. 437)
2. A (p. 442)
3. B (p. 446)
4. A (p. 449)
5. B (p. 417)
6. C (p. 417)
7. C (p. 420)
8. D (p. 421)
9. C (p. 422)
10. B (p. 422)
11. D (pp. 422-423)
12. D (pp. 423-425)
13. E (pp. 426-427)
14. D (p. 431)
15. D (pp. 431-433)
16. B (pp. 433-435)
17. E (p. 435)
18. A (p. 442)

Short Answer

1. Frustration is the feeling that you are being prevented from obtaining a goal. According to the frustration-aggression theory, frustration produces anger or annoyance and a readiness to aggress. Likelihood of aggressive behavior depends on: (1) how frustrated you are (frustration increases the closer the goal is), and (2) situational factors conducive to aggressive behavior (e.g., the victim's ability to retaliate, the perception of the legitimacy of the situation, the presence of an aggressive stimulus). (pp. 425-428)

2. The most effective means to reduce your own aggression when you are angry is to avoid engaging in aggressive behavior. Instead, express your anger calmly. To defuse aggression in someone who you have frustrated, apologize for your behavior. People can be taught nonaggressive behavior by imposing swift yet mild punishment, by exposing people to nonaggressive models and by reinforcing their nonaggressive communication and problem-solving behaviors. Finally, by building empathy in people, they are less likely to dehumanize individuals and behave aggressively toward them. (pp. 445-450)

CHAPTER 13: PREJUDICE: CAUSES AND CURES

Answer Key

Practice Test 1

Fill in the Blank

1.   prejudice (p. 460)
2.   stereotype   (p. 461)
3.   discrimination (p. 465)
4.   out-group homogeneity (p. 469)
5.   illusory correlation (p. 477)
6.   bookkeeping (p. 479)
7.   conversion (p. 479)
8.   subtyping (p. 479)
9.   ultimate attribution error (p. 481)
10.   blaming the victim (p. 483)

Multiple Choice

1.   D (p. 461)
2.   C (p. 464)
3.   A (p. 467)
4.   B (p. 470)
5.   D (pp. 474-475)
6.   B (p. 479)
7.   A (p. 481)
8.   C (p. 483)
9.   D (p. 486)
10.   D (p. 491)
11.   B (p. 479)
12.   C (p. 460)
13.   A (pp. 463-464)
14.   A (p. 469)
15.   B (p. 472)
16.   C (p. 478)
17.   D (p. 484)
18.   B (p. 489)

Short Answer

1.   According to Devine (1989), stereotypes that we all know come to mind automatically when we encounter members of the stereotyped group. People who are low in prejudice are likely to suppress or override the stereotype by consciously telling themselves that the stereotype is inaccurate and unfair. People who are high in prejudice are less likely to entertain such thoughts consciously. Consequently, their thinking is more likely to be ruled by the stereotype. (pp. 474-476)

2.   The ultimate attribution error is committed when we make dispositional attributions for entire groups of people and leads us to expect them to behave in stereotypic ways (for instance, lazy or stupid). Such biased expectancies are perpetuated by the self-fulfilling prophecy when we interact with out-group members in a manner that elicits behavior that confirms the stereotype. (pp. 480-481, 484-486)

3.   Modern racism is prejudice revealed in subtle, indirect ways because people have learned to hide their prejudiced attitudes in order to avoid being labeled as racist. Modern racism can be revealed in voting trends. Also, consider the following example: while it is not acceptable to overtly criticize people on the basis of group membership, it is generally acceptable to laugh at jokes that do so. Racial jokes seem especially acceptable when the comedian is a member of the group he/she is derogating. (p. 492)

Practice Test 2

Fill in the Blank

1.   realistic conflict theory (p. 486)
2.   scapegoating (p. 490)
3.   institutionalized racism (p. 491)
4.   institutionalized sexism (p. 491)
5.   normative conformity (p. 491)
6.   modern racism (p. 492)
7.   mutually interdependent (p. 496)
8.   jigsaw classroom (p. 498)
9.   stereotype threat (p. 482)
10.   self-fulfilling (p. 484)

Multiple Choice

1.   D (p. 491)
2.   D (pp. 496-497)
3.   B (p. 465)
4.   A (p. 479)
5.   B (p. 480)
6.   D (p. 481)
7.   B (p. 482)
8.   C (p. 482)
9.   D (p. 485)
10.   C (p. 493)
11.   D (p. 496)
12.   C (p. 496)
13.   E (pp. 498-500)
14.   D (pp. 500-501)
15.   C (p. 499)
16.   C (p. 492)
17.   B (p. 460)
18.   B (p. 467)

Short Answer

1.   Rational arguments are not effective in changing prejudice since it typically has a strong emotional component. Moreover, schematic processing does not favor the consideration of disconfirming evidence. For these reasons, any quick and easy one-shot attempts at presenting disconfirming evidence (e.g., conversion model) will be unsuccessful. Making the individual aware of disconfirming evidence that is concentrated in only a few members of the categorized group will create a sub-stereotype leaving the original stereotype intact (subtyping model). Hence, the best strategy for modifying stereotypic beliefs with disconfirming evidence is to make the individual aware that such evidence exists in many members of the categorized group (bookkeeping model). (pp. 479-480)

2.   When discrimination attains the status of a social norm, it is taught along with other social norms to members of society from their earliest years. The desire to "fit in" and to be liked by others ensures that people will exhibit normative conformity to society's rules. In this manner, institutional discrimination is sustained. (pp. 490-492)

3.   Compared to students in traditional classrooms, students in jigsaw classrooms exhibit decreased prejudice and stereotyping, increased liking for groupmates both within and across ethnic boundaries, increased liking for school, better performance on objective exams, increased self-esteem, intermingling, and empathy. (pp. 497-501)

SOCIAL PSYCHOLOGY IN ACTION 1

SOCIAL PSYCHOLOGY AND HEALTH

Answer Key

Practice Test 1

Fill in the Blank

1. stress (p. 510)
2. perceived control (p. 512)
3. self-efficacy (p. 516)
4. learned helplessness (p. 517)
5. stable attribution (p. 517)
6. internal attribution (p. 517)
7. global attribution (p. 517)

Multiple Choice

1. A (p. 506)
2. D (p. 510)
3. B (p. 512)
4. C (pp. 513-514)
5. A (p. 515)
6. B (p. 517)
7. D (pp. 532-533)
8. D (p. 508)
9. C (p. 511)
10. B (p. 510)
11. B (pp. 514-515)
12. B (p. 517)
13. A (p. 517)
14. A (p. 528)
15. A (p. 527)

Short Answer

1. Stress, which lowers the responsiveness of our immune system and makes us more susceptible to disease, can be reduced by increasing people's sense of control and by getting them to explain negative events in a more optimistic way. Social influence techniques can be used to get people to change their health habits. Cognitive dissonance techniques seem particularly effective in getting people to change intractable, ingrained health habits. (pp. 530-534)

2. Research finds that giving residents a sense of control over their lives increases both happiness and health. As director, you should stress to residents that they have the ability to make decisions about their lives at the home and should present them with options from which they can choose. You must be careful, however, not to repeal these changes once implemented. Research finds that instilling a sense of control and then revoking it has more negative consequences than never instilling it in the first place. (pp. 512-515)

Practice Test 2

Fill in the Blank

1. coping styles (p. 522)
2. Type A; Type B (p. 527)
3. social support (p. 524)
4. buffering hypothesis (p. 525)
5. fight-or-flight (p. 522)
6. tend-and-befriend (p. 523)

Multiple Choice

1. D (pp. 524, 529)
2. D (pp. 512-514)
3. B (p. 516)
4. B (p. 516)
5. C (p. 517)
6. C (p. 520)
7. D (pp. 522-523)
8. C (pp. 522-523)
9. C (p. 524)
10. A (p. 525)
11. B (p. 527)
12. D (pp. 531-532)
13. E (pp. 512-514)
14. A (p. 517)
15. D (p. 529)

Short Answer

1. Situations themselves have less impact on people than do people's interpretations of the situations. If people who have recently broken up are as likely to interpret the event negatively as positively (e.g., they finally got out of an unsatisfying and suffocating relationship), then we would expect the correlation to be low. Rather than measuring the recency of breakups, the researcher should have measured how the participants felt about the breakups. (pp. 508-512)

2. According to learned helplessness theory, depression may result from explaining negative events as due to internal, stable, and global causes. You would recommend that your client adopt an optimistic attributional style and explain negative events with external, unstable, and specific attributions. (pp. 517-519)

SOCIAL PSYCHOLOGY IN ACTION 2

SOCIAL PSYCHOLOGY AND THE ENVIRONMENT

Answer Key

Practice Test 1

Fill in the Blank

1.   density (p. 543)
2.   crowding (p. 543)
3.   sensory overload (p. 544)

Multiple Choice

1.   B (p. 539)
2.   C (pp. 539-541)
3.   B (p. 542)
4.   A (p. 543)
5.   C (p. 546)
6.   D (pp. 550-551)
7.   C (p. 552)
8.   D (p. 554)
9.   D (p. 538-539)
10.   A (p. 539)
11.   D (pp. 541-542)
12.   B (p. 543)
13.   A (p. 544)
14.   C (pp. 547-548)
15.   C (p. 546)
16.   D (p. 554)

Short Answer

1.   Your example should depict a situation in which the most beneficial action for you will, if chosen by most people, have harmful effects on everyone. Some common examples are driving to school, littering, and failing to conserve resources. (p. 546)

2.   The failure to conserve water is a classic social dilemma. In large groups, like an entire community, communication between members is an impractical means of resolving the dilemma. It may be possible to send committee members door-to-door, asking people to sign petitions condemning wastefulness while making them mindful of their own wasteful behavior. Because such dissonance arousing techniques require an initial behavior (e.g., signing the petition), they may also be of limited use on a large scale. Making selfish behavior public is likely to be an effective strategy in this case. Your committee might decide, for instance, to publish the names of water gluttons in the local newspapers. (pp. 549-550)

3.   You might remind people of socially sanctioned behaviors (evoking injunctive norms) by using the waste can or by displaying anti-littering posters. You could change people's perceptions of people's littering behavior in the park (changing descriptive norms) by removing the litter. In the long run, evoking injunctive norms is likely to be most effective since the effectiveness of descriptive norms depends on everyone's cooperation. (pp. 552-554)

Practice Test 2

Fill in the Blank

1.   injunctive norms (p. 552)
2.   descriptive norms (p. 552)

Multiple Choice

1.   A (p. 554)
2.   B (p. 554)
3.   D (pp. 539-541)
4.   B (p. 554)
5.   C (p. 543)
6.   B (p. 544)
7.   D (p. 548)
8.   A (p. 556)
9.   E (p. 539)
10.   B (pp. 540-541)
11.   C (p. 541)
12.   B (p. 542)
13.   C (pp. 543-544)
14.   E (p. 544)
15.   A (p. 546)
16.   D (p. 550)

Short Answer

1.   Experimental research has demonstrated that when people are exposed to uncontrollable loud noises they experience learned helplessness, which leads to depression, decreased effort, and difficulty in learning. Field studies demonstrate that children attending noisy schools had higher blood pressure, were more easily distracted, and gave up on difficult problems more easily. Likewise, children living in noisy apartment buildings do more poorly on reading tests. (pp. 539-542)

2.   Communication fosters trust and cooperation among members and allows members to persuade each other that selfless behavior is in the best interests of all. Communication, however, is a strategy that is necessarily limited to small groups. In larger groups, such as entire communities, nations, etc., making selfish behavior public evokes normative pressures against such behavior. Another proven technique is to change the way in which people perceive themselves and their social behavior by first evoking cognitive dissonance. (pp. 546-548)

3.   Researchers have used dissonance techniques to make people interpret their failure to engage in safe sex practice (Aronson et al., 1991) and to conserve water (Dickerson et al., 1992) as hypocritical behaviors which gave rise to dissonance. People in these studies were motivated to eliminate dissonance by buying condoms and taking shorter showers. (pp. 548-550)

SOCIAL PSYCHOLOGY IN ACTION 3

SOCIAL PSYCHOLOGY AND THE LAW

Answer Key

Practice Test 1

Fill in the Blank

1.   acquisition (p. 562)
2.   storage (p. 563)
3.   retrieval (p. 563)
4.   reconstructive memory (p. 566)
5.   source monitoring (p. 567)
6.   polygraph (p. 574)

Multiple Choice

1.   A (pp. 562-563)
2.   C (p. 564)
3.   D (p. 566)
4.   B (p. 570)
5.   C (pp. 575)
6.   D (pp. 579-583)
7.   A (p. 580)
8.   C (p. 581)
9.   D (p. 570)
10.   D (p. 563)
11.   E (p. 565)
12.   B (pp. 566-567)
13.   C (p. 575)
14.   A (p. 580)
15.   C (p. 580)

Short Answer

1.   You would tell the court that people's heavy reliance on eyewitness testimony should be tempered by the knowledge that they often overestimate the accuracy of such testimony. The problem, you would explain, is that people assume that eyewitness confidence is indicative of accuracy when, in fact, the things that make eyewitnesses confident are not the same things that make them accurate. For instance, viewing conditions that decrease accuracy do not generally decrease confidence. Likewise, rehearsing testimony increases confidence but not accuracy. (pp. 562-570)

2.   Requiring unanimity makes the jurors consider the evidence more carefully. Furthermore, while a minority is not likely to reverse the majority's verdict, the minority may change the minds of the majority members regarding how guilty the defendant is. For instance, a majority that maintains the guilt of a murder suspect may agree to second- rather than first-degree murder if influenced by a minority. (p. 583)

3.   An eyewitness must first acquire the events witnessed. That is, the eyewitness must notice and pay attention to the events (acquisition). Memory of the information that has been acquired must then be stored (storage). Finally, the information that has been stored must be recalled from memory (retrieval). Eyewitnesses can be inaccurate because of problems at any of these three stages. (pp. 562-563)

Practice Test 2

Fill in the Blank

1. own-race bias (p. 565)
2. cognitive interview (p. 576)
3. deterrence theory (p. 584)
4. procedural justice (p. 588)
5. recovered (p. 577)
6. false memory (p. 578)

Multiple Choice

1. B (p. 583)
2. A (p. 576)
3. C (pp. 583-584)
4. D (p. 578)
5. D (p. 565)
6. A (p. 567)
7. C (pp. 569-570)
8. E (pp. 570-572)
9. D (pp. 573-574)
10. A (pp. 573-574)
11. A (p. 574)
12. C (p. 576)
13. D (p. 581)
14. D (p. 584)
15. D (pp. 586-588)

Short Answer

1. Less-than-perfect remedies for the tendency to render a guilty verdict after exposure to emotional publicity include voir dire and instructions by the judge to disregard. Research indicates that jurors who claim that they have not been influenced by publicity nonetheless render more guilty verdicts when the publicity is emotional. Research also shows that instructions to not think about something often have the opposite effect. For instance, trying NOT to think of a white bear evokes images of a white bear. Another problem with pretrial publicity is that people are likely to form negative impressions of individuals whose name appears in a newspaper article along with a negative stimulus even if the article explicitly denies the association. The remedy to this problem is to permit people to serve on the jury only if they have heard nothing about the case. This may require a change of venue in well-publicized cases. (p. 580)

2. Deterrence theory and procedural justice offer the reasons used to explain why people obey laws. Deterrence theory explains obeying the law by focusing on the importance of the threat of punishment. In order for deterrence to be effective, however, punishment must be perceived as severe, certain, and immediate. Procedural justice focuses on how people's judgments about the fairness of the legal system influence whether or not they obey a law. The perceived justness of the law and of legal proceedings are important aspects people consider. (pp. 584-588)